The New Librarianship

A Challenge for Change

The New Librarianship

A Challenge for Change

Paul Wasserman

R.R. Bowker Company
New York & London, 1972
A Xerox Education Company

XEROX

Published by R. R. Bowker Co. (a Xerox Education Company)
1180 Avenue of the Americas, New York, N.Y. 10036
Copyright © 1972 by Xerox Corporation
Printed and bound in the United States of America

Library of Congress Cataloging in Publication Data
Wasserman, Paul.
  The new librarianship.
  Includes bibliographical references.
    1. Library administration.   2. Libraries and
society.   I. Title.
Z678.W35   025.1   72-8621
ISBN 0-8352-0604-1

Contents

Preface

The present volume is an outgrowth of a detailed and comprehensive program of research into manpower issues in librarianship, conducted at the University of Maryland and elsewhere by a number of scholars with support from the Office of Education, the National Science Foundation, and the National Library of Medicine.* This broad-scale inquiry was directed toward examining the field's manpower problems with a view to making policy recommendations for the field. The study design called for the problem to be approached from a number of vantage points—sociological, economic, political, organizational, psychological, and educational. The investigators commissioned to conduct the studies were, therefore, drawn from the range of relevant disciplines, with only the project directors coming from the field of librarianship.

Among the avenues explored were the following: the attractions the field holds for those now in it and those who might be drawn to it; the personality of those in the occupation and in its various subfields and work roles; the characteristics and perspectives of the institutional administrators; supply and demand facets of the manpower problem; or-

---

* The technical reports growing out of the research and submitted to the Office of Education are the following:

August C. Bolino, "Supply and Demand Analysis of Manpower Trends in the Library and Information Field," July 1969.

Mary Lee Bundy and Paul Wasserman, *A Study of the Executive in Library and Information Activity*, September 1970.

Edwin E. Olson, "Interlibrary Cooperation," September 1970.

Robert Presthus, "Technological Change and Occupational Response: A Study of Librarians," June 1970.

Stanley J. Segal, "Personality and Ability Patterns of Librarians," October 1970.

J. Hart Walters, Jr., "Image and Status of the Library and Information Services Field," July 1970.

Rodney F. White and David B. Macklin, "Education, Careers and Professionalization in Librarianship and Information Science," October 1970.

ganizational relationships in libraries and information centers; library education as a professionalizing and socializing force; and the implications of network development for manpower planning. Central to the study rationale was the notion that librarianship should be viewed not as a static institution committed solely to traditional objectives, but as one with the capacity to be responsive to changing environmental requirements. It was hoped that from the intelligence gathered from these inquiries certain of the significant dimensions of the field's manpower concerns would be illuminated and proposals to influence future development would be drawn. Thus, while the investigations were in the nature of more basic research, their ends were committedly pragmatic.

This book, then, owes its genesis to the study of the executive in library and information activity which was pursued as one salient means of perceiving the field's manpower situation. It was in the course of this investigation that the conceptual and philosophical perspectives of the writer shifted from the focus upon the administrator himself to the broader questions of leadership and of the leadership potential of the discipline.

DR. PAUL WASSERMAN
Professor and Former Dean, University of Maryland
School of Library and Information Services

Acknowledgments

No work of this nature is based upon the ideas of one individual. It is a synthesis, a reconstruction, and a blending of elements, sometimes traceable, often simply absorbed without any possibility of their attribution to a distinct point of origin. The principal sources of behavioral insight which have conditioned the writer's views are identified through the course of the book.

To one person the author must, however, express a basic intellectual debt. Mary Lee Bundy, during a professional association of half a dozen years, served as catalytic agent, colleague, provocateur and imaginative contributor of many of the ideas which have found expression in this volume. Indeed, many of the issues treated here have been so much discussed between us, in formal course offerings, seminars, conferences, and private debate, that it would be impossible to say who inspired which thoughts. But that is not to suggest that we are always in agreement. I do not speak for her in this book, only for myself. Still, my debt to her incisive mind is very much reflected in these pages.

Jeanne O'Connell's important contribution ranged from editorial to bibliographic assistance through every stage of the work. Carolyn Forsman also assisted in these ways with a portion of the manuscript, and Gayle Araghi aided importantly in tracing citations. Other colleagues have aided me in avoiding errors and confusion about facts. They were particularly helpful in their review of chapters VII and VIII on Spheres of Leadership Influence, and chapter IX on Prototypal Forms of Librarianship. These associates included Ralph Blasingame, Kurt Cylke, Henry Dubester, Paul Vassallo, James Welbourne, and Bill Woods.

Finally, I wish very much to acknowledge the exceedingly valuable efforts of Effie Knight who not only typed manuscript at every one of its complicated stages, but took responsibility for many other facets of the manpower study at considerable personal cost. Without her committed and intelligent contribution, not only this book, but many of the other efforts upon which the writer has been engaged since 1965, would have been impossible to achieve.

Introduction

The New Librarianship: A Challenge for Change is written during a time of crisis in the American society. Its author comes to the task convinced that the talents and energies of every concerned individual must be enlisted in the task of creating a better society. One cannot be of this culture, and particularly of the university community within it, without awareness of the deep-seated problems which face the nation and of the necessity for significant changes in the institutional structure and in the social system, if matters are to be set right.

In such a cultural context, the fair-minded observer of library institutions and library practice perceives how libraries, like many of the institutional forms in the culture, are failing. Libraries are failing because they are tied inexorably to the past. They are failing because they are a design of the conventional wisdom and so reinforce their values and their stale ritual without question, without remorse. They fail because they are morally and psychologically bound to physical plant and to physical objects, rather than to clienteles and to problem solving. They fail as they identify with the status quo rather than with the forces of change sweeping our planet.

It is very difficult, it may be impossible, for a conventional, passive, and complacent professional discipline to break dramatically with the past. Yet, precisely this is necessary if librarianship is to survive as anything other than a custodial function. If there is to be further development and evolution, collection development as its loftiest ideal must be challenged. A role positively linked with the achievement of specific and viable ends identified with human needs and with human aspirations must be conjured. For not until then does the concept of librarianship transcend the system of procedures, buildings, and of institutional forms and become a unity, constructed of the human beings who make up its practice and of those for whom it exists.

Essentially, our concern through this volume is to articulate the arguments for and the need to redirect the field. We are concerned not only with the product of library service, but, just as fundamentally, with the process. Put in its simplest term, the appeal is to fashion a proactive institution, a proactive discipline, as a substitute for a reactive one.

While this book proffers certain alternatives to the present mode and pleads the case for a different future, we are acutely conscious of the difficulty of converting the views of a field deeply rooted in its traditions and in its time honored values. The prospect of change is painful—as much so for the author as for others in the discipline. For the profession of librarianship has rewarded him too well; too many habits of mind persist, too many emotional ties and loyalties enter in. To confess this is not to try to escape personal responsibility for the implementation of the ideals suggested, nor to implore others to do what he cannot or does not choose to do himself.

The ideas offered here are directed to those capable of moving the field, and, in consequence, the society forward. As one looks with confidence to the future, hopes and aspirations must be tied to the young and rising generation who will be able to view all sides of the question with impartiality. This book, then, is most intended for and dedicated to those coming new to the scene, those without the same commitments to the status quo of librarianship and of the other institutional forms of the culture, to those whose primary personal and group loyalty demands and engenders, rather than inhibits change.

PART I

A Theoretical Analysis of the Change Process

CHAPTER 1

The Need for Change

W̲e live in a society whose only constant may be change. In this mass, complex, technological society the average citizen and his family find themselves engaged in changing jobs many times, perhaps even shifting careers, and adapting to the cultural, educational, and economic implications of new geographic locations. To function in new and strange surroundings we must respond frequently to unanticipated events and situations. No territory is inviolate. The campus, the school, the city streets, are all staging areas where different dramas are acted out every day.

THE CULTURAL IMPERATIVE

Institutions must cope not only with increased numbers requiring their services and with constantly shifting clienteles, but with new types of people sometimes fundamentally different from their traditional clienteles. One prevalent response is to increase the size and scale of the bureaucratic form. This often contributes to further alienation and to the failure of the large anonymous organization to work appropriately with clientele. In spite of growth in work force and resource base, the needs of particular groups often remain unattended. Demands for redress, protests against the social order in the city, in the university, and in the school, increasingly are mounted by those who feel disenfranchised, frustrated, and humiliated by the institutional forms which seem unmoved and thus irrelevant to their requirements.

In this time of social upheaval, how institutions in the culture respond to such issues is critically important. Failure to respond adequately contributes to individual and group distress, and violence seems to be the only palliative. Within each of the professions, the forces for change range from the protests of the active members boldly committed to a revised ideology for their profession to new experiments which depart from convention in such a way as to challenge the prevailing values of the field.

At root are the basic moral and ethical questions which confront the nation translated into each profession's own terms. In librarianship, restrictive forces are always abundantly evident, yet the countervailing liberalizing influence is powerful. To equate each profession's service in ways congruent with the common good is becoming more appealing. Yet to translate the rhetoric into institutional logic and expression remains a formidable task. For there is no assurance that change to service for the common good is the highest priority, nor is such a change viewed unanimously or even consensually within the library profession.

While present cultural conditions are critically important to every institution, they have particular meaning for the field of librarianship. For the fact of change itself, causing the turbulence which characterizes the nation, calls for appropriate support in the interest of a healthier social and political condition. The situation poses a particular challenge to an institution charged with responsibility for information dissemination. Information access is of more importance under conditions of change than in a time of stability. However, if the facts are separated from fancy, the slogan from reality, the ideology of librarianship is still reflected in the passivity of its institutional forms. For libraries remain predominantly passive agencies, overwhelmingly responsive to traditional demands and oriented powerfully to the book rather than to the client. Such an ideology tends to seriously foreclose the institution's options to perform otherwise. Moreover, the consequence of past choices has noticeably linked libraries to the requirements of particular segments in the culture —in the public library to the literate middle class, in academia to the humanistic professor. Those voices now clamoring for redress—blacks and students, to mention two—have not been perceived in the past as significant constituencies. The institution and those who practice in it have identified libraries as the servant of scholarship and they have been astonishingly indifferent to perceiving alternative responses and responsibilities.

The overwhelming majority of the profession does not appear to perceive a different role for libraries, not even the relation of social movements to libraries' activities. For them, the ends of the institution are the collection and organization of books. The history of the institution reinforces such a continued course. Yet if this is where the institution now stands in the culture, we hope that its position is not irrevocable. The task here shall be to explain why such an attitude has prevailed and how libraries might become more responsive to a changing society.

The Context

In this time of uncertainty, rational men have begun to question how and whether institutional forms are to survive. The orderly and accepted social arrangements of society, so logical for another time, now seem more doubtful. Even if there is no clear-cut danger to traditional social and political forms, the challenges of modern times are evident daily in the streets and on the campuses.

The most pessimistic suggest that the revolution has begun, that survival is a matter of reconstructing institutions out of the rubble of present-day forms. Such a view may seem unrealistic, perhaps even farfetched, as we survey the placid world of libraries. Only the glimmerings of any threat are perceptible. But warning signs are visible for any but the most myopic. They are visible in sporadic community disavowal of responsibility for burgeoning costs of service in the public library, in the voices of conscience-torn younger librarians striving for relevance, and in the assaults by dissident students upon the card catalog as a symbol of the impersonal and impenetrable bureaucracy.[1]

Contemporary society is a composite of all those organizational arrangements which make a civilization. The survival of this or any culture may be seen as the capacity of each of its institutions to formulate or to reformulate its program and services in ways which relate genuinely and unequivocally to the realities and the needs of the times. The fact that libraries have survived as long as they have in their present condition and with their present commitments makes them no less vulnerable. Those who question and who demand more of society reason that institutions exist solely to satisfy their expectations. Our concern here is to show that the process of bringing down an institution and leaving nothing in its place gives a false sense of progress and perhaps will ensure retrogression. Our concern about librarianship is not to perpetuate

1. All three events are amply documented in the 1969 and 1970 volumes of *Library Journal*. Reports of local funding difficulties appear in the following issues: March 15, 1969, p. 1083 (Newark, N.J.); April 15, 1969, p. 1565 (New York City); September 15, 1969, p. 2992 (Oakland, Calif.) and p. 3000 (Farmingdale, L.I.); May 1, 1970, p. 1694 (New Britain, Conn.); May 15, 1970, p. 1791 (Detroit, Mich.); and August 1970, p. 2757 (Newton, Mass.). The concerns of the young librarians are well summarized in the August roundup issues on American Library Association pre-Conference and Conference activities, particularly "The New Constituency," August 1970, pp. 2725–2742. Details of estimated $50,000 damages to the card catalog by University of Illinois students are included in March 15, 1969, p. 1086. See also April 1, 1969, p. 1401, for a report on the solicitation of volunteers to guard the card catalog at the University of California, and "The Ordeal at San Francisco State College," April 1, 1970, p. 1279.

a value-neutral technical discipline nor to buttress an institutional form with a majestic history but without a modern soul. It is rather to reinforce the importance of the information service which is at the core of its purpose. We wish to suggest the dialectic for the transformation of the institution in a culture and at a time when information has become indispensable—for decisions facing individuals, for intellectual discourse, for the development of technology, and for the evolution of the human condition.

Change Conditions

Change has ever been characteristic of the human condition. What is different at present is the pace of change. Such truisms are widely accepted; what is less widely accepted or understood is that the turbulence in the culture cannot be dissociated from the need for institutional responses. To accept change as the overriding societal condition, to perceive that political and intergenerational ferment is the present culture, to be sensitive to the passionate strivings of social movements without perceiving the need for congruent institutional contributions, is to be disoriented.

Library leadership needs not only to perceive the cultural condition, but to calculate a strategy for linking organizational forms to the pace of change.

The climate for change in a discipline is influenced by many forces. Two very powerful ones are interrelated. The first is the set of perspectives shared by the leadership structure of a profession. The leaders either actively urge the field forward or reinforce the sanctity and sanity of traditional response. The second force which determines the climate for change is the attitude of the leadership in individual institutions. The choices leaders make determine the performance of their organization.

Philosophy and values revolve about ethical issues. These then become choices, at least when choice has not been foreclosed or provoked by external factors. Still, to be adaptive is to take initiative, which may be uncommon in many professions. There are those who argue that change may be retrogressive. There are many who argue that the rate of change in librarianship is no worse than in any other institution. They claim that those who criticize are merely carping, that the critics' demands are too harsh and that they are too demanding in their aspirations for leadership. They argue that to change for its own sake or too quickly, leads only to a type of dysfunctionalism in organizations which reduces their equilibrium and effectiveness. They argue that institutional leadership responds ideally by adapting only very gradually and prudently.

They argue further that dramatic change may seem attractive in an immediate sense, but over the long run will prove too costly or inappropriate for the institution. This is the "wait and see" philosophy, so characteristic in librarianship of administrators facing automation implementation.[2]

Still these are uncommon times, and perhaps the need for change can be put in terms of the question of societal survival, with its resolution ultimately seen as the capacity of its institutions to be responsive. When organizational forms in a culture begin to be viewed as irrelevant for those for whom they are intended, the culture is in danger. It would be naive to suggest that libraries hold the balance for the survival of American society. Yet libraries share responsibility to meet human need with other cultural inventions and must undergo the same public scrutiny.

For the most part, libraries have been committed to the kind of gradual change which occurs over the course of history. The precise variations are imperceptible, and the equilibrium of the stabilized forms and conventions remains unaffected by the process. More rapid change has been introduced into librarianship only through technology which merely affects procedures and work flow. The typewriter, the photocharger, and the computer are among the more dramatic illustrations.

The present is an era of radical change, but libraries have not moved with the same momentum. Radical change comes about when values are reconsidered. The values of librarianship remain fundamentally unaltered. The change process may be influenced by environmental pressures or by revolution within the organizational form. None of these conditions have been pervasive in libraries. Those who reject the partisan role in change argue that the more conditions change, the more they remain the same. Conversely, they comfort themselves with the notion that the future will inevitably be unlike the past and because direction of change is not discernible, the means of transforming the present conditions are beyond control. In either case the responsibility of leadership to promote the process of change, and to achieve a change strategy so that the organization may survive, is absent.

It is striking in this time of ferment in higher education among administration, faculty, and students and in cities, changing in such dramatic ways, that the relation between the library's possible contribution and such disruptions is so little understood. It is not that innovation is not a catchword in the field, for it is. But innovation is more talked about than carried out. The evidence from another field, drawn from

2. Paul Wasserman, *The Librarian and the Machine* (Detroit: Gale Research Co., 1945), pp. 125–127.

the American Council on Education's study of undergraduate curriculum trends between 1957 and 1967, could be applied directly to librarianship:

> Despite all the talk about innovation, undergraduate curriculum requirements as a whole have changed remarkably little in ten years . . . in many cases, the minor changes in requirements, amounting to no more than a reshuffling of credits, can only be characterized as tinkering. . . . It is also clear that innovation is relative. One institution claims as innovation what others are discarding. . . . Most of what passes as innovation is not really new. . . . The significant area for innovation lies in rethinking the total undergraduate program in an attempt to restore unity and relevance. The evidence on such activity is discouraging; there is too little of it.[3]

Institutional Complexities Affect the Current Scene

The American library as an institutional form was begun in another time, a simpler time. It was a time when all of man's knowledge was recorded in printed books and when the rate of production of new ideas was less overwhelming. Over the institution's life span libraries have been transformed into more complex forms, so that the bureaucracy and the technology which growing size have engendered commit libraries to patterns which make them less viable than when they began. Institutional history and tradition impose ritual processes and a ritualized sense of library purposes. Ritual translates into apathy and ultimately many concede that nothing very much can be changed. Failure, it is rationalized, is caused by lack of material or resources, rather than by limited imagination or enterprise, which are the more genuine constraints.

Often those associated with the institution confuse the evaluation of achievements with the organization's wholesome mission. The goodness of books and reading is held as the pious justification for an organizational form. And even many others among its users who are not tied personally to the institution, but to the abstract idea of the worth of the book and of reading, also treasure the institution. It is only those who hold the pursestrings who are recalcitrant and who submit the enterprise to more calculated measures of achievement.

Arguments about the health and vitality of organizations are fruitless. Those involved are defensive; those for whom they are intended are critical. Yet the difference between organizations which are healthy and

3. Paul L. Dressel and Frances H. DeLisle, *Undergraduate Curriculum Trends* (Washington: American Council on Education, 1969), pp. 75–76.

those which are moribund can be measured without refined evaluative machinery. The university president can identify departments which are exceptionally vital and differentiate those which are pedestrian and ineffective. In the same way the undergraduate or the faculty member can characterize his institution's library—his measurement is his satisfactory or frustrating experience.

When young, libraries, like societies and very much like the other institutional forms within the culture, are flexible and opportunistic. They are as yet unparalyzed by the rigidity of specialization and they are willing to try new things. As they grow older and more complex, their traditions solidify and their vitality diminishes. Their creativity fades with the loss of the capacity to meet new challenges. With the years flexibility is lost, as habits, attitudes, and opinions inevitably give rise to concomitant organizational and institutional lore and ritual.

When organizations begin they exist in a climate of confusion and variation in which the prime task is seen as the achievement of maturity. As organizations mature there is an inevitable narrowing of their scope and perspectives. Few and particularized organizational interests are centered upon in a pattern of relatively fixed relationships. Aspirations tend to be established and perpetuated. Methods are fixed and modifications uncommon. Accommodation is only the consequence of unusual or dramatic events because there is a vested interest in what has worked in the past. As the organization matures, it solidifies in its ways, and less and less does it have the capacity or the courage to try alternatives through enduring risks or by functioning entrepreneurially.

As the organization endures and expands, even when inspired out of social conviction or motivated by the loftiest intent, its structure grows larger, its inventory mounts, the scale of work force increases, while its enthusiasm tends to wane and its original spirit to thin. For it evolves into a system which is more preoccupied with continuity and perpetuity than with adaptation of responses to the beat of a contemporary measure. The organization thus becomes an accepted way in which things are done, with experimentation and radical departure from past practice gradually eliminated or continued under the most careful set of controlled conditions.

What is true for the individual organization and the individual institutional form is also true for the total society. For the social system is constructed out of the logical need of another time in a way designed to ensure social and political survival. But the same syndrome which assaults the individual organization and the institutions in the culture operates across the social continuum as well. The social system is the sum of the organizations and the institutions which make up a society, and the characteristics of its response and of its responsibility are the correlate of all the forms which exist within it.

The tasks of library leadership one hundred years ago were to design the institutional form and to derive its technology. The pioneers of the period fit the entrepreneurial model of the middle and late nineteenth century as the educational counterpart of the industrial leader.[4] These were individuals of vigor and imagination, enterprising men with a capacity and a spirit to carry out social and technical invention, all in the context of the literary and educational milieu of their day. It was their efforts in organizational craftsmanship, their bibliographic cunning, and their vision of the necessity for standardization which brought into being the prototypes of librarianship which endure into the modern era. There was, in the late nineteenth century and on into the twentieth, no professional class. There was only a leadership and an employee class who were their followers. The measure of a library's worth at that time was the size of its inventory and the capacity to identify items within it. The modern library is often similarly measured.

It was not until much later that the earliest professionalization began, first with the perception of need to differentiate specialized clientele requirements, later with the specialization of functions within libraries. Still, almost until the post-World War II period, it was only in the uncommonly large and complex libraries where leadership was perceived to call for more than the capacity to know books, to know how they should be identified, to have the carriage of a man of refinement, a scholar. Well into the 1940s and the 1950s libraries still bore the traces of a peasant culture, with growing numbers of employees performing routine repetitive tasks, with only a small elite differentiated as its leadership class.

The picture has changed—somewhat. Libraries have grown dramatically in the past two decades, keeping pace with the generally advancing scale of organizational phenomena in the culture. The factors leading to their resurgence corresponded to a renewed societal concern for the expansion of the formal and informal educational structure, both as consequence of the increased numbers engaged in educational efforts and of the affluence of the times which could expand its investment in such enterprises.

But the caliber of library leadership which characterized the early and classic phase of American history was no longer in evidence. Institutional arteries had begun to harden, bureaucracy was entrenched, the habituation of ritual response made more difficult for libraries and for

4. See Reinhard Bendix, *Work and Authority in Industry* (New York: John Wiley, 1956), chapter V, for generous coverage on the nineteenth century industrialist.

librarianship the calculation of original strategies for handling new problems. The consequence may be seen in the evolution of new information technologies, organizations, and competitive disciplines outside libraries and librarianship. For as libraries and librarianship grew in size, in scale, in terms of support, they held fast to their historic values, traditions, and commitments, and they have been content to maintain their historical image. Naturally local library developments are highly variable. But in the main, the characteristic response in the face of the new and untried has been that of caution and reluctance. Bureaucratic inertia, lethargy, fear of the uncommon, are widespread.

The need for change in modern libraries is conditioned by many factors. It is conditioned by the changing physical characteristics of modern intellectual property, by the dictates of economy and efficiency in workflow systems of ever increasing scale. Most significantly it is conditioned by the human and the intellectual requirements of clientele. This is then more than simply a matter of procedure, of technique. It is a matter of purpose. For new social needs arise and intellectual requirements change. And the conventions and the programs of another age demand reassessment.

The responsibility of the viable organization and profession is to calculate strategies appropriate to the times and to the more particularized situation so as to ensure their sustained viability. An unresponsive institution, an unresponsive discipline, ultimately is perceived to be irrelevant. It is at that point that the culture calls the institution into question. In a volatile culture, programs and services committed to the ends of only one small segment in that culture; programs and services which neglect, dismiss, and alienate particular groups; and programs and services in which the ritual requirements transcend client need are all in jeopardy. Those institutions which concentrate upon the artifacts and rituals, which fit its history but do not mesh with the intellectual and cultural requirements of the here and now, no longer suffice. Activities which simply reinforce the status and image requirements of those who ply the institutional craft, without congruence with the culture for which the organization's products and services are intended, run the risk of extinction.

CHANGING A FIELD

If the logic of change need is accepted, it must still be specified that change can be retrogressive, as well as progressive. Particularly in those instances when limits of financial or human resources are present, the climate may condition practices which may ultimately retard organizational effectiveness. The use of volunteers may be a case in point. Cost-conscious administrative strategists would be unlikely to perceive the lessened capacity of organizational responsiveness in the differences in the attainment between staff efforts and those of well-meaning amateurs.

The rhetoric of change, as it is heard in the pious espousals of organizations and professions, may often be concomitant with negative change or a well-nurtured posture of resistance to anything which challenges the equilibrium. For to change from one set of conditions to another runs against the grain of many of the most cherished forces of the organizational form. Organizational characteristics are imbued with the need to derive a kind of mechanical system which will respond in familiar ways, in which organizational life is a sequence of anticipated successive states modified only by limited degrees. Under these terms, the strivings of yesterday are seen as very much like those of today and tomorrow. Predictability is kept high, since perceptions of the future are believed to be clear. Under these terms too, controls are exercised in order to keep affairs in balance and to ensure the perpetuation of the form without breakdown or crisis. And so change is minimal, closely controlled, inconsequential.

Only in its technical concerns has librarianship come to accept adaptation. The reasons are several. The quality of publications has grown so that the number of transactions which arise in their wake to identify and detail their movements has come to be commonly perceived as a problem. Order and precision occupy a high place in the litany of the discipline. The threat of inundation constitutes a forceful propellant. Moreover, the technical and mechanical problems of libraries have been identified by outside experts in operations research and computer technology as amenable to solution. Thus it tends to be here, in classification questions, acquisitions, cataloging, circulation procedures, and the technical processes of the enterprise, where adaptation finds most ready acceptance. Thus the application of technology comes to occupy the highest place in the hierarchy of status in librarianship, and its partisans are the modern heroes of the discipline.[5]

The characteristic phenomenon of an entrenched field such as librarianship in resisting change is seen in the construction of a kind of mystique about its institutions, in the reverence for the conventional, and in the subtle construction of barriers to that which might disturb its own sense of identity and significance. The form which such restriction takes may be seen in monolithic resistance to a new ideology which might require dramatic shifts in orientation, jurisdiction, and the professional

5. These issues are more fully elaborated in Wasserman, op. cit., pp. 87–96.

balance of power. It is manifest in a deep-seated reluctance either to hear criticism of the existing order from those in the field, or to develop feedback machanisms which call for honest and unbiased dialogues with constituencies about the limits and the failures of the organizational form. Through manifold devices, but notably in its professional forums, education, and informal exchanges, it shapes the collective mind and spirit of those identified with it to the virtue of the existing order. And thus reality is confused with imagination, and there is only a filtered perception of the truth based upon romanticization of the discipline or upon the illusions arising from profession-wide self-deception.

In their past, libraries have calculated a strategy built upon a very simple model. They have acquired book collections and provided users access to them. In each context where they perform, their propensity has been to orient themselves to the requirements of a particular class— in the city to the reading middle class, in the university to the faculty, in the school to the reader. Larger questions of informational responsibility and responsiveness will engage our concern later. Here the question of change relates to the possibilities of fashioning strategies for reaching others at different points on the human scale. What is requisite is a re-vision of the library model to provide clear and unambiguous rights for those who have yet to enjoy substantial values from the long-standing system. The constraints to such reconstruction are many, not the least of which may be the self-identification of librarians with the elements of the cultures they have sought to serve and the congruence between such service and their own aspirations.

To adapt genuinely to the requirements of variable subcultures so that they would find their needs reflected in the patterns and programs of libraries would also call for an experimental stance. For differences from past practice are distinctly implied, and their precise shape is un-certain. Experiment threatens ritual. It implies openness and adaptability, the design of new roles and new procedures for different clientele. Such change for those who hold fast to tradition is repulsive. These are moral issues for the profession and for its institutions. This is why technology may be so much more readily and pervasively acceptable.

There is no morality in technology. It is directed at process. Only when it interferes with the human options within the internal system is there threat or strain. But the technical or means change is as nothing beside the responsibility of choice about ends, as the professions and the institutions select the response which they will fashion from the mosaic of variable options. Libraries have come to exist within the context of a culture which gives high place to institutional forms which, through formal and informal mechanisms, reinforce going values. The public library is an illustration for it does precisely this. To change, to alter its commitment in fundamental ways, would be to perceive the immorality in past choice of an option which foreclosed upon specific elements in the culture outside of its traditional following. It would call for a redress which would put into political jeopardy all of the comfortable, time-honored alliances out of which the base of support has been sustained. In the academic setting, the library would transcend the boundaries of common bond with the campus elite in order to identify more genuinely with the intellectual requirements of the most transient in its culture—the students.

To condition such change calls for perception among the professional class and institutional leadership that there is a societal mandate to alter the usual responses. In short, that not to do so would threaten institutional and professional perpetuation. Such a perception is linked with leadership capacity and imaginative professionalism, and such professionalism is uncommon. For the institution and its practitioners identify with the values and the symbols historically associated with libraries and librarianship.

The academic and corporate setting tends to find libraries principally enlisted in the service of the organizational elite, with both librarians and library administrators identifying with and aspiring to share in the status of those whom they serve. Long habituation to this condition renders exceedingly difficult the transition to alternate strategies of library response for other individuals and groups and so to the devising of different activities less congruent with the strivings of librarians. Still, not all are ever sanguine about the existing condition. In times of turmoil and disciplinary uneasiness it becomes possible to fashion alliances for change. As the basic premises of the institutional and disciplinary system come into question, greater willingness to work for the construction of alternatives may be engendered. Those who actively seek change and those who although more passive perceive benefits in weakening the established order may hold the key in combination. So long as the institutional forms are secure, so long as there is no external threat to their continuity, advocates for change can be ignored or squelched. But in other times, in these times, a rising chorus of discontent can call into question the commitments and the contribution of a single institution and, beyond, to those of an entire field of practice. This then leads to the substantive issue—the need to proffer viable alternative goals and strategies for the classic ones.

A significant impediment to change in librarianship is the consequence of what has been until the very recent past its exceedingly low level of economic development. Meager resources have limited the forms of specialized professional roles, and this has been countenanced in view of the lack of adequate remuneration for such work. Administrative roles are thus the premium ones and are so perceived by those within and those outside its practice. Held then to the level of a marginal economy, it has been only those who assume managerial responsibility who hold power and prestige. In organizations and in cultures where such conditions prevail, the bureaucracies which arise tend to orient their services to the benefits of those who are seen as their own group and with whom they identify; they tend to be alienated from other groups in the culture with whom they do not feel a kinship. The goal of service for all is displaced by the goal of service to an elite and to the social strata which best reinforce the self-perception and the cultural self-interest of the members of the bureaucracy. Seen thus the professional class is a weak political group, dependent within the framework of the institutional and professional bureaucracy upon those who hold power. The administrative class can readily divert the activities of the individual bureaucracy and the professional discipline to its own purposes and prevent it from upholding any general responsibilities for providing services to other strata in the society. Thus again, it is only in troubled times when the capacity for upsetting the status quo is most opportune. For it is at such times when the professional class and the administrative class may perceive societal strain short of the crisis level and, in league, strike out for adaptations. Indeed, once it is seen within institutions and within professional disciplines that there are those who are alienated from the group which holds power and that political action threatening to the existing order is possible, conciliation becomes a more adroit alternative than the prospect of revolution and change. Such sensitivity may be seen to inspire present efforts within rigid library hierarchies to move toward shared decision-making mechanisms and, at the disciplinary level, to explain the establishment of national policy committees representing the alienated in concert with those who would staunchly perpetuate the status quo. The possibility that such devices may be cynical ploys to pacify insurgency, buy time, or even to co-opt those who represent the alternatives cannot be dismissed lightly.

Relation of Education and Practice

As technical disciplines arise, they make alliances with other institutions which reinforce their survival capacity. The success of the educational element in a discipline is measured by its congruence with the aims of the organizations for which the education is conducted. The educational forms require the help and protection of the practicing institutions in order to establish and maintain their proprietary right to the educational sequence. The practicing institutions need the kind of legitimation and support that can be provided only by the educational interests, which offer a type of latter-day religious induction rite. Such mutual interdependence can and does create tensions, because each faction would like very much to control the structural position of the other and thereby provide for the satisfaction of its own needs. Yet whatever the scope and condition of such tension and conflict, the usual modus vivendi is established, constituting a basic aspect of the institutionalization of the educational process and vice versa. This happens in spite of the carpings of those who lament the condition of the other camp. The very astute perceive in these exercises the relief value of such letting-off of steam without losing sight for a single moment of the firmness of the mutual bondage.

While criticism by the practitioner may even be vitriolic, it is directed to issues involving means and seldom to fundamentals. For the educational interests uphold the legitimacy of the practicing institutions and of those who direct them and, in consequence, their political orientations and their policies. It is not uncommon for there to be active participation from members of the educational segment in the political processes of practicing organizations through common efforts and national societies and sometimes through personal involvements in the affairs of individual institutions as board members or consultants. The converse is also well known. In technical disciplines like librarianship, many practitioners play pronounced roles in the formulation of educational policy and in its practice, as advisors, alumni, occasional faculty. Such interchanges can provide the climate for change both within the educational and institutional worlds. For contradictions inherent in such a tenuous relationship can give rise to more serious questioning on both sides. The traditional orientation can be seriously debated and, if found wanting, assaulted. Thus education can become both an intellectual and a moral force. On the other side there is the capacity to engage in serious discussion to question whether educational stress upon the perfection of idealized and theoretical constructs is viable in an educational sequence which ostensibly leads to a more active and pragmatic responsibility for helping to reshape an institution in a time of change. And of whether educational responsibility is not abdicated in the perpetuation of selection standards oriented to criteria which ensure hospitality only to the same people with the same common attributes which have brought the institutional form to its present condition. Thus the very institutionalization of organizational and educational processes can be seen to hold the seeds of their reconstruction.

Institutions establish client systems in which certain norms and expectations are set up and the policies through which these norms can be held and applied to a large and relatively complex variety of situations are implemented. The values and the goals which the organizations follow, and which the professionals of the discipline who practice within the organizations follow, are purportedly shared to a considerable extent by a large part of the culture in which the organizational form exists and in which these values presumably are binding upon those who have responsibility for the conduct of the organizations' affairs. Yet the establishment of such values and their legitimation in terms of generally agreed-upon goals and symbols, even though they may be perceived and understood, are never fully accepted by all. For it is understood that there is a willingness and an ability of certain cultural elements to provide the resource base which the system demands. Frequently it is the case that over periods of time the majority of the members of a societal group may identify with the values and aspirations of the system and thus be willing to provide the resources necessary to sustain it. This will be true until the time when other cultural tendencies develop. The present may be precisely such a time.

In a period of basic questioning, new premises can and do arise. These may come to be forcefully shared and opposed to the long-standing and accepted bases which gave rise to the earlier institutional system. Then the values upon which the institutions were maintained at another stage are no longer seen as binding upon all those in the culture who are needed to support them. There may even be questioning about the interpretation of the values; whether in fact the institutions are conducting programs and services genuinely reflective of such theoretical values—as, for example, equal services to all. Still others, both within and outside the context of the institutions, may derive new interpretations of existing values and seek change in the basis of the institution. For it may be that the initial attitudes of the culture toward the premises upon which libraries were begun have begun to change and that it is no longer so obviously simple to maintain the legitimacy of the earlier values among all the groups and individuals in the culture who must now be supportive. This may be one lesson of the Newark, N.J., Public Library episode,[6] and of the attempted destruction of the card catalog at the Uni-

6. On February 11, 1969, the Newark City Council voted to shut down all activities and facilities of the Newark Public Library as of April 1. After considerable protest from—and dissension between—both inner-city and suburban residents, the council voted on March 11 to reverse its previous action and restore funding for at least nine months. See *New York Times*, February 12, 1969, 78:6; February 14, 38:1; February 21, 45:6; March 1, 30:3; March 3, 12:3; March 12, 96:1.

versity of Illinois and other campuses. The continuous implementation of earlier policies and procedures may no longer satisfy the aspirations of the different groups in the society at a time when continuous shifts in the balance of power among them, and in their orientations to the existing social system and to the organizational forms within it, are subject to drastic reconsideration.

The process of change tends to be intensified as there are variations in the balance of the relationship between institutions and the cultural conditions to which they relate. That is, the institution as a political and economic entity remains intact to the extent that its commitment and thus its processes remain congruent with the political and economic ecology which gives it sustenance. When, for whatever reason, there is disequilibrium between the institution and the ecology, change is an increasing prospect. Seen in library terms, to the extent that there are serious reductions in the economic bases for the support of public institutions, academic programs, or educational efforts, library programs are adapted to the limits of resources. As constituencies grow or diminish, inevitable responses arise from the library's revision of its strategy for maintaining a carefully modulated interplay between institutional contribution and the cultural segments with which it must correspond. In cases where there is disequilibrium within the institutions themselves, when the ideology and the agenda, as perceived by significant elements in the organization, are incongruous with contemporary need, once the threat is recognized of such divisiveness being brought into focus in the outside culture, compromise and ultimately change come to be inevitable.

Every sensitive institutional system, conscious of the resources needed to protect and perpetuate its prerogatives, zealously monitors its relationship with all the forces in its environment which are seen as powerful in ensuring its survival. Still, certain organizations either through an inflated sense of their own intrinsic worthiness in perpetuity, or in consequence of a myopic misreading of what they perceive as a monopolistic mandate to perform distinctive, irreplaceable services, fail to conjure with reality. For the community can disinvest, invest elsewhere, or ultimately lose interest in any but the most essential services for which it may not easily find substitutes. The possibility exists that parallel and competitive programs will be fashioned. Adaptation and change are the normal devices for warding off such competition. In a marketplace economy the very existence of parallel alternatives is seen to reinforce the capacity of an institution to adapt to changing times. But this presumes an organizational propensity to react to competition. Self-righteous organizational forms remain oblivious. They do so, however, at considerable peril to their survival. An organizational climate open to alternatives, and

schooled in the technical discipline, from whom approval and ultimate support is sought. The new propositions which are formulated eventually meet their test in the marketplace. The consumer of the service, the client, decides. Yet in those emergent fields, those in flux or characterized by a quickened tempo of change, constituencies have neither the experience nor the technical capacities to make evaluations about new evolutionary stages. The professional discipline itself is relied upon for the expertise in finding the most logical new direction. Thus it is only at the point when cultural recognition perceives the incongruity of the technical choice with client aspirations that disillusion and dissent may ensue. The critiques of modern educational method written in recent years by aroused contemporary nonprofessional observers illustrate how this can come to pass.

The development and the acceptance of a new paradigm results in a new perspective. It is for this reason that the conservatism of professional practice counsels prudence and guards carefully against acceptance of novelty. Herein lies a very heavily loaded instrument for fending off alternatives. In the hands of the adroit it may be seen as an ideal self-defense mechanism to ensure continuity of tradition whatever the cost.

Debates over paradigms are not only about the relative problem-solving ability of the discipline, even though they may be so disguised in the rhetoric of discussion. The circumstances of the decision to revise the ideological basis for practice must be grounded less on the issue of past achievements than on the promise for the future. Those who offer a new paradigm at an early stage have limited evidence of its problem-solving ability. They have only their passion and commitment and the faith that the new proposal will find success in solving many large problems with which the field is confronted. They are certain only of the fact that the traditional paradigm has failed. Herein resides the most powerful argument of all for proposing alternatives.

Our task in this volume is to try to help design a strategy to revise the leadership structure of librarianship so that the profession and its institutions can change. Librarianship is now a learned profession only to the extent to which it traffics in the artifacts which support others who are learning. A truly learned—or, more properly, learning—profession seeks to perceive, to understand, and ultimately to practice the means whereby its knowledge base evolves and matures, all the while remaining responsive to the several cultures within which it fashions responses. Its point is thus to derive the modifications which reasonably and rationally re-orient the institution in its contemporary design. It is no easy matter to chart the conceptual territory of what leadership is required to propel a discipline and an institution toward what it must seek to be and to explain why this must be so. Essentially our perspective arises from a sense of the need for change as a present imperative for the field. As the issues are complex and subtle, they are often shrugged off and resisted. The propensity to conduct business as usual, to resist adaptation, is overpowering. Still the crisis of the times, translated into the crisis in librarianship, serves as a powerful and irreversible lever for change.

CHAPTER 2

The Dynamics of Change

The argument to this point has specified why librarianship must calculate strategies of change, and I have attempted to identify the mechanisms the profession needs in order to encourage innovation instead of offering ritualistic responses. The discussion which follows is drawn mainly from social science literature, and is based upon my observation of individual institutions, notably business and government. To consider the discipline we must focus on the institution itself, as well as on those who practice librarianship, for this is a culture of individuals drawn together by the characteristics of the field. The institutional form gives shape to their occupational lives and occupational expectations. The inclination to change is the prime question for the individual as well as for the organization. It is the leadership role that distinguishes professionals where the desire for change is expressed both in professional ideology and in institutional stewardship.

Many disciplines prefer to view change as an evolutionary process rather than revolutionary, as long-term adjustments caused by subtle environmental factors outside the ability of professional leadership to inspire or accelerate. When this attitude prevails, ritual is sanctified. Change mechanisms result from attitude and behavior change in people. While the tempo may vary among disciplines and among organizations within a discipline, if change is the objective, the first strategy must be to encourage those in the discipline to perceive the need.

Evidence from librarianship suggests that there is no consensus on the critical need for change. The field may still be distant from the very first strategy level, the perception of the need. None of the portents—a decline in the use of city libraries, competition for the information function, alienation of particular classes of clientele, collective-bargaining efforts by professional personnel—are seen as fundamentally threatening. Not all individuals or specific institutions are complacent, but the mood of the profession is not of anxiety or peril.

Readiness for change may not equate with action. Perceiving a problem is not the same as having a strategy for implementing a change that will solve it. In part, the limits of capacity or imagination of librarians to delineate alternatives may explain why the uneasy feelings of many about the state of the discipline fail to translate beyond this feeling and into action.

The history of a discipline is another determinant in its disposition to find tolerable the idea of alternatives. The prospect of the new or the unknown arouses uneasiness, particularly in those disciplines with long-standing folkways where tradition and stability are everywhere reflected in practice, in physical arrangements, in status systems. Since libraries deal in one of the most significant representations of past heritage, the book, the psychological constraints against change may be great.

Librarianship is captive of its past. Its testament to history is a tradition which honors as heroes those who have built the great collections of books. The commitment to what has been continues to condition contemporary perception. The dynamics of a constantly changing environment, shifting values, and habits of work and leisure are blinked away, while the attendant risks to institution and occupation remain imperceptible. It is as if the practice of the discipline were somehow impervious to all but the constants of its past contribution—the collection, the keeping and the lending of books.

Comparing librarianship to another field one could look upon aeronautics as if its parameters were those of the conventional aircraft. While the original organizations and the discipline of the field involved the construction of airplanes, long since has its strategy embraced new technologies, new elements of flight. As librarianship traffics in knowledge and information, so does this corollary field center upon transport forms. And the difference between the perception of the need for change of these two fields may reflect the willingness or unwillingness to conceive of new organizations arising as competitors or alternatives. It is only when the self-perception of a discipline is one of monopoly control that it can self-righteously disregard the changes which have come to pass in the contemporary world.

The perception of need for change is lent powerful impetus when environmental pressures reinforce the professional and institutional conscience. Constituents may bring to a higher temperature the flames first kindled by professional ardor. Conversely, however, the detachment and unconcern of real and potential clientele may reinforce the complacency of those who will not be moved.

FACTORS WHICH CONDITION INNOVATION

Change which reconstructs organizational strategy beyond the modification of routine or procedure may be termed innovation. Innovative propensity tends to correspond to attitudes. Satisfaction with existing organizational patterns, involvement with professional ideology, trust of possible alternatives—each is a factor. Certain individuals are more committed to the zone of the customary than are others. The degree to which librarians as a group, and library leadership as a class, are committed to traditional methods and views seems germane. I believe that many individuals are drawn to librarianship by the appeal of the order, the arrangement, the procedural ritual which governs its activities. This is how the occupation is perceived—tidiness and preference for books. The seedbed of innovation is never so tidy.

Depth of personal knowledge and experience with particular ranges of problems are important factors in innovation. The greater the number of individuals committed to problem solving, the more likely it is that something can be generated. In collaborative effort there is not only the pooling of ideas, but an increased probability that one of those engaged upon the task will identify the best solution. The interaction of many serves as stimulus. The ideas and views of collaborators and colleagues, just as in scientific advance, give impetus to new ideas. There is also competition, abrasion, criticism, and the demand for evidence of any claim. Collaboration, professional discourse, and open forums do not happen by chance. They are either encouraged or discouraged within the context of individual organizations of particular disciplinary groups. The evidence seems to suggest very limited support of such collaboration in librarianship.

The one notable instance of recent library history which has been supportive of innovation is the adaptation of computer technology to library processes. Institutional efforts have, on some occasions, been correlated.[1] A new grouping in the American Library Association, the Information Science and Automation Division, has come into being, and the technical medium to support regular discourse, *The Journal of Library Automation*, has begun. The consensus which led to these developments was born out of the common concerns of all those straining to cope with the problems of work flow in organizations of growing size,

1. For efforts in this direction on the part of Columbia University, Stanford University and the University of Chicago see Allen B. Veaner and Paul J. Fasana, eds., *Proceedings of the Stanford Conference on Collaborative Library Systems Development*, October 4–5, 1968 (Stanford, Calif.: Stanford University Library, 1969).

scale and complexity. The housekeeping ritual at the core of the system was seen as amenable to modern technology, if the tools for these specific library tasks could be fashioned. I am forced to ponder whether the application of some of the discipline's richest talents to what are its procedural rather than substantive concerns may not be a costly diversion. In order to calculate the advantage or disadvantage it would be necessary to measure its utility against the opportunity costs.[2]

Innovative strides are more common when the conventional idea-system of a field is widely questioned. For instance, a growing professional consciousness of responsibility to unserved clients evokes a clash of ideas and provokes comparisons and discussion of what practice is and what it might be. It is thus that innovation is born. The individual professional and the individual administrator may move first from apprehension to self-defensiveness and finally to new means of expression.

There is imitation as well as innovation, and what is imitative in one context may be innovative in another. Moving technical methods or ideological values from one setting to another can constitute innovative contribution of considerable value. This imitative drawing in of perspective and insight from spheres outside the traditional boundaries of a field can enrich institutional and disciplinary capacity. Imitative models within a field tend to be those with prestige so that emulation is above reproach. The idea of an undergraduate library as developed at Harvard, and the Greenaway Plan[3] fashioned by Emerson Greenaway, celebrated former director of the Free Library of Philadelphia, are two illustrations. However, computer technology aside, if we are looking for external prototypes to adapt from within the library field, the innovative propensity does not appear to be very pronounced.

Professional practices in other lands sometimes serve as models. But American librarianship is little disposed to concede that there may be lessons to be learned from the library efforts of other cultures. Comparative librarianship is viewed as a one-way street, with American experience the only conceivable universal model. And so the balance of payments grows ever more lopsided. The experience, the perspectives, and

2. A widely employed concept from modern economic theory, the opportunity cost of any particular course of action is the amount of gain which could have been obtained by pursuing the next most desirable alternative. Clearly the opportunity cost doctrine is most applicable where choice involves closely competing alternatives.
3. During 1958 Greenaway worked out a plan with the J. B. Lippincott Co. whereby the Free Library would receive before publication one copy of each trade title. By allowing librarians more time for reviewing, selecting, and processing, the arrangement sought to make new books available for use as soon after publication dates as possible. With some variation, the plan has been adopted by a large number of publishers and libraries.

the imaginative advances of Great Britain, Scandinavia, and others are seldom given credence.

THE EXPECTATION OF CHANGE

If members of a profession expect change, it is far more likely to occur. Change frequency is augmented in proportion to the numbers of individuals who expect it, somewhat like the prospect of witnessing flying saucers being a function of the number who are looking for them. In some technical fields there is widespread and active expectation of change. In other fields anticipation may exist at a low level because of prevailing attitudes. The question essentially is whether there is a pervasive view that change is natural, inevitable, or morally and professionally good. The expectation of change is cultivated by a conceptual ideology which conceives of problem solving as the ideal mode of human behavior. Groups are indoctrinated with such perspectives.

America as a nation has been accustomed to striking out forcefully at problems, whenever experience has been seen to be in conflict with hopes and expectations. It is only in recent times that discouragement about the entire system has set in as a result of the complexity of the problems of the day. Ironically enough, the notion of progress itself is a stimulus to the expectation of change for the better; as this is so, such conceptual ideology impels a culture forward. When an optimistic outlook is replaced by a feeling of doom, human beings resignedly accept the workings of their relentless fate. This latter ideology of pessimism has been characteristic of librarianship, accustomed over its history in consequence of its passive disposition to accept the limits of an underdeveloped state. As with others in the culture who are demanding redress of inequality, professional and technical groups also hold the capacity, if they believe they do, to reevaluate their condition and to work more aggressively for reconstruction of their future.

There is a correlation between the enterprise of individuals and the potential of a field for innovation. History suggests that the greater the freedom open to the individual, the surer the likelihood that new ideas will be engendered. One constraint of the hierarchical, bureaucratic structure typical of librarianship is that individuals are not permitted to explore their world of experience and evaluate perceptions. They are indoctrinated to accept authority as the ultimate source of truth and so can be little expected to pursue notions variant from organizational norms. Indoctrinated with the virtue of bureaucratic dependency, the individual's propensity to engage in inquiry and evaluation is diminished.

Dependence upon authority is in part conditioned by the development of specialized knowledge. In many lines of specialization, experts concentrate upon complex matters, the details of which remain mysteries to the uninitiated. In librarianship, the intricacies of data processing serve as one illustration. The voice of authority thus becomes more audible in consequence of mystique and of facts to which only a few are privy.

I believe librarianship is like a systematized creed functioning within the context of an institutionalized hierarchy. The essential condition is unified control and dedication to the unquestioning support of the system. The pronouncements of leaders are due to divine inspiration. Still questions are now being raised even in what have heretofore been among the most rigid of hierarchical orders—universities and religious bodies. Social and political strife can be seen to inspire the emergence of new ideas and variations in response. The very instability of such a time offers opportunities for the exercise of ingenuity and places a high premium upon initiative and resourcefulness.

Another element in the dynamics of change is competition which may serve as a powerful incentive in stimulating innovation where it is related to economic rewards, prestige, power, or professional recognition. In industry, when a company maintains its place as innovative leader, economic advantages are often assured. Universities attempt to do likewise by attracting outstanding professors and supporting means to ensure that original ideas will follow from study, teaching, and research. Librarianship, on the other hand, has distributed its rewards and incentives less on the basis of any innovative capacity of its leadership and more nearly in consequence of dramatically increasing the size of book collection and physical plants. This is due to the widely shared view in the field that the essential contribution of the library is in building collections. The penalty and reward system fails to perceive innovation as meritorious. Library administrators are reluctant to gamble the time and the resources to change alternatives. As they see no threat in exploiting only the conventional measures of library success, the existing arrangements remain undisturbed. Only the most entrepreneurially disposed, impelled perhaps by the lure of peer rather than institutional acclaim, form the thin vanguard.

For innovation to stem from competition, it must afford the innovator a basis for his claim to the superior performance which is ultimately his goal. What constitutes superior performance is determined by the discipline's scale of values. So long as traditional values are unthreatened, and physical plant and number of volumes remain the chief determinants, innovation will continue to be seen merely as novelty.

The notion that deprivation may be an ingredient in innovation and that adaptations are accelerated by the futility of the present condition seems not to be borne out by reality. For while deprivation is being suffered, it is not always perceived as such by the victims. This is one reason why the riots in the cities are a latter-day phenomenon, reached only when those who have far less had achieved access to media which demonstrated in explicit detail what they were missing.

It would appear that for innovation to take place a degree of leisure to think, of time to ponder and to manipulate new ideas, is necessary. Freedom from pressure extends the boundary of new ideas. Yet it is true that crisis frequently creates emergency conditions which give rise to ideas and activities. Past wars serve as an illustration. Still crisis elicits varying responses. If librarians are like other groups which have been studied under crisis, some would react with frenzy, others with belligerency, while only a minority would remain cool and rational. Under the terms of such stress two potential types of innovative action may be brought about. The one will contribute to survival and advancement and the other give only the illusion of doing so. The one will fashion the requisite instrument to achieve and accomplish rational ends, the other resort to fantasy thinking. Until crisis is real, forecasts of prospective behavior can only be conjectural.

A crucial question in the dynamics of change is how recognition is accorded in a specific discipline. In certain contexts the innovator seeks prestige by choosing variation as his means to success. He may be interested in change only incidentally. His primary urge may be for recognition, and the exercise of creative ability may be the most suitable device at his disposal. In some fields originality tends to be highly prized, as for example in the arts and crafts. In other fields—perhaps librarianship is one—there would appear to be few rewards for creativity and thus less production of new ideas.

Career choice would be expected to mesh with self-perception, with fields perceived as tradition-bound receiving less than their share of creative individuals. Many at the point of occupational choice have yet to perceive fully their intellectual and ideological personalities. Consequently, fields not celebrated for their tolerance of originality attract some proportion of innovative individuals. Moreover, the business cycle and thus competitive opportunities play a role. During the 1930s, I believe many who might have made a mark through the stamp of their originality in other fields were drawn into librarianship—perhaps because this field was one where the uncommon contributor would be more certain to receive rapid acclaim under conditions of competition less intensive than in parallel lines of pursuit.

Where a field continues to demonstrate that it is not genuinely hospitable to the innovative mind, the individual who perceives himself to be odd-man-out has two options. He can drop out by selecting another career, or he can shift to an enterpreneurial role outside the formal apparatus of the discipline. Those who have gravitated to the consulting or publishing worlds would fit these terms.[4] The other choice is to conclude that the playing ground for creative efforts is not the formal work place and so to husband resources for the hours away from the formal organization.

In a professional practice carried out essentially within the context of large public or quasi-public organizations, the incentives which normally accrue to creativity are not so prevalent. Neither the individual nor the organization controls new intellectual property and thereby realizes a profit from it. Thus the value of a new idea is its acceptance by others, for here is where prestige lies. For many who innovate in such settings, the fundamental striving which must be satisfied is that of being imitated. The final expression of such emulation is translated into followings or schools of thought which the original innovator may recognize as a consequence of his effort. This is clearly the case of those in academia who advance their own ideas in order to persuade others to spread these ideas to wider audiences. But librarianship, constituted as it is in more pragmatic than intellectual currents, holds little promise of even such proprietary potential.

Not all ideas are welcome. Frequently the richer a disciplinary history, the firmer the bonds of convention. Thus many ideas are rejected, and their proponents become the target of hostility and reprobation. Innovative ideas may ultimately achieve recognition, but they may require reinforcement from successive proponents plus supportive pressure from the general culture. Time to absorb innovation is often a prime requisite.[5]

The individual who is freest of all to suggest innovation is one drawn from an alien discipline. He is not constrained by knowing too much about the bias of the profession. The freewheeling interpretations of an "ignorant" person may be more acceptable to the members of a group. Also, ignorance of tradition often facilitates fresh insight.

The ultimate irony of innovation is that while the discipline and its institutions may need to undertake adaptation, change is destructive of

4. Their number are legion. Among the better known, present-day names in librarianship who might be so characterized would be Saul Herner, Dan Lacy, Eric Moon, and Stephen Salmon.
5. The research center in library education, as formal concomitant of the library school, may serve as an illustrative case in point. The first center was begun at the University of Illinois in 1959. But it was not until almost a full decade later that the efficacy of such a design had come to be accepted widely by a significant number of institutions of comparable purpose, with programs at Case Western Reserve University, the University of California, Drexel Institute of Technology and Indiana University, among others.

stability. The result is an ambivalence toward innovation. On one hand there is a theoretical commitment to change tied to the belief that innovation is essential to professional and organizational growth. At the same time there is fear that its consequences will upset the harmony. The notion of innovation in an orderly, goal-directed, risk-reducing process remains an abstraction, while the discipline and its organizations combine in practice to make innovation unlikely.

One view holds that skilled professionals can anticipate and control the risks of innovation. Phrases like "the management of innovation" suggest that it is somehow possible to foresee the risks and rewards of alternative efforts. By selecting only projects whose benefits would justify their anticipated costs, by playing risks off one against another, it is assumed that the risk of innovation is tolerable. But risk is never so susceptible of calculation. To calculate risks when the odds are known is not the same as to deal with uncertainty. In this situation the innovative efforts of disciplines are to convert the level of uncertainty to a level that can be foreseen. This process of conversion of uncertainty to risk takes varying forms, depending upon the kind of uncertainty to be dealt with. Some of the more important issues relate to the technical feasibility of the innovation, the novelty value and the nature of the innovative contribution itself, and the potential market value for it.

Even those skilled in assessing problems are not always clear as to whether one is working on a minor problem of adjustment or a major problem of goal strategy. For technical feasibility frequently resists the definition required to perceive clearly the investment significance of the activity. It becomes a matter of who has done it before and who is doing it now. In a field where there is no competitive edge to turning out work ahead of another, it is possible to collaborate and cooperate as efforts are moved along. In a competitive ambience, on the other hand, the ultimate achievement, with its promise of commercial success, will spur on activity in ways not in evidence in fields where there is no great advantage in being first. The consequence is that except for the presence of uncommon individuals, or a critical problem, the same impetus to be innovator in the noncompetitive disciplines is outweighed by the benefits of working cooperatively. Such organizations, on the whole, usually adopt a "wait and see" policy. Library administrators tend not to be risk takers—the payoff is seen as not worth the gamble.

The questions of marketing, most germane in commercial contexts, also obtain in innovative efforts in noncommercial cultures. Innovation must be assessed against the question of who will want the product, that is, what is the consuming group and how useful will this market find the innovation as a function of the cost and the alternative investment made to produce it, compared with other alternatives. The uncertainties of marketing are especially pronounced in a field where there is no obvious constituency clamoring for a new design. Moreover, the implications of acceptance may pose problems for the capacity of the organization to deliver if the demand soars, since no economic incentives accrue as a result of successful innovation. A hypothetical illustration is a public library offering a new information service on automobile repair. Increased demand for such service would necessitate greater input into that activity. Demand could rise steeply, forcing an increased investment in the new product to the detriment of other services. The same psychology which keeps small business small can thus apply to market innovation in librarianship.

In principle the uncertainties which innovation imposes may be resolvable, but the cost may be high. Innovation within an organization and within a discipline poses the problem of decision in spite of uncertainty. This uncertainty calls for a genuine commitment to the importance of change. Yet the rational view holds that innovation is manageable. Specifying the rational view, exhorting others to innovate, or telling them how to do it is not the equivalent of actively participating, sustaining, and supporting such effort. To hold to the rational view may simply be self-deluding in the way which many employ as convenient disguise for their genuine position in other spheres where posture and practice depart. Freedom from prejudice might be an illustration.

To hold to the rational view of the controllability of innovation makes uncertainty seem less frightening, for it plays down the economic and personal pains with which new developments may be fraught. The surprising, the uncertain, the fuzzy and dangerous elements of innovation are suppressed. The rational view of innovation holds for only the most marginal of changes. The less significant the variation the more the process seems to be orderly and predictable. The more radical the innovation, the greater the potential conflict. For to move along the continuum from minor modification to major variation is to come closer and closer to changes in the basic assumptions and theoretical perspectives of the field. Dramatic variation calls for revision of professional and institutional ideology.

It is one thing to replace a procedure and quite another to disrupt the contribution of an organization. Under the latter terms, elements of organizational and professional technology will be rendered obsolete, and individuals who have built up technical or craft skills over a professional lifetime may suddenly find their skills irrelevant. The whole construct of organizational life will be subject to review for the organizational contribution will no longer be the same. The effects of innovation will be felt throughout the organization. The cumulative effect of change will also be overwhelming for those who direct the organization. Those who lead organizations base their confidence on an understanding of the details of the existing operation. Modifications of a fundamental nature put them on unfamiliar ground. If this is so, how can the leader be expected to lead? Where is he to draw the resources of experience and expertise to trust his own judgment? Is he to become completely dependent upon the proponents of the new? The leader would thus be faced with a crisis of self-confidence.

Thus fundamental innovation may be seen as a disruption of the stable basis of the organization even by its leadership. Here is the source of efforts to maintain things as they are. A whole range of strategies has been developed to sustain the equilibrium. Efforts at innovation are rejected. Individual organizations do not tolerate discussions of nontraditional mechanisms. When such efforts are permitted to continue, they tend to be isolated, so that their contribution can be contained and kept from truly changing organizational or disciplinary life. When tolerated, the innovative activity is kept on such a level that it is always in jeopardy. Efforts at public library services to the disadvantaged serve as one illustration. There may be an oscillation between support and resistance, giving rise to confusion among those in the discipline or in the organization. Indeed, innovation may be most strenuously resisted at the very time when every outward appearance proclaims the virtue of innovation as official doctrine. While seeming to encourage the development of new ideas, these ideas can be relentlessly struck down.

The stable and traditional profession thus seeks most to stand fast. The effect is a kind of dynamic conservatism. Resistance patterns are not themselves obstacles to innovation so much as processes of conservation which are viewed to be essential to the survival of the basic organizational and professional forms. The current condition in libraries requires the undertaking of dramatic change which in itself is destructive of the stability to which such organizations cling. This is the paradox which makes libraries so vulnerable. In spite of the ambivalence toward innovation, the crises of the times require the adoption of new forms and new styles.

PERSONALITY DETERMINANTS RELATING TO CHANGE

The behavioral sciences have succeeded in perceiving some of the psychological propensities of the human mind and organization so I will draw from such sources, particularly upon the work of Barnett,[6] and fit these propositions into the context of innovation in the library field.

6. H. G. Barnett, *Innovation: The Basis of Cultural Change* (New York: McGraw-Hill, 1953).

Differences in cast of mind are evident between those who design and adapt and those who accept change. Some seek to design originality while others who prefer the new require a prototype. Many innovators require advocates to put their ideas into practice. While imitation of a nonstereotyped pattern is an innovative perspective, it is not motivated by the same urges which are characteristic of the original designer. Change is not influenced without advocates. And without the application of the innovation, those who originate fail to receive the feedback necessary to improve upon the design. With discouragement, innovators, like others, tend to lose their enthusiasm. Many innovators are aware that to accept openly their proposals may reflect discredit upon the follower who has not conceived of the idea himself. But few innovators perceive how they may be little honored, and perhaps even be damaged, because of their identification with unconventional ideas.

The most sophisticated are often willing to leave the hardships of proselytizing to others. The capacity to be creative may be intrinsic to the makeup of some who are at the same time indifferent to other people or without the zeal for carrying the banner of reform. In certain disciplines, perhaps excluding librarianship, there is a relationship between master and disciple under the terms of which particular methods and interpretations attract a following. There is no necessary correlation between the mind equipped to pursue difficult intellectual propositions and the ability to influence others to the same persuasion. Put another way, this is to say that there are those who are primarily thinkers and others whose contribution is to execute the designs of others. Such a dichotomy oversimplifies. Yet many disciplines attest to such a relationship between creators and proselytizers.

A particular kind of change advocate appears to be common to developing fields like librarianship which have a well-entrenched characteristic of accepting adaptation from outsiders. Such individuals tend to straddle two professional ways of life. They may have been drawn positively to the new discipline, but they do not appear to be completely content within its culture. And negative aspects of the earlier discipline from which they came may provide explanation for why they have left it and come to the new. Those in library education drawn from the technological or behavioral sciences, those in data processing, subject bibliography, or specialized administrative roles, would be illustrative of the breed. Any number of reasons may explain why a particular individual would have found it expedient to gravitate into the library milieu. The more obvious might tend to be reasons of economics, limits of technical capacity, or constraint upon mobility. But the characteristic state of this class of individuals is ambivalence. In the instance of the displaced academics, they are not fully prepared to expatriate themselves to the new discipline. This is often the posture of the behavioral scientist, the technologist, or some other member of the library-school faculty who makes clear at only the slightest provocation that he really is not in or of librarianship. Many prefer the prestige and incentives which the new culture affords and the absence of the type of peer competition which the earlier setting imposed upon them. They are encouraged to introduce to librarianship those ideologies and constructs which are more to their liking and which represent their earlier disciplinary roots. And they can be selective and choose what they believe is best out of the two systems and attempt to fuse them. The role appears to appeal to increasing numbers.

To speak of classic types in the matter of change and change ideology is to oversimplify for the purpose of clarity. Each person is conservative in some regard as well as change-oriented. Nor does passionate proclamation of individual position always conform with behavior. As the next generation stresses and presses for change the very process enforces upon the older generation a concomitant pleading for stability. Out of this process the latter are drawn to conservatism. What is true inter-generationally in the culture at large may doubtless be as true for the professional disciplines.

Certain individuals in certain institutions are viewed as models by others. Their capacity to influence the acceptance of innovation is thereby enhanced. It is not always those with the greatest prestige who will be seen as the model. The copying of styles of dress and speech and musical patterns of the black community in the United States illustrates the point. While prestige may be exclusively the property of an elite and coexist with authority, it does not work perfectly. Thus no leader, whether individual or institutional, is universally revered or perceived as a model by all. Individuals and institutions are free to select among competitors for their attention. Complex fields like librarianship thus boast models of automation, of subject bibliography, or of building expertise. There is variability among the models both substantively and ideologically.

Political and technical identities overlap. Those who emulate can select as model the individual or the institution based upon the prestige of rank, office, or standing. Such recognition can also be accorded in consequence of substantive contribution. Frequently there is confusion about this or, perhaps more commonly, unawareness. In a complex and specialized professional world, the culture tends to make assumptions about individuals so that simply to occupy a certain role is automatically to be imbued with certain presumed virtues. For this reason, organizations when seeking library administrators usually choose from among those who already occupy such positions even while there is no assurance that they are effective at the tasks.

Acceptance of innovative ideas is associated with the degree to which proponents and potential partisans share common values. Those of an independent cast of mind may tend to embrace new ideas simply because they are advocated by those out of power and because the added prestige of those who do not hold power becomes an indictment of the existing leadership. The moves in the councils of the American Library Association by those associated with social responsibility questions might reflect this. Many reject new ideas when advocated by one of their own since they jealously perceive that to follow such a banner would be to identify a leadership role for the person who proclaims it. Still others are prone to reject anything sponsored outside their own identifiable group. Librarianship tends to reinforce its own values and commitments and to repulse any new ideologies which might arise from within. A kind of obsequious deference attends those from outside the field who may proffer ideas and suggestions. Perhaps this stems from awe in the face of alien terminology. More likely it may be traced to the deference librarians accord the authority of other disciplines since virtually all are self-consciously perceived as more potent intellectually than librarianship.

One grave difficulty in acceptance and advocacy of new ideas is that those who are esteemed by a field are so esteemed because of past performance and past behavior. Such a process may be a liability. Those who have achieved distinction have a loyalty to those who admire them, and they are obliged to meet the expectations of their followers. Such expectations constrain and so forbid radical departure from expected behavior norms. Thus the very reputation achieved as a consequence of past actions may limit the capacity to advocate revolutionary ideas, even when, ironically enough, the reputation itself may have been founded upon originality. Radical ideas which exceed the bounds of expectation may be advocated only at the risk of loss of prestige by the proponent. This may be why the professional elite are seldom found in the vanguard of change, why radical change is seldom inspired by those who hold preeminent positions.

An impediment to influencing adaptation is sometimes seen in the personality characteristics of those who propose change. Those who in manner, dress, or attitude create antagonism, as do many who wage war against the status quo, may be rejected without serious attention to the merit of their proposals. For their behavior offends the congenial atmosphere and thereby engenders antipathy. While the individual and not the idea is the offender, both become the targets of those who are offended. In a culture which extols the virtues of marketing, the appealing personality is the correlate of acceptability of new ideas. Appealing personality is often a more valuable asset than prestige, since it is flexible and can be manipulated with ease. It does not depend upon past accomplishment, is adjustable and dynamic, and can reflect the circumstances of the moment. Its immediacy gives it precedence over estimates made on the basis of other, more rigorous criteria. Its overriding influence is reflected in the way in which such high premium is placed upon personal relations. Evaluations of candidates for posts in libraries or on faculties are often based upon observations drawn from temporary interviews as much as from the concrete evidence of a life's work.

The acceptance of ideas prevails more readily when a majority of any group is ready to be convinced. It is not that an absolute majority is needed, but only that impression makes a new idea seem inevitable. Advocacy is thereby strengthened by the notion that opposition to the idea would be futile or unreasonable. Under these terms, the technique of those who advocate change is to attempt to overwhelm those who object to it by calling up a mass opinion, the logic of which is allegedly irresistible simply because it tends to be consensual. It is clear that many accept the new idea mainly because everyone else appears to be doing so. What better explanation for the pervasiveness of changeover to Library of Congress classification in academic libraries. The multitude is right where it must be right, even if it is not, and there is no use in contending with the weight of the consensus.

Innovation is often assessed on the measure of its compatibility with existing practice. The optimal alternative is seen as that which is not only feasible but comfortable. The less displacement caused to human beings in the acceptance of new models, the greater propensity for accommodation to change. In this, the practical utility of ideas is of paramount concern. Many innovations, simply because they have not been fully explored, may be seen to be inefficient and awkward. If performance is uncertain or disappointing under tests made by those who would employ them, skepticism and reluctance are common. Even highly prospective acceptors are not often willing to take a chance or to serve as experimental subjects or to run the risk of being duped—that is, unless they can be made to understand the utility of participating in such experiments. There is an appeal in the opportunity to identify with an experimental school with its promise of prestige and of external resources. The prospects for improving personal and institutional reputations argue powerfully for making adaptation. Even so, except in disciplines and institutions where experimental design and laboratory efforts are indelibly a feature of professional norms (and librarianship cannot be so characterized), individuals and organizations prefer to invest in fully tested products. And furthermore, they want the tests to be developed elsewhere so that when the innovation arrives it is in perfect operating order. The delay can be drawn out until total efficiency has been assured. This is the argument advanced by all who hold off the moment of adaptation interminably since the ideal pattern is never quite within view, but their own retirement is.

A key deterrent to the adoption of the new may be cost. The practical realization of a new idea is often a costly undertaking. The tendency of the organization is to use labor and materials and other resources in ways in which they have always been utilized rather than to experiment. For this reason, libraries do not move with dispatch into specialized information services to new constituencies except when there is available either external funding or special appropriation. It is only the uncommon organization which is prepared to revise its arrangements to deploy existing resources and personnel in new patterns not yet fully tested. The cost of the new idea may be seen to be so great that it simply cannot be afforded. Or else the idea may seem acceptable and appear to have important implications, but the expected returns may not be viewed as commensurate with the investment. But cost arguments may be spurious. Indirect costs often are not reckoned with in naive cost-accounting situations. For instance, the library which opts for sending inquiries for free copies of college catalogs each year and which pays for housing them as alternative to subscribing to a microfiche service simply does not accurately gauge all relevant costs. For it may pay heavily in client dissatisfaction in the face of missing copies.

It is an easier task to get people to do something if doing so appears to entail no loss to them and if, in the consequence of doing it, they are not required to give up anything. For while they may not even think it is especially good, just because it costs them nothing, they are more likely to accept it since it is free. If trying a new product does not commit the user and if he does not have to pay for it, he obviously has nothing to lose. Cost is a relative question. It is related to an individual or an organization's economy of preferences. The cost of a new program must be measured against the overall resource position, the cost of alternatives, and also the pressure of need. Pressure and need are the key words. When an organization desperately needs to do something to adapt itself to new terms, it will be far more prone to accept an innovative prospect, even at a cost. Political consequence of action or inaction must be reckoned. The equation must also include calculations for reconciling the cost of not accepting an innovation. If the perils are seen as great, if the need to be responsive is fully perceived, then the organization must fashion a response even at a cost of subtracting something from ongoing commitments.

Some innovations are received more readily than others because they are viewed as providing a material advantage. The advantages may be direct or subtle. Some innovations are accepted because they give priority over someone else. This is most pronounced in competitive fields. Sometimes novelty will give political advantage to those who embrace it. Library automation reflects this. Application of technology is thought to be reflective of the disposition of the library or of its administration to move forward. The effect may be calculated to offer an image of modernity and contemporary understanding. This is precisely the explanation for widespread acquisition of computers in business and government before they had been programmed effectively to provide efficient and economic return. The lure of prestige may be as attractive as material advantage.

New usage makes performance demands upon those who adhere to it. It is inevitable that such requirements are seen as a central consideration in determining whether or not to accept new practice. Those changes which require prolonged effort to master are at a competitive disadvantage with alternatives which do not make such demands. For the difficulty of individual or organizational relearning is a powerful obstacle to change, no matter how desirable. Change demands personal and human response which must first overcome the constraints of habit. Still another deterrent to acceptance of innovation is the fear of adverse public reaction in the form of ridicule or blame from clients or sponsors. The converse may operate even more powerfully. The nonacceptance of innovation at a time when all the pressures militate for change can make the unresponsive suffer consequences just as great as the penalties imposed on those who act too soon.

THE INNOVATOR CHARACTERIZED

In many instances the innovative type wants what he cannot obtain. Such an individual may come to view himself as responsible for establishing an unattainable kind of aspiration. Yet this does not prevent him from being frustrated and even refusing to relinquish the impossible or unrealistic. There are such perfectionists in every field. Doubtless librarianship has its share. Professional problem solvers of many kinds repeatedly and deliberately set goals for themselves which keep them and others moving forward in a cycle of never-ending frustration, and yet of continuing accomplishment. Oftentimes, the frustrated individual feels that his level of aspiration is imposed upon him by circumstances, but still he feels he must strive for nothing less. Such aspiration may be the consequence of group conventions, but far more often they arise out of an individual's personal history, perhaps even from a sense of divine prescription.

Some of those who fashion innovation derive their formulas by consciously inquiring into the wants or needs of others. They strive to discern and perhaps even to invent wants where none exist. Under such terms, the inventor voluntarily assumes the role of needer of information and calculates a strategy or tool which will be useful to the hypothetical client. The same strategy for developing a product and matching it with a client where none had existed is employed in marketing. Motivationally, such a capacity is a correlate of entrepreneurial propensity since it is proactive rather than reactive. I believe that, in the main, people attracted to the library profession are reactive types and that this explains why the invention of novel information services in librarianship remains uncommon.

Some innovations arise as one group or one individual will equate with another and project into the behavior of that class. The imitator will sense what this group requires or prefers. This is frequently the stance of the academic librarian and, when managed adroitly, may lead to implementing new ideas and services. But such a performance is by no means assured. The academic librarian may perceive himself as colleague, enjoying a climate of comparable interest with faculty, a client himself, not a professional or administrative functionary.

Disciplinary preparation may influence the propensity to innovate. For instance the fundamental method of humanistic scholarship is book-based. If one is schooled to perceive the existence of a strong book collection as the paramount good in which a library traffics, it would likely be this value more than any other which propels behavior. Thus the enthusiasm and zeal of the professional contribution would receive strongest impetus here, with the book collection the locus of innovative advance. Yet the technological and problem-solving disciplines indoctrinate new entrants to a different persuasion, wherein information may take other forms and arrangements. The emphasis on collection building and attendant record-keeping problems, rather than on innovative services, might thus be explained by the disproportionate number of librarians who are educated to the values of humanistic rather than technological or behavioral scholarship.

Certain determinants identify the characteristics of those who are more likely to be innovative. Perhaps the most apparent is a lack of defensiveness. Such an individual demonstrates also a kind of freedom from rigid ideological constraints. There is the capacity for tolerating a high degree of ambiguity, where there is ambiguity in the potential explanations for phenomena, so that conflicting information can be received without distress. The innovative individual is self-evaluative so that his contribution is not necessarily based upon the praise of others, but on a need to satisfy his own standard. This does not preclude the judgment of others, but the appraisal process is more nearly one of a realization of his own potential. Lack of rigidity implies the ability to deal spontaneously with conflicting elements, to reconstruct them in new relationships and to transform from one form to another without feeling constrained. It is out of such processes that the creative design is shaped. Such processes are the antithesis of the drive toward routinization which characterizes organizational forms and the bureaucratic mentality—and often libraries and librarianship.

An innovation has far less appeal for those who enjoy the benefits of presently existing alternatives than for those who do not enjoy such prerogatives. Put in a library context, this would suggest that if a novel program were to be established in a public library, it is likely that the individuals who have been enjoying the previous program would be less attracted to the innovation than those who had not. They would more closely consider how or whether the innovation encroached upon their interests. Nor does this necessarily suggest that the more likely acceptor is the one who is dissatisfied. It implies only that, for whatever reason, he does not get the satisfactions from a situation that others in the culture do. In contrast with others, he is unsatisfied. He may simply not know that any alternative exists until the time when it is made available. Unserved elements of library constituencies in public and academic settings might fit these terms.

Acceptability of new designs is related to the individual's conception of himself, as a consequence of experience. To predict potential for the acceptance of new constructs would thus call for knowledge of the specific human being. Many accept innovation because their peers do, because they are convinced by an eloquent spokesman or by their own personal assessment of the utility of the idea. Others stand against an idea they may like, as has already been mentioned, simply because of its sponsorship. In some individuals dissatisfaction may be a pervasive cast of mind which colors their view of large sectors of the culture. Such a disposition may have had its origins in disappointments in life, indoctrination, or prolonged disillusionment. And it may be consciously or unconsciously bred by the unexpressed ideology of a discipline which induces docility, passivity, or marginal expectation in its members. Still no one is completely or persistently an accepter or a rejecter; he is simply more or less so with reference to a specific idea.

The overpowering potential of an idea, an ideology, may be seen to sway many, given the proper climate and the proper spokesman and the proper timing. For any given idea, the incidence of acceptance may be high or low. But there will always be some who lag behind others in giving their approval to it and some who perhaps never do and never will. There are recalcitrants in every sphere; the essential task is one of finding the proper levers to manipulate in order to ensure acceptance from all but the most unwilling. For there are relenting as well as diehard conservatives, slow and reluctant as well as quick and eager accepters. The lesson of recent months on college campuses has abundantly demonstrated that it takes relatively few to provoke change and that those at either extreme who doggedly remain there need not be drawn to a particular side in order for action to be furthered.

Further Personality Dimensions Related to Change

Insight into change propensity is facilitated by the categorization into ideal types advanced by social psychology in an attempt to explain organizational behavior. Here we rely upon the constructs employed by Bass and others as the point of departure.[7] The rational, objective advocate of change may be characterized as one who responds to pressure for change within the organizational context and does so based upon information and a carefully plotted strategy of evaluating the information. Such individuals may be seen to respond favorably to pressures for change from outside the discipline or from outside their own organizations. While they do not initiate change themselves, they are among the first to recognize change proposals and to support the initiators of change once they have fully understood the implications. It is they who will personally test and observe the merit of the new design. It is they who will begin to work committedly to bring about change in their own areas of responsibility.

The radical change advocate bases his point of view primarily upon emotional influence and nonrational appeal. His advocacy of change is complete, dependent entirely upon subjective identification rather than objective analysis. He tends to support change movements almost regardless of whether specific proposals have intrinsic merit or not. He is simply for change for its own sake. Implicit is a view of the failure of existing forms and institutions, with any possible modification seen as potentially promising.

The rational resister opposes change based upon what he presumes to be a genuine, analytic assessment of the facts. Motivation to resist may, at core, reflect a fear of status or prestige loss or reduced influence upon

7. See for example, Bernard M. Bass, *Leadership, Psychology and Organizational Behavior* (New York: Harper & Row, 1959).

the nature of the organization as a consequence of proposed change or even personal pessimism about one's capacity to carry out change effectively. The organizational consequence is that such individuals make it necessary for change advocates to provide an effective rationale and data-based appraisal of the program for change before they can be won over. Thus rational resistance may be seen as a mature response to change advocacy, posing the greatest problem for its advocates. However, by constantly defending the status quo, the rational resister may also hasten the chances of his own defeat, for his survival in the new and modified set of conditions may not be feasible as a direct result of the ardor of his earlier resistance.

Traditionalists resist change simply because they respond conservatively to almost anything which represents a variation from the way things have always been. They cling to traditional practice for its own sake. To return briefly to the radical change advocate, he tends to be a dissident and one who refuses to identify with the conventions of his own group. Such an individual may be a traditional alien, thus inclined almost by definition to be an accepter of change. The characteristic is most often attributed to the young of whatever age, not yet ground down by the weight of experience, years, responsibilities, or shattered illusions or to the attendant cynicism to which these attributes are thought to give rise. To the extent that the disaffected in librarianship may comprise such a group, it is among them that there is the highest proclivity to nonconform and to accept new alternatives, whether in work with the deprived or at the other end of the scale, computer applications. Obviously the dissenter is more likely to be attracted by a new alternative than is the person who is satisfied with custom. That is not the same as saying that the nonconformist will embrace any new alternative, but rather that he is more likely to accept original perspectives on established practice.

Many individuals are prepared to accept new ideas simply because they have never dedicated themselves completely to a custom or to an ideal within the cultural context in which they practice. Thus their receptive attitude to change may not be due to a dislike of existing arrangements, nor can it be said that they fail to participate in them and receive gratification from them. But while they are participants, they tend not to be enthusiastic participants. And, therefore, they do not achieve complete identification with the ideas and the behavior expected of them, nor even experience lasting satisfaction from them. As a consequence, they tend to be more open-minded and objective than are their opposites, the traditionalists or rational change resisters who are committed, and who have committed themselves, to ongoing practice. Receptivity to new ideas and to novelty may correlate somewhat with tenure of professional indoctrination, but mere youth itself does not automatically equate with openness to experience of the unknown or the untested.

An important difference between passive and active participation is seen in the difference between wanting something to happen and even appreciating it when it does and wanting to bring it about oneself. Perhaps the distinction rests upon personal preference and personal tolerance, and even upon the differentiation of emotional and rational predisposition. This is somewhat akin to individuals recommending certain things but not practicing these things themselves. The active participant is a protagonist for his ideology, and he is therefore ready to perpetuate and to defend his interest in it. On the other hand, passive acceptance is apparent in attitudes displayed toward many new ideas, and it is sometimes possible to avoid objection so long as no pressure is placed upon the accepting individuals to practice the ideas. Many will tolerate it if, in their opinion, only a few are foolish enough to want to have it. Some libraries may well illustrate this point.

Laissez-faire organizations offer an open climate for the proliferation of new designs within them. For if the organization does not restrict the performance of an individual, it becomes possible for him to accept and introduce innovative ideas once he understands there is tolerance for such activity. The indifferent organization is like the indifferent individual. Since organizational indifference is reflected in general passivity, this very condition may provide the widest opportunity for the introduction of variation. For while an organizational ethos may not be strongly and firmly behind the notion of innovation, its very neutrality can serve as fruitful seedbed for such modification. It is only required that those who would bring it about are unmolested in their efforts to advance changes. Conversely of course, such an environment holds potential for negative or dysfunctional action as well.

Behavior can change and does. Some start out by being active participants in their organizational lives and later acquire a distaste for it. Some experience a change from positive to negative attitude as a result of the effect of personal events. The cause of estrangement may be either a definite situation or be more complex and the result of a cumulative sequence of events. It is not always possible to distinguish between the individual who has achieved and repudiated his identification with an ideology and the one who has never identified himself with it at all. It is the difference between disaffection and dissension. Because organizational crisis, when it is clearly perceived, affects both those who respect the status quo and those who are less constrained by tradition, acceptance and tolerance for new measures is possible among all. For very sick human beings and very sick organizations, when they understand that this is their condition, are obviously more likely to try unfamiliar remedies than are others. Human beings and human organizations are predisposed to act in accord with their own self interest and their vacillation in the face of change can be an opportunistic strategy. For they are attracted and they are repelled, they accept and they reject, in accord with their own immediate situation.

The most highly valued goals for individuals who seek change reach this value possibly because they are viewed as attainable by only the limited few who come to share them. Many play out their organizational lives by accepting their place within the structure, but there are others who feel unfairly treated and never quite accept their assignment and the lesser rewards consequent upon it. Their dissatisfaction arises not because they object to the values of the culture, but because they are personally denied esteem within it. They are distinguishable from the indifferent in that they are not uncaring, but simply have not made it. So they will tend to be negative about their roles and jealous of those who are in more favored positions. When they are resigned to their fate they become indifferent, but when they are not, they may well be receptive to change. For the prospect of change may be seen to equalize opportunity or to affect them in such a way that they may enjoy a more opportune relationship with those who have been their superiors. Perhaps this explains in part the attraction of union activity among those in the professional ranks of librarianship who have not successfully negotiated the normal career structure. For the union may even be perceived as a strategic device for catapulting such individuals into situations which attract attention to them, ultimately influencing their shift into the regular hierarchical structure at a more advanced level, at the point where they may be ready to be coopted. Unlike the indifferent, the resentful individual may be more susceptible to the suggestion of change because he has nothing to lose by accepting and, in extreme cases, everything to gain.

Those who perceive themselves as members of the more privileged groups have a clear-cut interest in the existing system in which they thrive and therefore will resist change which might deprive them of their advantage. Any change which might threaten the social, economic, or political prerogatives which they enjoy would be unwelcome. Consequently, pronounced organizational adaptation, and certainly organizational reconstruction, holds little appeal for them although it may be very attractive to the dissident, the disaffected, and even the indifferent, who may hope for rewards denied them under existing conditions. To attempt to explain and to correlate change propensity with sex at this time[8]

8. These words were written on the eve of "The Women's Strike for Equality," the fiftieth anniversary of the women's suffrage movement in America.

is most hazardous. Yet one or two important points are germane to the present discussion, particularly when it is related to what can only be characterized as a male-dominated female profession. The issue relates to the degree of restraint or freedom to act imposed upon members of one sex compared with the freedoms and prerogatives afforded to the other. What is true for the culture at large is as true in the professional context. Conservatism or activism may be seen as a question of which sex appears to have an advantage and which one wants to get it. Thus women may be more receptive to change than men in one situation and just the reverse in another. Men, however, seem always to have been contracting agents in the transmission of new ideas except, perhaps, for those which pertain exclusively to women. Men have, of course, had the greater opportunity, not only to observe and to adopt new ideas pertaining specifically to male behavior, but also to exercise options in interpreting and accepting those changes which affect them. This may explain why the males are so much in evidence in library professional meetings, while the women, disproportionate to their numbers, tend to remain back in the library. To the extent that men, by virtue of the traditions open to their sex, come to have greater familiarity with individuals in other settings, they have been first and more frequent to accept imported ideas since they have access to them and learn about them faster than women. Still the common feminine propensity for the new is a far more pronounced disposition toward change than the well-known masculine tendency to cling passionately to familiar ways.

Change takes place more readily when those who were once satisfied become dissatisfied. This will happen either because of personality requirements or because of the external environment. A genuinely persuasive advocate can influence someone to accept a new idea even though that individual thought he was happy with the one he had. Moreover, a new idea, expressed in superior performance, can impress itself upon human beings who had no reason to complain about that which would be replaced by the new. Yet the dissatisfied individual is seldom an indiscriminate accepter. Only uncommonly can it be said that one who is a malcontent will accept anything from anyone under any conditions. He, just as others, is influenced by the auspices of the innovation, by its meaning and value as he sees them, and this is a matter of how he sees them affecting himself personally.

Individuals may also respond to innovative proposals not in absolute acceptance or rejection, but in some degree of one or the other. Propensity to accept change is thus not necessarily an either-or proposition, but may be seen relatively. One may be rigid, and resist change in specific instances. Or one may be dogmatic, which is to resist any change in the total system of beliefs. That mind which is not open, through fear of the new, is a passive mind. Such a mind achieves its systematic character through the efforts of an external authority rather than its own. Dogmatic thinking refers to a total cognitive configuration of ideas and beliefs which are organized into a relatively tight and closed system. Rigidity, on the other hand, identifies the difficulties of overcoming single beliefs encountered in attacking, solving, or learning specific tasks or solving new problems. One can be rigid without being dogmatic, dogmatic without being rigid. The individual totally identified with a particular line of thinking may not only resist some kinds of change dogmatically, but may change very easily when the authority upon which he is dependent does or says something to influence him. If the source of authority is a national professional association, the American Library Association for example, one might postulate that the most dogmatic would not shift their stance until the association had expounded its views. This would undoubtedly be less pronounced in matters relating to the affairs of a scientific discipline than in those characterized by ideology of a political, social, or religious nature.

The obvious pitfall in all the hypotheses which build upon individual psychological differences to explain change propensity is that they do so at the expense of the situational determinants of behavior. A complete concern with personality ignores the importance of the context. On the other hand, a concern centered solely upon the context leaves the observer embarrassed at not understanding individual differences. It may be as justified to criticize the one-sidedness of personality approaches to political and professional issues as to deplore the pondering of situational factors without calculating personality into the equation. A reasonable position would appear to accept the notion that even while a person's belief system is a relatively fixed and enduring structure, the extent to which it will influence behavior and the extent to which it is either an open or closed system at a particular point in time will be jointly influenced by situational factors and by personality traits. The individual who plays out a role in an organizational drama is as much politician as he is personality. Thus the realities of the organizational and cultural condition may be as prominent in influencing his behavior as the determinants of his own nature. It is to these conditions that our attention will be drawn next.

CHAPTER 3

Bureaucracy and Professionalism as Change Issues

Since organizational structure provides the framework in which change is treated hospitably or not, the differences in the formal arrangements for work may be seen to influence change propensity. In an organization characterized by centralization of authority and responsibility, latitude in decision processes is foreclosed to those in lower-level positions. The consequence is conforming and noncreative response throughout the organization. The decentralized structure provides the prospect for greater scope in the decision process through its emphasis upon problem solutions at different hierarchical levels, closer to the environments which act upon and are acted upon by the programs. Delegation of authority in the decentralized power mechanism affords broader latitude to those who can thus more swiftly shift formulas in response to environmental dictates. This is why a specific public library branch or a departmental library in the university may frequently be a spawning place for creative departure from institution-wide sameness. Even under such terms, because the central repository of power will so seldom relinquish its control, there is proscription governing many organizational arrangements in order to ensure standardization and routinization, particularly in matters of procedure, cost, and personnel. The latitude in selecting and implementing alternatives is reduced, and the innovative potential of the decentralized unit is constrained. Still, with a tendency for the decentralized distribution of decision making authority, creativity and innovation may far more nearly be perceived, and thus chanced, if the mandate is responsiveness to performance rather than to administrative imperative.

In the marginal organization, the slack needed to absorb the costs of any but the most modest adaptation in design is frequently absent. The more limiting the financial or human constraints, believed or real, the less favorable the climate for innovation. In some ways the mythology of penury serves to assuage the conscience of those who prefer to see options foreclosed; their energies must then be dedicated to immediate needs and safe programs since there is no money to do otherwise. If resources are severely restricted, there will be only limited organizational tolerance for chance-taking behavior. Although, under such terms, there is not much to lose either! One might assume that the large, well-financed program would be less constrained toward new departures because its regular day-to-day activity would remain adequately supported, and the testing of innovative ideas should not normally impinge upon such activity. Yet the most imaginative ideas are not necessarily born in the large, well-financed institutions. The untested, the novel idea, often comes into being simply to test its utility and value in a marketplace. The larger and more secure enterprise, in its self-consciousness, may be reluctant to put itself to the test. However, the large organization has the money without which experiments might be difficult to support. With some extra resources risk-taking comes to be seen as a more legitimate expectation. This is particularly true when the cultural terms make the chancing of new alternatives the only feasible route to perpetuating the institutional form. Some see this as the present condition of the public library.

In those organizations in which the principal business is conducted by members of a self-conscious profession unhabituated to risk-taking behavior, where the professional ethos is an economy of scarcity rather than abundance, the norms are preset in such a way that every experiment must smack of success. There can be no talk of failure, since success means that institutional resources were well used and that those responsible for these resources have not misappropriated. This is one explanation for the fact that much of the literature of librarianship is an unending recital of the testimony of success and does not document the projects that failed.

As there is little slack in institutions in the present stringent economy, there is only the most limited risk-taking mandate perceived, and consequently the slimmest prospect for innovative response. Yet paradoxically, it is precisely when constraints are imposed by the environment that the adaptation and alteration are most desperately needed. The alternative may be even more marginal existence. Just as corporate advertising budgets are reduced in recessions and, in consequence, further limit market potential, so service organizations may reinforce their own marginality by subsisting in unchanging ways when resources are cut back.

Within the constraints of the bureaucratic form, and perhaps because of such constraints, organizations develop accommodations which provide a limited kind of tolerance toward those who incline to a variable view of the organization's contribution. The king's jester poked fun at the court and the kingdom; even the public university can tolerate a Marxist. Thus organizations tend to be tolerant of such individuals so long as they are few in number and can be observed. Moreover, the authority configurations of organizations in fields where it is necessary to ensure a stream of innovative advances may legitimatize creative, questioning roles by forming departments with the mandate to provoke and to stimulate alternative answers to organizational problems. In so doing, they facilitate the inventiveness of those who ensure the steady flow of intellectual and technological output without which organization's continuity would be less assured. Furthermore, through compartmentalization, innovative effort is coopted to the purposes of the organization, and creative propensities are thereby channeled into tolerable organizational forms. There is small danger, then, that the whole organization, or any but those elements clearly designated for this purpose, will become the seedbed of alternative strategies. Seen negatively, this puts the innovative destiny of the organization in the hands of a specified few. The pitfalls are apparent. Where such talents are scarce, and during periods of high mobility and institutional auctioning for such services, in-progress designs became highly vulnerable as individuals are lured to competitive institutions. A more basic drawback, however, is the fundamentally mistaken thesis that one individual or one group in isolation, without the immediacy of regular and intensive immersion in the organization's problems and external environment, can succeed in shaping innovative strategy sufficient for moving forward effectively in response to changing needs. The view allows an organization the comfortable but false illusion that it is satisfying its needs once it has provided bureaucratic accommodation for perceiving them. Moreover, when such responsibilities are wholly vested in those encouraged to see themselves as the mainstay of the organization's innovative thrust, the natural tendency will be to narrow the range of their concerns, to seek out opportunities in which the risks are far more limited than if they were to give free rein to imagination. As such individuals are identified and identify themselves as organizational problem-solvers, it will often be likely that the immediate needs of the organization receive highest priority. In consequence, the broader, the more fundamental, the less obvious conditions will go unnoticed and unattended as the organization falsely assumes otherwise.

A paradox of the organizational culture is that the act of creativity tends to be the reserved domain of a limited few—those who manage or those charged with the design or research and development function.

The largest proportion of those engaged in organizational efforts are simply expected to conform, to carry out the ritual without originality or creative question. The conformity norms of organizations mirror the pervasive cultural tendency. In private life just as in organizational life, to be original, to be different, may be perceived as a somewhat dangerous stance. Yet when the rate of change is at an incredible rate, to merely conform may well be to invite destruction. For the problem of the organization as the problem of man is to adapt to the new cultural condition lest the traditional program and services be swept aside as irrelevant in the face of contemporary requirements. While it is in the organizational context that originality and innovation are most desperately needed, bureaucratic constraints foreclose such options. The creative role is more often than not displaced to outside the realm of the workaday world. The businessman writes his novel in the evenings; the librarian expresses himself in musical accomplishment or horticulture. The bureaucratic culture seldom allows for the fact that creativity is inspired by man's need to express himself and to demonstrate his potential or that the need to be expressive is often deeply hidden behind many psychological veils which inhibit the individual from identifying his need for such expression. As this is so, the organizational responsibility includes specification of the high occupational and social value of the creative act in the work place. For organizational culture will inspire innovation only when it projects itself as a culture within which new ideas and insights are not only acceptable but encouraged. Yet this posture flies in the face of the ritualistic proposition that organizational effort is measured as quantitative, undifferentiated production aggregates. It is doubtless more nearly true than not that the more original a proposed new idea, the more frequently bureaucracy views it with apprehension or disdain. In a contemporary organizational and cultural context which identifies powerfully in its main thrust with the stereotype, the greater the degree of novelty of any proposed innovative offering, the greater the discomfort provoked by such prospect.

BUREAUCRACY VS. INDIVIDUAL CREATIVITY

The very nature of the bureaucracy provides little support for those behavioral characteristics and conditions which encourage innovation. For as the hierarchical structure is anxiety-producing, it will set such severe limits on the personal security of the individual that the risk of failure is a substantial threat. If failure in the attempt at experimentation punishes the transgressor, then it is hardly worth the personal calamity to be so vulnerable in a culture which best rewards stability. The kind of freedom needed to attempt the new simply cannot thrive. Or if the chancing of new alternatives subjects the innovator to the same tight and rigid measures of observation, control, and evaluation typical of the standard production process, risk-taking behavior may entail such insuperable hazards as to become all but impossible.

Inherent in the hierarchical framework is the vesting of greatest status in the individual at the topmost point of the pyramid. The capacity to influence the organization is not spread among all members and thereby forecloses the easy traffic in ideas which might be construed as the threats of subordinates to managerial structure. Furthermore, stress upon specialization as an additional consequence of bureaucratic arrangement concentrates expertise in a very narrow sense. The particular capacity of the generalist, who almost by definition may be naive about specific operational details but nonetheless genuinely creative in posing novel questions about an entire process, receives small recognition. There are few generalists in bureaucracy, and their perspectives are inevitably suspect. Indeed, for the nonexpert to counsel in technical processes and processing strategy in a library may be considered as rude as for the citizen informed only through the media to question the purpose of the war in Vietnam.

Hierarchical structure imposes authority lines which are precise. The legitimacy of conflict is ruled out in a system which does not even recognize the possibility, although it is only through conflict that problems are genuinely revealed. But because conflict implies the possibility of pluralistic perspectives, it is seen as potential prelude to the dispersion of hierarchical authority in power and so is intolerable. Just as bureaucracy concentrates power and authority and thus delimits the potential for objective difference, so does it reduce or squelch the capacity for innovative contribution. If surface conflict is suppressed, hostilities are played out in ways which do not publicly bare tension or distress. And the culture of libraries and other organizational forms remains invariably one of good manners and superficial gentility.

To achieve success within the constraints of the bureaucratic form is to behave in ways which do not threaten the authority base. The ideal cast of mind of the bureaucratic man is a conservative orientation, since novel responses to problems are a threat to the existing order. The safest pattern of behavior is then that which conforms. Yet conformity is the precise opposite of innovation. To achieve creative contribution, the individual is required to concentrate less upon negotiating his way carefully through the success structure and more to center his zeal upon those activities which give him intrinsic as much as extrinsic rewards for achievement. But the organizational structure is basically concerned with power and status, equally as with organizational attainment, and there political ends are always in evidence. Even the organizational entity specifically set up to spawn new design achieves an acceptability rate for its product which is congruent with such reality.

Bureaucratic structure facilitates the means whereby particular departments seek out their own identification, effectively competing with others within the same organization in ways sometimes marked by passionate internecine rivalry. Hostility between the catalog and the reference departments is comparable to the infantry-paratroop rivalries. The units of work are clearly delimited and differentiated; the organizational boundaries drawn. In consequence, the purpose of the entire organization may be dismissed or lost sight of as such jurisdictional battles rage. Further, since the specialization of function which specialized units facilitate may result in increased productivity, fundamental questions about the absolute efficiency or net contribution of organizational units may be ignored. Sometimes defenses against these perils are found in the devising of units with overlapping responsibilities in which there is a deliberate organizational obfuscation of the line of responsibility for given problems. President Roosevelt may have displayed imaginative creativity in a cabinet structure on just such a political model, but whether it represents the ideal solution to jurisdictional differences between catalog and reference departments awaits the revelations of a statesman of librarianship.

Innovation requires acceptance of the individual and his ideas regardless of his status. It is only when an individual is less apprehensive about his own security that he can be what he aspires to be, attempt what he aspires to attempt. This is virtually impossible in an organization grounded in status differences as a consequence of hierarchical placement. Moreover, in an innovative culture the process of external evaluation is ideally held to an absolute minimum, once again antithetical to bureaucratic norms of exact productive measure. An atmosphere which is evaluative and measured tends to intrude upon freedom of options and to introduce constraints and pressures inimical to the exploration of original alternatives. For evaluation carries with it potential threat, conditions a defensive posture, closes down upon openness of experience through chance or opportunity. The very judgments imposed by external standards, too heavy-handed, too precise, too soon, can stringently delimit and desensitize the striving toward creative or innovative performance.

The repugnance of innovation to bureaucrats is often seen in the way in which they only most reluctantly allocate resources to attempt new designs. To tamper with resource allocation within the rationally formed organization by seeking that which has not yet been proved to contribute to the organization is considered questionable behavior. Attempting innovation and the chancing of resources in the process may be more a matter of attitude than of availability of resources. But in any event, the cost-conscious ethos, the evaluative devices of accounting and scientific management, while enhancing efficiency and rationality in the production process, may equally be seen to constrain creative effort.

Still the new organization or the newly reconstructed one may condition bureaucratic norms to allow a climate which encourages a high-level creativity. Innovative perspectives engender the type of internal competition which facilitates functional responses. Creative leadership attracts peers who share the values of novelty and the heightened pace of organizational action. When organizations are young or small and bureaucratic lethargy does not yet dampen creative ardor, problem-solving is seen as the most highly valued form of behavior. The dilemma of the bureaucratic form is seen in the attempt to conserve momentum once leadership charisma, original enthusiasm, and the creative flow which arises from its inspiration give place to scale and ritual and the state of organizational equilibrium which ultimately comes to pass. Without the most remorseless passion and zeal to assure its perpetuation, the earlier condition seldom persists. And organizational reality seldom equates with the romantic memory of days when the institution was in its stride.

PROFESSIONALISM VS. BUREAUCRACY

The capacity of the bureaucratic organization to be innovative is, at least in some measure, enhanced by its potential for structuring itself along lines which give place to the professional contribution. Because professional values call forth a set of internalized considerations which are reflected in the behavior and the norms inherent in the profession rather than in the bureaucratic form, members of full-fledged or aspiring professions tend to enjoy a high degree of autonomy of work, both as to the process and as to the purposes of their occupational role. Professional contribution and development may thus be as much a measure of success as hierarchical attainment, and for this reason evaluation by the discipline, in some ways, is viewed to be as significant or more so than organizational acceptance. In the ethos of those disciplines wherein research and intellectual productivity are important benchmarks, high professional values are accorded to the advancing of new ideas and to the introduction of new knowledge. However, there is great variability among the different bureaucratized professions in supporting such values; librarianship for one has yet to display that it honors contributions which are deserving of recognition as much along peer lines as in the local institutional context. Until the disciplinary culture, reinforcing of and inculcating an innovative bent, supersedes narrow production goals in the calculation of professional contribution, innovative zeal remains in conflict with organizational norms.

There is no professional ideal at sharper variance with the institution than the ideal in organizational relationships. Inherent and basic is the conflict between the bureaucratic view of employer-employee terms governed by hierarchical norms and the disciplinary model of a professional class which is self-monitoring, subject to performance standards which arise in response to peer-derived measures. To the extent that bureaucracy succeeds in a preoccupation solely with its own affairs, with little attention paid to the broad sweep of events and the ideology of the discipline, the capacity for innovation is inevitably constrained. The lethargy of any number of libraries which might be so characterized affords ample evidence for this thesis. The Chicago Public Library of the 1960s perhaps serves as a striking case in point.[1]

In an earlier period, the technology and organizational processes were so simple that managers could master all. Thus it was seen as fitting that power and responsibility throughout the organization would be closely held.

As the substantive and technical content of work grows more complex, the professional effort is predetermined less by the organization than by individual technical capacity. Professionalization tends toward the inspiration of new roles and relationships; individuals who have specialized functions are no longer perceived simply as interchangeable parts. Thus professionals tend to develop associations which protect the integrity of their work and their standards from the encroachment of organizational authority and that bias toward local opportunism which flies in the face of professional standards and values. To the degree that professionals are oriented toward their work and toward their discipline rather than to their particular local situation, their reputations and recognition are based upon evaluations of a more subtle order. In this manner, professionalism is a potential countervailing alternative to bureaucracy. It tends to be pluralistic and collegial rather than autocratic and hierarchical. When these two patterns are drawn together within a

1. The need for change in this instance received abundant testimony in Lowell A. Martin, *Library Response to Urban Change: A Study of the Chicago Public Library* (Chicago: American Library Association, 1969).

single organization numbering a variety of specialists, as is the case in libraries, basic changes in management practices become inevitable. The social system resulting from a marriage of control elements should be pluralistic, since there is more than one source of authority, loyalty, and command and thus negotiation and compromise are far more requisite. However, this calls for a more drastically revised perspective on personnel arrangements and upon power than is yet the case in many of the organizational forms which employ professional personnel. In librarianship, there are only isolated instances of such experimentation with authority structure.[2]

Still, professionalism is not an organizational good without limits. Another side of the coin perpetuates the protectionism of the medieval guild and forcefully protects entry from interlopers who have not been indoctrinated in the process professional ritualism demands. Entry barriers exclude the uncredentialed who may well have contributions to make to institutional purposes. Or, when tolerating competitors, the institution may consign them to an organizational limbo which receives neither the rewards nor the status inherent in the position of the true initiate. Those in such ambiguous roles in libraries at present may include systems analysts, subject bibliographers, and community workers. Even more ironic, at the very time when the aspiring professions (librarianship is one) are straining for bureaucratic tolerance to adapt to the peer evaluation systems of other disciplines, the evidence of the times is that such devices may be as faulty as hierarchical review. The most dramatic illustration, and the one which academic librarians long so desperately to emulate, is the review system of teaching faculties which leads to tenure. The dysfunctional consequences of the tenure system, a product of peer evaluation, have long been known to include all the syndromes which assured permanency spawns. But the issue which fixes tenure decisions at storm center on a growing number of campuses is the fact that the value commitments shared by the professional peer cult do not necessarily coincide with those of an increasingly vociferous constituency—the students. Because the evaluative criteria may sometimes be in direct conflict, the sanctity of peer review is threatened, and new models may be born. For the emergent professions, not yet fixed rigorously into a single pattern, the challenge is to derive a new scheme which leapfrogs from hierarchical evaluation over the stage of peer

2. The Cornell University Library appears to be one place where such ideology of professionalism is being evolved. See "Report of the Committee on Continuing Education and Professional Growth," *Cornell University Libraries*, August 1969; also David Kaser, "Modernizing the University Library Structure," *College and Research Libraries*, July 1970, pp. 227–231.

evaluation and into the next form. To soar successfully this far would be to transcend both the narrow limits of bureaucracy and the self interests of professionalism, and to arrive at a type of postprofessional evaluative device which invites, in the same method of review, both client judgment and peer assessment.

In those disciplines where members are permitted to practice only after they have acquired a shared knowledge base and a shared set of assumptions and ethics, there is inevitably more autonomy in the work setting. The true professional is allowed to use his judgment to make decisions which affect the work of the organization. Thus professional attitudes and values may be seen to influence the behavior of individuals within organizations in important ways. Still the work situation controls the degree to which professionals can be autonomous. In the most highly professionalized fields, the professional is subject far more to his own than to external monitors. In others, which have more normally functioned within the institutional setting—social work, education, and librarianship would be illustrative—professionals are seen most typically as employees subject to organizational requisites. The effect is for professional performance to give place to extensive organizationally derived requirements which may negatively affect the professional contribution. At issue is the integrity of the discipline and its legitimacy as a profession. The evidence for librarianship, albeit limited, suggests that in spite of a high sense of personal identity with the aspirations of the field, the reference points for the occupational group stem from the national organization as the authority base, rather than from any fundamental belief in self-regulation.[3] If there is conflict between local bureaucratic prescription and association standards, it is a salient issue for librarians, while possible encroachment upon their own professional prerogatives is seldom a burning issue.

Those attitudes which look toward a national association or a local bureaucracy as authority bases tend to be a function of the socialization process which takes place both during professional education for librarianship and in the work place itself. Libraries and library education are infinitely more reinforcing of bureaucratic and associational authority than of individual professional integrity, capacity, and disciplinary concern.[4]

It is true that organizational structure renders professional activity

3. See Richard H. Hall, "Professionalization and Bureaucratization," *American Sociological Review*, February 1968, pp. 92–104.
4. These issues are considered at length in Mary Lee Bundy and Paul Wasserman, "Professionalism Reconsidered," *College and Research Libraries*, January 1968, pp. 5–26.

feasible and that without it the option to practice would be effectively foreclosed. But more critical is the inherent negative consequence of conflict between a potential professional contribution, contribution as innovating force and an employing organization concerned with and committed to the perpetuation of organizational values. The librarian in his bureaucracy, like the teacher in his, functions in an environment which seldom solicits or rewards innovation. Librarians are rewarded for keeping accurate records, maintaining their areas of concern in tidy fashion, and exuding gentility and orderliness while not threatening the status quo. The role definition which an individual ascribes to himself under these terms is not to be that of designer of strategy, but rather of performer of set tasks laid out within a hierarchical structure of proscriptive limits. If this is how one understands his function, if this is how one behaves in response to it, then he sees himself not as professional practitioner but more nearly as minor functionary. This is how he is perceived by others who are less subject to self-delusion about the importance of minor clerical tasks. In consequence, those with innovative potential who might be drawn to the field are turned away and libraries change little except in minor ways.

To the extent that professionalism represents an alternative control to bureaucracy, it has potential in counterbalancing the authority ethos. The negative aspect of professionalism inculcates values which are often retrogressive, self-serving, and protective and which reduce the capacity of the discipline to respond to crisis. Perhaps the most dramatic current illustration is medicine's reluctance to support universal government medical insurance. The consequence may be seen in an alienation from the rest of society.

With increased complexity of information and information processes, to remain viable in the professional role calls for continuous growth in personal understanding and for greatly broadened perspectives of disciplinary responsibility. Yet library professionalism tends more often to reinforce narrow perspectives to protect itself as it is and to draw an ever-shrinking circle around its area of proprietary concern. Indeed, the very process of indoctrination which stems from an educational sequence terminal in nature reassures the credentialed that they are fully equipped for lifetime roles.

To the degree that professionalism retains for itself prerogatives and forecloses such options to others, professionalism may even inhibit the bureaucracy. This may be precisely the result of requiring libraries to screen out individuals who possess ability but did not enter the field according to the usual educational route. This is a direct effect of professional pressures upon organizations to adhere to association standardization devices; the Master of Library Science degree from an accredited library school being one such device. The cynicism of this professional stance is even more pronounced when there is a scarcity of individuals with uncommon and much-needed skills and within a discipline in which the most widely recognized "in-joke" is how much of a farce most library education is. The capacity to deny place in the professional ranks reinforces the insulation of those who already have professional status; they do not perceive their own need to learn. For instance, professional protectionism is the cloak of academic librarians seeking shelter from the new technology or media, and of the city librarian unwilling or unable to attract nontraditional clienteles.

Another dimension of the same syndrome overstates the need for expertise in a particular work role resulting often in the placing of librarians in clerical roles. Such zealous application of professional control results in the placement of many in activities for which they are overskilled and overeducated. This is as much a drain on organizational capital in libraries as in other organizational forms. Related to this are the protective constraints placed upon a particular work role. A jealous professionalism guards against intrusion by others into overlapping zones of interest as in admonishing any but librarians to assist clientele. Professional aspirations might more legitimately consist of an insistence upon enlarging the role potential of professional positions in order to utilize fully individual educational preparation and imagination. But it is relatively easy to specify limits; to influence an occupation self-consciously clutching at professional recognition to behave in ways more in keeping with the responsibilities of professionalism than with its superficially perceived rewards, is a far more difficult task. The problem is most acute at a time when many in the disciplinary ranks, much as they bewail the limits of their present condition, are quite comfortably fixed in the situation as it is and do not seem to relish different alternatives. Ultimately, cost-conscious management perceives the incongruities and speculates about the means of alleviating the condition. If the consequence is not to be a profession denatured, left to a class of low-level functionaries without capacity or vision to fulfill client requirements in meaningful ways, more responsive and responsible professionalism must be called forth.

CHAPTER 4

Strategies for Change

From bureaucracy and professionalism, we turn to issues inherent in considering change strategies within specific organizations and disciplines. Once more the design rests upon a foundation drawn from the behavioral sciences, but the discussion extends into librarianship where abstraction may be translated into concrete illustration. Time is the crucial element in the equation of change. Change may appear to happen at once, but it is the result of a continuing process. Awareness of shortcomings comes first, since it is not before then that the change process is set in motion. Even with the recognition of need, time is necessary for calculating strategy. And time is needed to move from strategy to implementation.

There are differences between the way in which change is wrought in a specific organization and in a discipline. The organization identifies first with its own unique problems. Disciplinary thinking is at best a very subtle influence upon local aspirations and thus upon the realignment of priorities. Yet just as the history of an individual organization will condition the nature and the limits of its change potential, so will the traditions of the profession find expression in the choices of the organization. The institution and the profession are thus intertwined. Beyond this, however, local determination is sensitized to the distinctive strains within the organizational form itself, to the administrative echelons, and to the constituencies to which it is responsible.

ORGANIZATIONAL STRUCTURE

Prime responsibility for sensing the cues from all parties in the change process resides with those who hold senior managerial positions. Still, it is seldom that a single individual decides the utility of a process which would justify all the risks which results from a change program. Personal commitment is not enough without some consensual base to help ensure the attainment of sought-for ends. The process of change can be difficult and unpleasant. The costs and the strains must be widely understood, for the power and prestige of the organization alone will not suffice without the support of those who must live with the change. Shared understanding implies a climate in which the reasons and values for considering change are honestly debated. Without such discourse, genuine support is doubtful. The communication process shares information about a potential future which may arouse anxiety among those who will be affected by modification in normal arrangements. To share information honestly is to reduce organizational uneasiness, or at least to bring it into the open where it can be considered rationally and humanely.

The precise specifications for change strategy may be designed by organizational administration. Many organizations, including libraries, rely upon professional consultants to indicate the direction and the formulas for change. But the actual change phenomena in organizations are the consequence of more than carefully contrived plans and procedures. Unanticipated adaptation interrelates with the planned sequence. The climate for change is enhanced when there is pressure for change and perhaps ideally when the pressure is from both inside and outside the organization. The result of such pressure may be the development of a series of ordered stages, with activities involving individuals at every level in the problems at hand. This is the planned part of the process. The unplanned is the way in which this very involvement of individuals can lead to perceptions and strategies which have not been calculated as part of the original design. In this way implementation may be as much influenced by the contribution of those who participate in its prosecution as by the original strategy.

Implicit in the change proposition is the need for modified or adapted roles by some, so as to improve organizational capacity to be responsive. Such role change carries risks which are lessened if there is genuine commitment from the senior level of the organization. It is for this reason that authoritarian inspiration tends to produce favorable response to change dictates. This is the familiar pattern of decree, characteristic of the autocratic organization. Its authority depends on the senior person in an organization who issues ultimata to others at lower levels who are then expected to carry them out. This assumption underlies a strategy of organizational change based upon the replacement approach. Under its terms, individuals are replaced by others who are deemed to have the capacity to implement change which their predecessors did not.

While such cases appear to have been relatively uncommon in librarianship in the past, they are not uncommon now.

A variation on the same theme is to modify the structural arrangements to bring new organizational terms into play. Through the process of altering relationships and the resulting adaptation of power and authority, behavior may be sufficiently affected as to make possible the kind of changes which would have been blocked by the traditional hierarchical form. The group or committee problem-solving approach which involves individuals drawn from different hierarchical levels, from line and staff, from technology and service, is one of the devices employed to accomplish this.

A serious problem in deriving change strategy for libraries is the scarcity of analysis needed to differentiate successful from unsuccessful efforts which have already taken place. In librarianship, the incidence of dramatic and major experimentation has been low, and the documentation of failure is virtually nonexistent. Reports of what could most charitably be judged as limited success are invariably described in terms of self-congratulatory testimonial.

Specialists derive their change methodologies by focus upon the levers which they regard as most strategic. Those who concentrate upon organizational issues look to managerial influences and to human relationships. Those oriented heavily to technology approach change from the perspective of the production process. The service-oriented see programs as the key. To shift the terms to the client and to perceive the total process from this vantage point tends to be most uncommon.

More and more the tendencies of the times seem to be moving toward the consensual base in organizational effort and, at least on the surface, even the most authority-oriented institutions appear to be giving ground. With respect to advancing change, there is a question whether an idea deployed against the norm of conformity and the reverence of the status quo stands a chance in a democratic culture where one man has one vote. Or whether, in the still developing professional culture, courageous advocacy in unilateral defiance of a consensus of naysayers may hold out much promise for betterment. The strategy of change calls for a partisanship grounded in determination to alter conditions and so to bring about a new state of affairs—one not always congruent with the ideal of a majority.

The charisma necessary to fire change advocacy in others is exceedingly uncommon in disciplines where leadership magnetism has never seemed requisite to a relatively stable institutional and professional form. Yet without such a spark, change disposition remains uninspired, whether in the advocacy of change by authority or by swaying consensus.

In the classic model the change process is always an approach to equilibrium, in which there is first an unfreezing of an old pattern, then the change to a new one and ultimately the refreezing into a new pattern. The most influential members of the organization must first be attracted by models in the environment which lead to the reconstruction of their perspectives. They will then identify with these models and try to become like them. An alternative is the design of an experimental plan as a means of problem-solving. In the first instance, the change agent identifies with a phenomenon discerned through experience or found elsewhere in the culture. The second addresses the situation through a testing process out of which new attitudes are formulated and new solutions to the problem are explored. Choice in change design may be as much a matter of opportunities perceived and of organizational propensity and tolerance as a function of the personality of the change agent; any or all of these factors may inhibit, prohibit, or further the acceptance of an innovative model or of original formulations.

In the typical model of change the effort is seen normally as a process of power allocation, with the change initiator a senior functionary—perhaps the senior functionary of the organization—and a crucial factor in the change equation. It is he who defines the power arrangements. It is he who exercises control in the organization and who thus enlists support of those sympathetic to change implementation. It is he who designs the program, involving task, people, technology, and frequently other organizational variables. It is he who forms the working team to implement the design, drawing upon capacities of those committed to change and devising the strategy to be used against those who resist adaptation. In the change process itself, goals are reshaped, new alliances formed, and the organization comes to a new state of equilibrium.

The change process has been little studied. Much of the evidence concentrates upon so-called planned changes, brought about in consequence of the utilization of individuals drawn to the organization for the express purpose of influencing change. Typically, planned change tends to occur as a result of managerial judgment and to cluster around problems of efficiency, internal structures, and procedures. But in a time when organizations are subject to more fundamental question than in the past, the lessons of the behavioral literature which focus upon planned organizational change are of only marginal value. For the process of change under revised perspectives of power, of involvement in decision-making by many who have traditionally been kept out, is a very different process. New configurations are being drawn at this time; there are striking changes in the power alignments and in the organizational response to priorities from nontraditional contenders in the decision process. The limits of understanding are reflected in the fact that the analysis, the empirical data, and the models of change have all been scaled to the normal bureaucratic condition.

The more uncommon motivations in influencing the organizational change process have yet to be conceptualized. But what is already clear is that organizations must fashion new designs for survival, if they are to survive, by deriving the terms responsive to shifting needs. The ritual responses of bureaucracy, shaped from patterns imposed by administrative hierarchy, seem inappropriate in the present condition. Commitment to the perpetuation of traditional values is inevitably reasserted, the calculation of change sharply delimited. Under these conditions no viable model can emerge to ensure survival by adaptive accommodation to current needs. If past models of organizational equilibrium and bureaucratic response no longer suffice then, new resources of creative human intelligence must be brought to bear within the context of the organizational and disciplinary setting; the task is to conjure more appropriate mechanisms of change which fully exploit the potential of many more parties at interest than the managerial echelon.

CHANGE DEVICES

In a social context, unlike the sciences, there is little ability to predict the future, virtually none to control it. Here lies potential frustration for those who attempt to emulate the pattern of science in spheres which are more a function of human conditions and aspirations than of physical laws. The impossibility of exactitude in deriving situations, in making forecasts and plans of high reliability, also occasions avoidance of issues, acceptance of limits and, in some cases, stagnation. But to be unable to precisely control the future is not to be powerless in its contemplation. By employing present knowledge it is possible to plot the future, to fashion a framework and a model as the basis for perceiving and influencing events to come.

Reasoned change effort must not await the certainty or exactitude of science, but can rely upon strategies which do exist. Among such devices is the simulation model which replicates in abstraction the realities of the operational context. A variation upon this theme is scenario writing.[1]

1. As with "gaming," the scenario approach to forecasting was first employed in the area of military-political strategy and has been highly developed by such think tanks as the RAND Corporation, Stanford Research Institute, and Hudson Institute. Discussion of its uses and purpose can be found in the writings of Herman Kahn and his associates at the Hudson Institute. See, among others, Herman Kahn et al., *On Escalation: Metaphors and Scenarios* (New York: Frederick A. Praeger, 1965); also Herman Kahn and Anthony J. Weiner, *The Year 2000: A Framework for Speculation* (New York: Macmillan, 1967).

This technique describes a set of conditions in the future not by giving free rein to the imagination but by constructing the picture through a step-by-step unfolding of plausible events which lead to a particular eventuality. Alternative futures are similarly plotted. While such constructions do not predict the future, they demonstrate how it might evolve out of a chain of events which seems reasonable to anticipate. Through the exercise of deriving probable indicators of future developments potential problems are brought to light. What is afforded is a sensitivity to the factors under human control which might be altered so as to adapt to options open to those who make the decisions. To improve the likelihood of understanding the stream of events calls for reliance upon experts who are better able to advise about the prospects of alternative actions because of their perception of the theoretical conditions which will give rise to them. Such efforts have long been employed by individual organizations who engage consultants to aid them in crystallizing their own judgments about the future. What is different in the present strategy is that the activity of exploring possible futures can be institutionalized through bringing together minds focused upon specific alternatives and thus better equipped to weigh the implications of present action for their future effects.

In the utilization of experts, informed advisors can be drawn from different specialties to comment upon distinct aspects of the same problem. Sometimes the discussion of alternatives is a matter of face to face discussion but not always. Debate can be replaced by a program of individual interrogation, in person or by questionnaire, with feedback employed at various stages so that the experts can revise their positions during successive stages of design development. Feedback may incorporate the positions of other respondents as well as questions about choice criteria. The experts are invited to reconsider their initial responses in the light of this new information and to submit a revised prospectus. Ultimately, the summary picture is compiled, and reveals such consensual bases as exist among the participants.[2] To calculate only alternative strategies is to postulate that there *are* alternatives to only a single future outside man's control. By making conscious choices, by influencing the flow of events and resources, it becomes possible to

2. This technique, the so-called DELPHI Method, was used in a recent study by Harold Borko, "Predicting Research Needs in Librarianship and Information Science Education," in American Society for Information Science Conference Proceedings, vol. 7, *Information Conscious Society* (Philadelphia: ASIS, 1970), pp. 27–29. The DELPHI Method was originally outlined by Olaf Helmer and colleagues at the RAND Corporation in the late 1950s. The state of the art is reviewed in Juri Pill, "The DELPHI Method: Substance, Context, A Critique and an Annotated Bibliography," Technical Memo no. 183, Department of Operations Research, Case Western Reserve University, May 1970.

attain, rather, a particular desired future. The utility of such devices is in constructing strategies of social intervention so as to increase the probability of future events, thus in effect, to invent the future.

VALUES RELATED TO CHANGE STRATEGY

The most fundamental questions which impinge upon calculating strategies for change are the same as those which make consensus difficult. There are conflicting values and theories about purposes and goals for organizations as for individuals. To construct a strategy for change, essentially, is to conjure with values different from those which have implicitly conditioned the organizational past. Differences can be extreme for they derive from deeply ingrained feelings. Some illustrations drawn from librarianship may suggest why this is so.

One view is that libraries function best when they aid clients to practice their own rational self-interest in a world which is competitive. Books are made available; people use them, if they choose to, under terms which are meaningful to them. This is opposed to an ideology in which service and unselfishness are the overriding societal goals. Under these latter terms, librarians are enlisted in the service of man and assist him to improve his condition by playing an active and partisan rather than value-neutral role. Conflict in the views of individual freedom and the need for discipline is another such issue. For some it is group effort which provides the power of regulating its individual members, with discipline emerging spontaneously through freedom. For others discipline is a precondition of freedom. The matter of values can be particularized to how the contribution of educational forms is conceived. That is, is the paramount concern the provision of specialized resources needed to sustain the technical, political, and economic order of things; or is it the provision of aid to as many people as possible in order to make them well-rounded human beings? Put somewhat differently, is the existing order of individuals working primarily for monetary reward the highest tenet of a culture, or might educational and informational forms assist in building a new social order, where individuals are seen as useful and important members of the community and where their contributions are a function of this rather than of their own private accumulative success? Even the sense of leisure is seen variously, with a preoccupation for recreation viewed by some as a positive value, and by others as simply the manifestation of hedonistic self-seeking. Libraries are caught up, too, in such value problems as the question of personal privacy and contemplation in competition with the value of mass use and group enjoyment. The consequence of these dilemmas is that in all of the essential views there are alternative value perspectives.

Those who shape institutional strategies are not even in agreement about whether the difference in opinion is valuable, to say nothing of whether reinforcing the notions of the past or emphasizing reconstructed perspectives is preferable in calculating organizational options. Given such grave complexities, there is an implicit clutching to the static condition. In view of the variety of alternatives which are possible, and which reflect themselves in decision processes about change, the tendency is to make no decision at all. Indecision is then reflected in a kind of drifting in which change comes almost automatically, but cannot be attributed to a calculated design. In this way no one can suffer recrimination for intruding his value perspectives in the formulation of a plan to alter the static state, and adaptations are only of the most gradual variety. Deliberate change calls forth clearly and unequivocally a particular value stance and demands its acting out by the organization. This visibility is often dangerous or repulsive to those who must choose. Yet consciously or no, values inevitably express themselves in the choices that organizations make. A stable social order remains thus only because established values survive. But a changing social context finds itself reflected in the adaptation of organizational values to match those of the culture generally. The reevaluation and redefinition of the organizational situation, however, depends upon the necessary understanding of the changing structure of the society and the changing balance of values in the society. When this is not clear, as it is not yet clear in the cities and universities, those who assume responsibility within these contexts are reluctant to depart from traditional values. The librarian remains undaunted in his concentration upon book collecting, rejects competitive values, or procrastinates against the time when emergent alternative values will be so deeply imbedded in his culture that their adoption is a foregone conclusion.

Fundamental antagonisms develop in value concepts as conditions and times change. In an earlier period, libraries collected books and made them available to their users in an undifferentiated way. The purpose was simply to collect much information and to organize it for use by library patrons. The system was uncomplicated. However, no longer can all the necessary material be easily collected, no longer does it take the same form, no longer is it so obvious that there is equal access. More sophisticated perceptions of how organizational arrangements and locations inhibit or facilitate use inevitably comes to be drawn into the equation of personal and institutional values; how some are advantaged in consequence of opportunity; how literacy and even perception of the utility of information is so differently enjoyed. Even habits of work are at issue. In an earlier time, the contribution of the librarian was reflected in personal attention and service, in a kind of craftsmanship now uncommon. Contemporary organizational value may inhere more nearly in efficiency, in production aggregates, in detachment and impersonalized relationships—in short, in bureaucratic norms. Yet unresolved is the question of the intrinsic logic of the organizational contribution through individual effort; how or whether traditional values are in conflict with current need; whether a counterweight to the inexorable influence of size and scale must reemerge as the mandate of the true service enterprise.

In modern context a range of disparate value systems are thrust into juxtaposition with each other and there is no easy means of mediating differences, or even the time for assimilating them. In prior periods, accommodation could be a gradual process carried out over time. Such procedures as mediation and assimilation, and ultimately even the devising and construction of new standards of acceptance, were then possible. The dynamic nature of the present makes the variety of responses to the changing environment so great that it is difficult for patterns to emerge with which different parties are equally comfortable. Choices are thus more strained and alternatives more at variance with each other. In the absence of an acceptable mediation process, the values of the past are more likely to be continued without change since they are reassuring and less threatening, particularly to many who have developed under terms which make old values more acceptable. An alternative is seen in a type of crisis-intervention strategy which is brought into play precisely when the system is at the point of disruption and when the dangers of inaction are dire enough to induce genuine aspirations for change. But such a point is exceedingly difficult to predict, especially by those directing the affairs of organizations where to concede crisis is to concede failure. It has been said that a library is at crisis point whenever a single client is dismissed, ignored, evaded, or unrecognized. But to recognize such possibility in a self-conscious discipline with a penchant for self-delusion is to strain professional credulity.

For organizations to perpetuate their values based upon customs which have been blindly accepted no longer ensures continuity of the organizational form. Ultimately institutional value preferences must rest upon debate and discussion, with persuasion the consequence of hearing all who have a stake in the organization's contribution. To innocently profess the value-neutrality of an institution, and thereby to plead for the simple reinforcing of what has gone before, is not sufficient. The logic and morality of program and service which orients to what has been and is, rather than to what may be, has come into question; indeed it is the central question. Evaluations and resultant change strategy are ultimately based upon consent and shared values among those who perform. If there is discord, this is inevitably reflected in programs. The ideal scheme for planning future strategy thus resists choice based solely upon the values of an authoritarian leader or upon a value-free system of competing and unreconciled options. Ideally, there must be focus, yet an organizational culture which is not over regulated. Clearly there is need for a relative degree of certainty, conformity, and continuity, yet not the imposition of value standards from above. The strategy of change in the professional organization thereby negotiates the twilight zone where both authority lines and individual choice are perceived and receive expression.

THE CHANGE CATALYST

In the drama of change the leading player, of course, is the catalytic agent. The commitments of those who tend to catalytic roles are inevitably suspect. Base motives of self-interest or worse may be ascribed to them. Moreover, disciplinary experience with those who have found expression of their ambitions in change programs but then left the organization in the middle of the process itself, lends credence to the theory of the cynical provocateur. Thus the ideological banner of the change catalyst must be unfurled for all to behold, while his protective armor needs to be strong.

Those who foster change must genuinely understand their own personal values and their motivations. The disciplinary and organizational requisites of change must be meaningful and relevant beyond the terms of the individual's personal needs and aspirations, must be translated into terms which are understood by others in the organization whom he attempts to influence. The value commitments which reflect his strivings must also be consistent with, or at least acceptable to, those who are to be participants in the change process. Furthermore, his professional competence must be relevant to the specialized nature of the change problem. As a principal in the process, he incurs responsibility not only for defining reasonable expectations, but for substantively facilitating the process as well. Without specialized competence, the capacity to spell out objectives and to achieve success in approaching them through a well-defined sequence of procedures is made infinitely more difficult, if not impossible.

There are other responsibilities. The organizational and individual costs and rewards must explicitly document that on balance the effort is worthwhile. Ethical questions of manipulation arise. Those with a vested interest in perpetuating the status quo question the morality of attempting to change their condition. The degree to which those who will be influenced by the change decisions are made parties to these decisions is also at issue. Involvement can take shape in debate about process or about goals and perspectives. Where a catalyst feels constrained to insist upon authoritatively maintaining his ideas as the overriding rationale, the capacity to function independently in the case of those who may be required to do so once the change has been effected becomes far more problematic.

Different situations call forth different mechanisms for adapting organizations to a new stance. The remedy is based upon a diagnosis of the organizational condition and history. Prescriptions may be a variation in the balance of power within the organizational structure, a reconstructed pattern of communication processes, a review and reevaluation of operational or procedural goals, a readjustment between the reality of the client response and the internal operations designed to bring it about, or simply the development of more effective problem-solving mechanisms. But the objective tends always to be modifications in the organizational apparatus. The organizational state and requirements, the capacities and style of the catalyst in the process, are the crucial factors. It is from these sources that decisions derive as to whether to emphasize method change through procedural variation or center rather upon goal change. The change strategy is also affected by differences between professional and client values. The traditional lore or professional strategy has held to a decision process which presumes that judgments made by the technically competent will be in the best interests of the clients. The assumption that they know what these best interests are in a time when the ethos of self-determination is in the ascendance, subjects such strategy to the risks of alienation as never before in the past. The most poignant illustration of this in librarianship may have been when an Indiana library decided to convert an old railroad car into a branch library for disadvantaged youngsters.[3]

ELEMENTS IN CHANGE STRATEGY

Change strategy is also a matter of style and often this has to do with timing. If the catalytic process is seen from the vantage point of the administrator, it is clear that some seize opportunity and move to imple-

3. With considerable community-wide involvement, the Vigo County Public Library (Terre Haute, Indiana) outfitted an eighty-ton donated railroad car to serve as a library for local youth in a predominantly black area. Almost immediately it was vandalized and became the subject of a petition for "The Rejection of the Train as a Library," by the Young Adults for a Better Black Community. In addition to the alleged paternalistic aspects of the endeavor, the black community claimed that it had not been sufficiently consulted at the grass-roots level and that the train was inadequate to meet library needs. After some futile attempts at reconciliation, the project was abandoned and the railroad car removed. See ALA Bulletin, January 1969, p. 8.

ment new programs swiftly, almost immediately upon the assumption of office. For others a calculated, slow, methodical process is followed. Delegation is another manifestation of style. Others in the organization serve either as levers for change or impediments. The existing personnel are examined in seeking out supporters or, when appropriate, new individuals unquestionably committed to the ideology of proposed change are drawn from the outside. The consequence of such choices, set against the temper of the organization, will tend to facilitate or reduce the capacity for adaptation to enter and spread through the entire organization. An alternative expression of style is in revising the pattern of communications. Individuals drawn from different parts of the organization, yet seen as strategic support elements and bound together in a freshly formed common alliance, prepare the ground for more active interaction and involvement of other individuals in the organization. That style succeeds best which matches the organizational temperament, or if it disrupts it perceives why and how and calculates the means for deriving an adapted organizational equilibrium consonant with the change strategy and change agenda.

Prior history influences strategy. The organization which is overcommitted, oversurveyed, overcommunicated, is less than ideal fertile ground for the individual attempting improvisation. Yet even this may be a more fortuitous proving ground than the immovable bureaucracy tied to venerable practice. Where there is prior experience without any important outcome, the reconstruction of a similar situation would be destined to hardship, if not failure. Difficult complications arise when those who hold key positions and are not susceptible to influence proceed to follow their own star. When such an individual occupies a sensitive post capable of furthering or retarding the adaptation of the organization, change strategy must somehow be adapted to take account of this block. The difficulty is that such recalcitrance may not always be foreseen until after the process has begun, by which time the capacity for shifting gears may be more difficult. Again since change propensity is seldom ideally clustered when resistance is expressed through covert tactics rather than public expression, the sensitivity of the catalyst is taxed to identify where in the organization such partisans are to be found. Hierarchical structure may also be an impediment, since individuals most susceptible to change efforts may be scattered through differing levels of the organizational structure. A strategy for change which follows from a revision of normal structural terms to draw in such advocates runs against the grain of authority lines, and the internecine consequences of new innovating alignments can be profound. This is but one of many powerful arguments which can be marshaled in favor of an understood status quo.

Change strategy devolves also about the contribution which the person who is attempting to influence the process assumes and the basis for making such a choice. The alternatives are many. They include mediation or counseling, demonstration, encouragement, resource-seeking, public relations. More than one role can be assumed during the sequence of implementation, depending upon the qualities which the catalyst brings to the role. Interrelating the program consequences through distinctive parts of the organization so as to ensure the spread of the ideology of change is essential. Without this element of the process, others in the organization and in the client group may never understand and appreciate the new perspectives. Without such shared insight, an altered picture of the enterprise is unlikely. For the process of explanation may ultimately lead to the development of revised insight into the organizational contribution with the effect of altering substantially the values and the attitudes and ultimately the activities of many both in and outside the organization. Collecting information from different points in the organizational structure and reporting it back to the whole organization may be another significant element in the process. To do so, in effect, is to mirror for the organization a reconstructed picture of itself, to afford a more widespread and accurate self-portrait during the process of change. A variation on the same theme is continuous self-examination, so as to modulate the process as the effects of particular efforts are perceived.

The variability of change expectations is very great, ranging from gradual and modest accommodation to drastic reconstruction of the entire organizational contribution. Under more critical terms, the change process may begin with a proposal for full reevaluation of programs and services. To influence such a procedure, the catalyst assumes a role well beyond that of neutral resource. He is change agent and committed partisan, attempting simultaneously to explain, to influence, and to introduce procedures and ideology which may be strange and unattractive to those within the context of the traditional organization. Not infrequently he is drawn to the organization because of these capacities. In such a situation, decisions are influenced on the basis of the authoritative position of the catalytic leader, the range and depth of his experience, the assurance and commitment which his personality and intellect instill in those who surround him. Charismatic qualities are frequently a part of the arsenal and, where they are not, they may be imputed to the individual in the leadership role as further reassurance for his followers. Charismatic leadership as the core of the change phenomenon in the recent history of librarianship has been isolated or unheralded. Perhaps Francis St. John in the Brooklyn Public Library of the late 1940s to mid 1950s would be one such illustration. The instances are limited because such a role demands more than expertise in the procedure. The prime requisite is some rare combination of power, will, charm, cunning, or vision to propagandize others to accept a view. Yet the process of initiating change does not necessarily assure the permanence of that which is modified nor even its continuity. As change becomes more familiar, as its consequence is more established, and as the catalyst withdraws and the system finds its own equilibrium, it is very simple for the past to recapture what has been lost, particularly if the partisanship of followers was more nearly opportunistic than genuine.

Pressure from outside the formal organization structure is one of the most powerful catalysts. Union activity would fit here as a device which provides political power not normally available to individuals functioning within a bureaucracy. With prospects of change representation through more normal channels foreclosed, collective bargaining becomes the alternate mechanism. Leaving aside the controversy of whether a union is an appropriate grouping for professionals, an interesting issue remains. In some small industries where the managerial expertise is limited, union experts have contributed technical and managerial insight to companies in order to ensure their survival and so to protect the industry. The International Ladies Garment Workers' Union is one instance. Beyond the point when library unions establish themselves as recognized bargaining agents, and once the grievance process is used only as a limited device and demands less attention than it inevitably does when unions come to power, the question of what role the union ultimately will play becomes more germane. It might be that unions will devote that proportion of their energy not committed to collective bargaining to issues of organizational goals, strategy, and service. It is conceivable that the union movement may eventually become a significant catalytic agent for organizational change in libraries.

A subtle but highly salient contribution of the change catalyst is the creation of a climate of belief that change is possible. Then a range of problems which might have been evaded can be brought forward for new study and attention. The effect inside the organization and outside it among those who relate to it is a revised and renewed sense that it is possible to identify problems and to calculate new strategies for resolving them. The appearance of accomplishment has a multiplier effect. It enhances the potential for further accomplishment. Most importantly, it furthers the process of self-examination, offering those connected with the organization a sense of assurance that it is entirely appropriate for them to look at the weaknesses of the system. Under these terms it becomes even more possible for the system to attempt something new. In such a climate of change, there is encouragement for new designs and alternatives to traditional practice. Authority is seen as committed to the process of change and the very authority of the catalytic agent is on seeking solutions to problems. This is not to say that devices of change are immediate or that somehow spontaneously solutions to all problems are found, but rather that such an organizational culture counteracts the brand of organizational despair which is born of a deep-seated conviction that nothing can or ever will change. It tends to sustain motivation toward change through periods of uncertainty and doubt. Even if those involved in the change process lose sight of the goal, assurance of support and organizational commitment tends to abet the process. The catalytic agent plays his most important role simply by inculcating feelings of security and self-confidence in those who are engaged in the process of implementing and testing change.

Those who catalyze change vary in their value positions with regard to the expectations they wish to create in the organization, and in their methods for inspiring expectation through the organization. Some play a powerful personal role. Others remain in the background. Some communicate through explicit discussion such facts as their anticipated tenure in the organization beyond the point where the change is operational; others give primary importance to the significance of the change rather than to their own relationship to it. The perceptions and thereby the potential contribution of those who participate in the process are very much conditioned by organizational terms and by the qualities of leadership imputed to the change catalyst.

ALTERNATIVE TO BUREAUCRACY— THE TEMPORARY SYSTEM

One significant form of change strategy is the devising of novel structural and environmental conditions for the purpose of problem-solving, using forms less threatening and more conducive to venturing into new idea realms than normal bureaucratic arrangements. Here we take the work of Miles[4] as the point of departure in considering the temporary system as strategy for change. Countless examples of the form exist, from conferences and committees, to presidential commissions, to consulting relationships. The common element is that they come into being for a temporary period. The identity is with a time span, the development of a specific end product, or the solution of an individual problem. The temporary system can be oriented to the work to be done during one

4. Matthew B. Miles, ed., *Innovation in Education* (New York: Teachers College Press, 1964), Chapter XIX.

time interval like a seminar, linked to a particular individual project such as in the formation of a research group or task force, or tied to a relationship built around a particular condition or state as in a consulting arrangement. By definition such forms tend to take place within informal contexts. The consequence is that the individuals and group, outside the bounds of the normal, formal, and structured organizational relationships, develop participation in different ways and at different levels. As such, efforts are thought to be more productive and efficient than under the more ritualistic methodology of bureaucracy. The group is formed to assault a particular problem on an *ad hoc* basis. When it has satisfied the purpose of its mission the effort is concluded. The weight of a permanent system with the self-conscious concerns of ordinary organizational life is not present, so energies can instead be directed in a more single-minded way toward the particular problem.

The most essential characteristic of the successful temporary system is in fostering a climate which furthers change capacity in ways often foreclosed in permanent systems. The concentration of attention upon carrying out the normal routine operation and maintaining the relationships which the latter impose are absent, and the energy required for this is saved. The capacity to diagnose, to plan, to innovate, and to deliberate change opportunities is enhanced as the pressures to maintain and to rationalize the system are relaxed. In short, the many reasons which cause inertia and the inhospitality of the bureaucratic form to innovative design tend not to be at work in the temporary system. In its very nature, implicit and built into the design, is a kind of openness to new perspectives, new attitudes, and new ways of assessing problems.

With its capacity to focus sharply, to apply in conscious effort the strategy and the attention of the group, the temporary system is unencumbered by the many potential problems of the workaday situation. Limitations upon goal requirements tend to reduce anxiety among members, increasing a sense of optimism about the likelihood of achieving success. The conditions of membership tend to be relatively clear, and group structure is related to the systematic requirements needed for problem solving. Those most likely to contribute are either selected or select themselves for participation. This concentration of individuals identified with a common goal reduces some of the socialization problems encountered in a different kind of ambience. Under its terms the traditional entrenched self interest in perpetuating the status quo can be much reduced. There is high probability that those most competent to deal with the substantive problems and favorable to honest consideration of alternatives would be included in such groups, but this cannot be automatically assumed. Perhaps the best illustration of instances where this may not be the case is in groups drawn together on the basis of political expediency. The President's National Commission on Libraries which functioned during the late 1960s, with its composition as much a matter of political, regional, professional, and private-industry representation as of abilities appropriate to the task, is the most striking recent case drawn from librarianship.

The nature of its design and a strategy of detachment from normal confines leads often to the social and physical separation of temporary groups, further engendering a spirit of innovation. Barriers to change are absent once individual or group preoccupation with traditional norms and ritual is reduced. The self-defensive mechanisms of the usual organizational structure, which result in reluctance to experiment, are relaxed. The converse is that the normal organization, by its detachment from the work of the temporary group, is insulated. Thus each has self-assurance and built-in protective qualities from the other. Proposed changes in the permanent structure need not be automatically accepted until some estimates of their success potential can be made, based upon experimentation or testing in the temporary system. Or such at least may be the predominant view of the permanent system. In a pragmatic sense, of course, there may be suspicion, hostility, even fear of the proposed outcomes and the consequent effects upon the organization.

The primary stress upon the temporary system is time. The highest premium is put upon accomplishing goals within the time allocated for the task and the inevitable consequence is heightened input of energy. Even if there is no precisely fixed terminal date for the completion of the work, the imminent fact of group dissolution propels effort to reach conclusions since this is the basis for the group's existence. A dysfunctional consequence of such urgency may be that it forces conclusions too soon. This may happen if the political requirements to conclude the work tend to overshadow the need for sophistication of results. This sense of urgency heightens perception of the passing of time, induces achievement among group members in sharp contrast to the normal bureaucratic sense of need for accomplishment without critical time constraints. In fact the temporary system is measured in terms of the creative problem solutions or innovative designs it proffers, rather than as in the usual context, in putting in time. As the work draws to a close, as pressure comes to be more acutely felt, the pace of effort inevitably accelerates to a high pitch.

The culture of the temporary group is also a departure from the norm. Temporary relationships, with emphasis upon substantive achievement, call forth roles which facilitate fruitful discussion in a climate open to free expression of differences. As the group becomes a group, as communication is enhanced within the system, the participants are forced to derive consensus about the primary goal toward which it is striving. With such a goal consensually determined, time pressure heightens effort to derive the decisions which will lead to it. Personal involvement in goal formulation tends to engender a sense of participation in the total group effort, adding meaning to each individual contribution. The group derives its sense of significance from the fact that it is engaged upon a special project. In consequence of the experimental nature of the situation, individuals tend to be under less pressure to prove unequivocally the value of their contribution, since the usual evaluative measures employed in the traditional structure are absent. The lessened self-consciousness and anxiety in the temporary group is often reflected in the permanent system since there is no demand that the proposals of the temporary group be accepted by the bureaucracy. Thus a kind of equilibrium obtains between the two. Yet the expressions of the temporary system may elicit acceptance in the regular group simply in consequence of its having been called into being; the assumption being that it must, almost by definition, have useful things to say to the larger body. This is somewhat similar to the situation of the executive who participates in a management-training program; whether or not his capacities have been improved as a consequence of participation, he tends to be viewed by his sponsors as having new abilities which he did not have before he was involved in such an experience.

Such factors heighten the sense of achievement anticipated by participants in the temporary group and seem to multiply the effect of the group's work, even perhaps to the point of distorting their perception of the value of the group accomplishment. A frequent consequence of participation is an expanded sense of personal worth, a revised self-perception as an individual who can play a key role in designing strategy or bringing forth innovation. It is this phenomenon which may partially account for the passion and zeal reflected in the behavior of persons caught up in the workings of a seminar or simulation exercise. The sense of importance may also be furthered by the feeling of being able to control the system in ways often foreclosed in the less transigent permanent system. These reasons may explain why the constraints and procedures of the temporary situation are abided. For it is clear that individuals are more disposed to tolerate controls upon their freedom and upon their living conditions within a temporary situation. The participant in the temporary system experiences a rational order in which he can behave responsibly; he is in a position to evaluate his own experience and he is himself valued for his participation in the goal achievements of the group. These conditions are a dramatic departure from the traditional bureaucratic milieu where feelings of alienation, powerlessness, and interpersonal strain are far more commonplace. The sense of personal freedom is also sharpened in a context where the individual can experiment in relatively risk-free circumstances. When the accustomed role definitions and requirements are not functioning, there tends to be a greater openness to change, in that the individual is removed from a structure in which paramount considerations relate most closely to authority deference, rather than to honest expression and interactions. The temporary system, as a general rule, encourages communication among participants. The language and form of discourse inevitably arise within the context of the group. The tendency is for its characteristics to be modified from those in the permanent system where, even if position and hierarchy are played down, status differences remain the true pattern of organizational communication. Relationships between individuals whose roles in the formal system might keep them apart are broken down in the temporary system, leading to the possibility of greater interaction and greater equalization.

A temporary system has the capacity to bring people together who might normally have little in common and even hostility to each other. The need to plan and work together in a common cause draws them together. Crisis elicits such cooperation most dramatically. Mixing people from different levels, of different life styles, with different views, may enhance prospects for change. Since the normal power arrangements are absent and a new structure is born, the contribution of each individual takes precedence in governance. A new set of relationships, understandable within the context of the group, arises as prelude to the constructive activity which is to take place. The likelihood is that this power distribution will more nearly be equalized than in a hierarchical structure. As consequence the effect of the group's work on the individual and the effect of the individual's contribution to the group may be more significant than would be likely within a normal bureaucratic framework. Group spirit is enhanced in ways also uncommon in the usual permanent system. For participation implies belonging in a closely knit group that has experienced something unusual and not understandable to any who have not lived through the experience. Among others, library school alumni and combat veterans share such a sense. The capacity for calling forth a high degree of commitment to the enterprise is often present as well. In those efforts where it is not certain that the goal can be attained or where there is substantial risk involved in the activity, the seriousness of the commitment may be most pronounced. With status differentials reduced and authority levels obliterated, the greater group equilibrium comes to extend the range of trust, the honesty of communication among members. As the types of defense mechanisms against openness which are common to the permanent system are absent, frankness based upon equality of membership and the capacity genuinely to address the problems of concern to the group are enhanced.

Because the temporary system is often designed to solve problems for which there is little factual evidence available there is a propensity to derive innovative solutions. Such change can be seen as change on its own terms and for its own sake. This is exactly the reverse of the way the permanent system resists modification and holds on to habitual responses. Thus those of the temporary group may be seen to ally themselves against the norms of the permanent system by proposing innovative remedies which can be viewed as antisystem. Time limits inspire energetic and serious concentration upon goals, born of the zeal to respond creatively to the needs out of which the temporary group was created. This is what makes the resolution of problems possible, sometimes under formidable odds.

While one consequence of the temporary system may be change in the human beings who participate in the process, perhaps the more significant outcome is the decision which changes the way things can be or are done in the future. This can result in products which go well beyond the anticipated limits of the original mandate, for it can trigger fundamental change in the structure or operation of individual institutions and organizations or of entire disciplinary systems. Moreover, by their nature such representations are far more likely to be treated seriously and to be accorded wide attention than any which are brought forth out of regular decision processes. Recommendations call renewed attention to the original problem and may be implemented with greater dispatch than routine recommendations because of the support which the temporary group has received throughout its working life. The pressure to do something about its proposals is enhanced simply as a consequence of having commissioned the effort. Those who call the temporary system into being understand this likelihood full well and this may be precisely their objective in setting the process in motion. It may even explain why special short-term retreats are held at which discussions can only begin to scrape the surface of major problems. Such events are more successful in underscoring the significance of issues than routine organizational discussions, even when it is clear that the attendant problems can hardly be solved in a weekend or four-day meeting.

Limits of the Temporary System

Like most devices, the temporary system is subject to limits and abuses. Unrealistic expectations, deliberately or naively drawn, perhaps rank highest. *Ad hoc* faculty committees of the 1969–1970 academic year drawn together on many campuses to attempt to solve the rampant political problems of that period, provided abundant illustrations of either failing. The frustration of overcrowded agendas and unrealized expectations, sometimes on the very heels of euphoria, brings high levels of fatigue and requires periods of readjustment in the wake of such strain. The disillusion which attends the eventual recognition that results may come to nothing serves to breed cynicism and mistrust and leads to perception of the exercise as merely a diversionary political tactic. Indeed some temporary systems may be brought into being simply to shelve a problem for a while, to reduce the pressure, when no genuine solution is really sought. Only those who are drawn into the engagement unsuspecting and who perform with passion are seriously disillusioned when the true purpose emerges. Some groups derive totally unrealistic schemes, too vague or inoperable to accomplish practical ends. Then the greatest frustration is borne by those who have held out hope for pragmatic rather than idealized solutions. Related somewhat is the possibility that the architects of change do not perceive that the imaginative design is only forerunner to the problems of implementation, that solutions without built-in follow-through as an integral part of the schematic may be doomed to failure. Here the pitfall of the temporary system may be seen as a consequence of its time limitations and its concentration solely upon highest priorities of concern. If implementation is not charted, if no strategy is drawn to bring the change to pass, there is no certainty that it will come to pass. Thus the salient problem of the temporary system, even when it functions admirably, is to devise the mechanism to assure close relationship between its contribution and the operation of the permanent system. This is simply another way of saying that the means must be calculated whereby the temporary system engenders a strategy for change clearly construed by all the parties at interest as furthering the ends of the operating system. In this way results will more assuredly be translated into the regular programs.

From the point of view of the permanent system, the temporary system offers the opportunity to observe and evaluate innovative changes. This is possible in circumstances which permit experimentation with uncertainty of outcome, in conditions where measurement is awkward, and when the permanent system might be vulnerable without such a project. Public library experiments with unserved populations can be rationalized in this fashion. Under these terms the risks which would need to be borne by the permanent system can be carried by the temporary system without necessarily committing the permanent system to perpetuating the design or ensuring that the process or the project will become permanent. Moreover, within the framework of the temporary system the permanent system can chance divergence from the usual ritual in order to study the value of this departure to the experimental design but without yielding such ground in its conventional efforts. Particularly at times where change is seen as essential, the permanent system requires a proving ground for experimentation. The temporary system is the seedbed of innovation, or it can be, testing change in ways seldom possible within the traditional structure. It is even possible that unless there is an overriding propensity to employ the temporary system strictly as a strategy for calculating the means for adapting the permanent structure, the entire permanent structure will ultimately come to be seen as itself a temporary system which has outlived its usefulness.

THE RATE OF CHANGE AS AN ELEMENT

There are alternative views of the ideal rate of change. One school holds with the gradual diffusion of ideas in an organization or into a discipline. The other tends toward rapid infusion with variation brought to pass within a relatively short time span. Historical perspectives based upon earlier anthropological lore identified how cultures could be and should be protected from attempts to change them through rapid coercion. Forcible introduction of change patterns compacted into the short run and not precisely suited to the cultural framework was seen as potentially fraught with grave difficulties and hazards. With this perspective, the only rational possibility becomes the long, slow, and very tentative process, allowing change to develop over time.

But a slow and gradual change process does not always square with present necessity. Individuals may sense the need for change and perhaps even want to change rather than simply accepting the gradual shifts which come over long time spans. In this situation, those who have the responsibility or the capacity to introduce change and who encourage gradualism may actually prevent a new pattern of activity with a higher value. Perpetuating the efforts of an organization or a discipline at a relatively low or backward level prevents the arousal of expectations in the larger culture and the placing of demands on it. For as new roles are learned and as new responsibilities are assumed, the resources necessary for continued output are different from those required before such modification. A library with dramatic and powerful contributions to make would not only alter the conditions of librarians within the organization, but help them to exercise more control over the organizational condition itself. The incentives they might receive for playing such a role would be increased and the demands made upon supporting agencies would be extended. To contain the effort, to play down the importance or the urgency of radical adaptation, permits rationalization of the fact that libraries and librarians are not truly interested in dealing with any more complex problems or service contributions than what has been traditional. The consequence is that librarians continue to function at minimum levels as they perceive that those who hold strategic responsibility in libraries and in supporting agencies are not genuinely interested in contributions at any higher level. For those in situations which they see thus constrained, appeal to high aspirations and goals for their practice is indulgence in the type of rhetoric all too commonplace in a world which naively or treacherously confuses reality with fantasy.

It may be a simple fact that many who appear to have little drive or ambition function this way not because of any intrinsic incapacity but because they are quite certain that any genuine aspirations they may have about their professional contribution will come to naught. The pervasive cultural condition is seen as an unyielding stability, an unchanging order, an ambience where energetic expressions of variation are not encouraged. Such perception is the consequence of personal experience. One designated a librarian quickly determines the outer bounds of his potential contribution as a condition of the constraints upon the organization in which he performs. Thus any change situation which serves to relax and adapt the potential of the work role can release great energy and passion into redefinition of the occupational contribution. This leads to the position that rapid change may not only be possible, but that in some ways it may offer inherent advantages. Particularly may this be the case in fields where new technology is arising and in which opportunities for new client relationships are possible.

Perhaps a slow and gradual rate of change serves only to convince individuals that regular patterns of behavior are really appropriate, thereby retarding adaptation all the more. To foster change drastically and completely is to precipitate transformations which permit less carry-over from the past, to heighten the need for swift accommodation to new ways so as to make learning rapid and behavior adaptive. When there are only partial accommodations, and when these are made at a slow rate, such change may not mesh successfully within a system in which all the parts are mutually reinforcing. The result may be a system in which certain elements outdistance and outpace the others, setting up variability of role and pattern within the context of the same organization. A computerized circulation system at the end of an order process that still requires months to acquire a book might illustrate this. Whenever it is possible to transform swiftly an entire structure or procedural system, this problem is less likely to arise. Moreover, to change at once across the entire spectrum of an organization affords the advantage that all members have an equal opportunity to move together in revising the system, without doing violence to the network of human relationships.

Conditional to such bold adaptation is a leadership capable of attracting all or most to the banner. When new ideology or technology is introduced, the enthusiasm necessary for its acceptance depends upon toleration and support if old patterns are to be rejected. When the leadership inspires such support, change accommodation becomes a positive act. The effect is to open the system. In an open system there is a climate of accommodation to new ideas, an enhanced prospect of attracting spontaneous participation, for it is a system no longer caught up exclusively in its conservative ritual. Whether change is introduced simply as a means of reinforcing the cult in its folkways or as part of a revised framework of ideological or technological perspective is closely related to the intelligence and the influence of leadership. It is this issue to which we turn our attention in the next chapter.

CHAPTER 5

The Leadership Role and Responsibility

Librarianship shall be treated in the context of both the organizational setting and the discipline itself. For distinctive leadership patterns and influence in a single institution bear powerfully upon profession-wide leadership performance, and it is abundantly clear that leadership at the national level exerts itself in the institutions which make up the discipline.

Leadership in librarianship is usually synonymous with managerial performance, with the level of expectation perceived as a kind of technical supervisory competence. This is really something quite different from leadership. Perhaps a manager can function reasonably as administrative officer when the goals of an organization or of a discipline are precise and when the decision process is based upon clearly understood technical criteria. Under these conditions the problem is essentially to work within defined bounds of known quantities, using well-established techniques to accomplish predetermined ends. Although these are not the conditions which exist in any fluid culture or where there is need for review of goals, it is enticing to this manager type to place undue stress upon means and to neglect ends. This is why such an option is invariably selected by those who are managers but would not or could not be true leaders. Yet this is a value choice to support preexisting conditions and arrangements toward which the organization has been oriented, by improving the terms rather than by the consideration of alternatives. It is not the end of the matter to impute leadership responsibility to only the calculation of ends. Leadership, of course, transcends technical concerns and demands responsibility in shaping institutional purpose, but even the most visionary leadership may be of small consequence without the organizational competence necessary to support or achieve the ideal design. Leadership responsibility under conditions of change must comprehend goal concerns as well as problems of technology and social system.

The disquietude of the times in a societal, institutional, professional sense appears to be a crisis of confidence. The malaise has been widely discussed, and the problems are complex and diffuse. Confidence seems to be inspired by genuine leadership ability. Uneasiness is often a reflection of doubt about the capability, the commitment, or the wisdom of those expected to take leading roles in resolving crises. Fundamental questions are now being raised about the ability of the leadership class. Those long insulated from strife, for whom decision prerogatives were held inviolate, are no longer so sheltered and are being held accountable for their conduct by both old and newly formed constituencies, all prepared and even eager to contribute their own assessment. If the failures of leadership are deeply felt, they are felt in all the disciplines and all institutions including political institutions, as well as the entire culture. Just as the college president is no longer insulated, neither are those who hold similar positions in other institutions likely to remain so very much longer. For it is clear that leadership is now in question and that leadership ability will be measured in new and in uncommon ways in the future.

CHARACTERISTICS OF THE LEADERSHIP ROLE

Without the differentiation of roles there would be no way for leadership to emerge. A group may or may not have a leader, but once it does then it can more nearly be characterized as an organization or discipline. Within an organization, certain members differ from others in that they accept responsibility for the general purposes of the organized effort. Leadership implies a following, yet there are limits on the relationship so that there may be interchangeability of roles depending on the situation. The common assumption is that leadership inheres in the topmost hierarchical level. This causes much confusion. To put appropriate demands upon leadership is first to understand that there is no necessary correlation between formal bureaucratic status and the assumption of a leadership role. When leadership is viewed as the central focus for group behavior, the leader is recognized as motivator or catalytic agent for achieving the group's ends rather than as administrative functionary. It is he who, regardless of formal position, has the most significant amount of influence over others.

Hierarchies designate as leaders those who hold the seniormost position, not those identified by members of the organization on the basis of potential contribution. Once a bureaucratic functionary is selected by other than the members of the group, goals are selected more nearly as a function of the commitments of that individual and of the hierarchical organization than of the members of the group. Perhaps the most fundamental difference between leadership and hierarchical authority is seen in the source from which such authority is drawn. The authority of the organizational manager derives from an external source of power which gives him dominance over the individuals in the group. They are thus lower-level functionaries, not necessarily genuine followers. An organizational head may also be a leader, but not necessarily so. To characterize the capacity of one in a leadership role is to attempt to evaluate his contribution as effective or ineffective with regard to a particular goal or purpose. Followers impute leadership only to individuals who will help the group attain goals which have value for group members.

The discussion of personal characteristics and other requisites of leadership forms a massive literature which has grown from long concern with this subject within such disciplines as psychology, political science, and sociology. Yet no consistent pattern of traits has been found to characterize leadership precisely. An individual who makes a significant contribution to the movement of a group toward an identified goal and who is so perceived by the members of his group can be characterized as its leader. Moreover, the capacities and attributes of group members make a difference in performance which in turn affects leadership behavior. An individual does not become leader by virtue of the possession of particular characteristics which are everywhere valid, but only when his qualities bear upon the needs requisite in the goal attainment of the particular group at a specific time. Leadership is thus a function of a particular set of variables operative in a specific situation. As the situation changes, as morale and composition change, the group will also alter its goals and there will be variation in the requirements and responsibilities of the leadership role. Different patterns of leadership style, behavior, and qualities are then required as change brings new elements into the situation.

There is inherent conflict in the leadership role in a culture which places high value upon democratic relationships. Because leadership operates within a formal system, organizational life is seen to impose structured terms. The leader is obliged to accept the value constructs of an overall authority system, to perform impersonally within its context as its agent. But without the following of those who identify him as leader, he cannot perform successfully. Thus there is incongruence, sometimes fundamental diversity, between those above and those below in the perception and what is expected of the leader. For the public library director to represent the interests of the professional library staff in collective bargaining at the same time that he functions as agent of the library board of trustees perhaps illustrates the dilemma. To assume leadership responsibility among the professional group imposes behavior which may conflict fundamentally with other elements of the same responsibility. The resolution of such incompatibility is to seek to identify the common ends of the two groups, to reconcile differing perspectives, and to accommodate within such a context. One test of leadership is seen in the capacity to attain goals. When the achievement of popularity or personal ambitions is seen as the overriding concern, leadership is absent.

The effectiveness of leadership cannot be measured precisely. The common method of evaluation is to focus upon performance. Perhaps the only genuine test is in terms of the group or organization in which the individual functions as leader. Accomplishments thus are measured in the language and the logic of the enterprise itself. Evaluations by subordinates may differ fundamentally from those of superiors. Still, cultural norms put greatest credence in the views of those to whom the leader is responsible, rather than in the views of his followers. This may be one reason why bureaucratic types rather than those with true leadership potential are nearly always selected for senior positions.

The pattern of leadership behavior required in one situation may be ineffective in another; the style of leadership needed at different points in the life cycle of an organization or of a discipline will vary significantly. But while change spawns revised leadership need, organizational constraints protect incumbents. Thus do organizations render themselves incapable of making needed adaptations. If a library at one stage requires leadership capacity linked to the building of book collections, at another to physical plant, and at still another to technological application, the incongruity of a system which simply perpetuates leadership incumbency is apparent. As formal placement high in the hierarchical structure is confusedly equated with leadership, leadership capacity is imputed to human beings so placed. But the match between the capacity to perform and the institutional need may very often be spurious. When this is so, there is no leadership, merely the holding of office. Such phenomena may be seen most poignantly enacted in colleges and universities where incumbent administrators are retained beyond the time when they are equipped to contribute to new and revised goals and aspirations of the organizational form. If the illustrations which might be drawn from librarianship are less colorful or are seen as less subject to contemporary strife, there is little question about the parallel between library administrators and college presidents.

To treat of leadership without reference to the composition and personality of those who follow is to neglect the side of the equation which sets it in balance. For leadership is a phenomenon of interrelations. The psychological propensities of a following give rise to ideologies and behavior patterns, and it is in these traits that leadership characteristics are also revealed. Groups in which an authoritarian or a passive cast of mind predominate appear to prefer status-laden leadership, tight control, and direction. Weak forms of leadership are thus subject to hostility and scorn. Among those oriented to a democratic ethos, powerful authority is accorded less hospitality, except that even here the exercise of strong leadership may be tolerated where the situation seems to demand it. Authoritarian personalities are little concerned with the manner of the leader toward them as individuals, but they do require that the group and individuals be moved toward their collective and individual goals. Equalitarians lean more nearly to evaluation as a function of the group process, with appropriate human relations seen as a prime requisite of leadership. They are less prone to accept rigidity or narrow direction. The authority-oriented are dissatisfied and uncomfortable without such direction. Such variability in psychological responses tends to determine which leadership style is viewed as comforting or frustrating. Undoubtedly it also influences the selection process of leaders and the style of leadership performance. Those who understand these matters either intellectually or intuitively are sensitized to the correlation of their own success with the effective conditioning of follower responses.

The physical characteristics, the economic situation, the social and political culture in which the group exists and from which its members are drawn, are only some of the elements which bear upon the leadership role. While situational variables impose unique leadership requirements, there are constants as well. The difficult task is to discern when stability of direction is more costly than alternatives in the form of a different leadership pattern. A group member is leader only during the time when he demonstrates his capacity for contributing more than others do to the attainment of the group goal. As the situation is adapted through goal change, through changes in the relationships and the composition of the group, through competition or pressure from external groups, leadership must remain congruent or it fails. As stability of direction is perceived to be more crucial to bureaucratic well-being than the inculcation of a dynamically responsive organizational climate, the potential for leadership is foreclosed.

FORMS AND STYLE OF LEADERSHIP

The ways in which leaders emerge are numerous. They are sometimes self-selected in consequence of their own determination to achieve within the framework of a particular organization or discipline. In other cases, they are lured from outside with incentives or uncommon problems as bait. Leaders also function in different ways. Some are outside men; their leadership is tied to the maintenance of effective relationships with external interests in order to assure the resources, the political base, or the client constituency which make organizational or disciplinary effort feasible. Others may be organizational generalists concerned with such internal affairs as staffing, technology, work flow, or other elements of process or structure. Still others provide highly concentrated technical expertise in which the distinctive capacity is to lead in the resolution of some particular set of organizational problems. Intellectual leadership, seen in the articulation and rationalization of the organizational or disciplinary contribution, is still another pattern. Often leadership attempts to express itself in a way which straddles across two or more such fundamental modes of performance, but the thrust tends to be most forceful in only one role. In addition to the organizational need which influences leadership style, self-perception of personal attributes and proclivity are also powerful determinants. At root is the element of values.

The type of leadership behavior is more nearly a device than an end in itself. The most idealized democratic forms may be unavailing when swift decisive action is essential, as in emergency or crisis. Still, whatever the ends sought, efficacy of method is a function of the acceptability of the leadership pattern to those who follow. Edicts do not implement decisions. Democratic style strives for maximum participation by group members with the end that decisions tend more to be the result of interactive processes. Individual responsibility in decision-making usually engenders more creative response, but only in an organizational culture where independence and initiative are seen as the occupational ideal. In libraries these norms have yet to be genuinely sought either among the led or the leaders. The authoritarian pattern withholds information, and actions are initiated from the central point by the leader. Conversely, the democratic leader achieves his strength by seeking to exploit the full capacity of the group. More coherence and integrity arise, generally speaking, under the conditions of democratic leadership, but responsibility is also shared in ways which are seen as less protective to the members. There is, in fact, always a kind of ambivalent perspective in the views of leadership and followership—a type of wanting to share, a reluctance to assume responsibility, a sense of need for control, a longing to have a voice.

The predominant tendency is to conceive of leadership in terms of involvement or autocracy, decision engagement or unilateral choice, harmony or conflict. Another way to view the phenomenon shifts it from the context of the interpersonal into the ideological realm. Perhaps this might be termed symbolic rather than human leadership. Such a design calls forth allegiance not through the acceptance of an individual, but rather through a set of principles which are commonly held. Thus, political and religious movements find supporters behind a banner which transcends specific leaders. Individual leadership in particular organizational forms or in a given discipline tends to be a substitute when it does not stand for a type of commitment to a cause or to a substantive ideal toward which it strives. For professional leadership uncorrelated with a recognizable pattern of ideas generates no firm identity; its responsibility is diffused. Followership under terms when the perspectives of action are articulated fires the imagination of those drawn to the cause. The intensity of commitment and the precise program for supporting the ideological goals become the important questions to address to leadership; they far overshadow the leader's style of behavior. With a consensual ideology of shared goals, librarianship and libraries—or any other discipline or organizational form—would tie its aspirations to these ends, with leadership manifested in the capacity to reinforce such ideological strivings. The design requires reconciliation of differences in professional perspectives, and in order to carry out the effort necessary to arrive at a consensual base the most uncommon leadership capacity is called for. But it would be a form of leadership linked with the intellectual and the substantive and not simply with power. For librarianship, this might be both unique and political.

WHY BE A LEADER

A whole range of motivational factors has been advanced to explain why individuals seek leadership roles. Economic incentives tend to be seen as equally germane in one sphere of activity as in another. Still, with a tax law that levies at a higher rate as income mounts, in view of the relatively minor real differences between the topmost rewards and those received at less lofty levels, there is obviously far more than financial improvement which holds allure. The salary differential between the Librarian of Congress and those who play secondary roles in the same organization illustrates the point. As of early 1972 the salary of the Librarian of Congress is $38,000. The Deputy Director, the Assistant Librarian, and most of the principal division heads receive $36,000 each. Furthermore, in a cultural milieu in which the young seem less than ever disposed to defer gratification over an appreciable span of time, the goal of ultimate high reward as spur to leadership aspiration seems doubtful.

If not economic incentive, such striving is often explained as an urge toward power and dominance. The prospect holds appeal in somewhat the way that submission to power, by those who are responsive, also provides psychological satisfaction. Such relationships depend upon the ability of those who lead to retain control of power and of the prestige which is its consequence. They retain this position only to the extent that those who are dominated by them accept the satisfactions drawn from their own status. The follower tends to identify with the group, perhaps vicariously through identification with its leader. Certain individuals need to feel a sense of power and tend to initiate conditions and gravitate toward roles in which they can lead. The desire for status and prestige is a factor since these are widely perceived and culturally acceptable satisfactions which derive from positions of leadership. The enjoyment of status as motive relates to the development of relationships which are supportive of ego requirements. Status determinants may be seen as enormously crucial in certain professional spheres. A leadership role may be so differentiated in status terms from the normal professional role that once leadership is assumed there is a deep abhorrence to revert. Once designated as principal or school superintendent, the professional teaching role might well be seen as anathema. But this may be occupationally differentiable and based on the hazards of particular leadership and on the relative prestige of normal professional occupancy. College presidents seem to be returning in increasing numbers to the classrooms of academia and with far less recalcitrance than might have been evidenced a decade ago.

Assumption of the leadership role need not always be the conscious goal which propels one toward leadership. Some are leaders as a consequence of their contributions to a discipline. This is frequently the case in intellectual and artistic spheres. A great scholar does not have the same kind of following as those who lead organizations. His status and his influence, however, may be even more powerful. In pragmatic and administrative cultures, the status and reputation of the scholar tends to be somewhat lower than the organization or political leader's. To the extent that this is perceived, those who consciously aspire to leadership roles, in the main, gravitate toward organizational positions rather than intellectual achievement.

If some leaders are less revered for intellectual than for organizational or political success, this may explain why followers in librarianship have a particular attitude toward their leadership. Perceptions tend to be emotional, to arise out of a need to feel affection for and be admiring and in awe of those who hold the reins. Leadership under such terms can be seen to placate the dependency requirements through which the organizational or disciplinary leader is seen as father surrogate and authority.

If it would be unfortunate to see the phenomenon solely as consequence of a predominantly feminine occupation with male leadership, in which there is acted out the traditional passivity syndrome, it may still be characterized as passivity and leader adulation for whatever reasons. In librarianship there is less conflict, less ambivalence toward those who play leader roles, than would obtain in another discipline where the acceptance of leadership might more nearly be conditional support, with serious attention paid to control of power to prevent invasion of freedom. It may be precisely a change in attitude which fans the flames of dissatisfaction among those who now assault the temples of librarianship. Still no leader-follower relationship is ever a smooth affair, for there are innate hostilities in the relationship. Under certain terms a leader will be an object of admiration, or again of hatred and scorn, paralleling the ways in which parental figures may be viewed. Group life, just as family life, is cyclical, with disappointments as well as satisfactions. And the lures of leadership succeed in enticing only those who perceive the balance sheet, in terms of intrinsic needs and satisfactions and of personal costs and deterrents, to be weighted favorably.

LEADERSHIP BEHAVIOR

In some ways performance may be differentiated between administration and leadership. The leader must focus upon goals; the administrator treats immediate concrete problems. The leader must express purpose and function in ways only dimly perceived by the administrator. The leader conceptualizes program goals, convinces others to carry them into effect. The administrator facilitates such design. Yet leadership and administration need not be mutually exclusive. For leadership is merely to comprehend both administrative responsibility and sense of purpose, the need to act with reflection on when and how and why, the power of office and the capacity to sway minds. Leadership is behavior in terms of time. Times of peril and confusion call forth leadership more than administrative capacities. In undemanding times when stability and perpetuity are unquestioned, the need for leadership is less acute.

Leadership attributes are reflected in subtle and symbolic ways. If the dean of a school does not behave in ways which suggest that this is who he is, few will accept him in the role, and none will take him seriously. The capacity to serve as leader is thus fashioned of self-perception, the defining of role with person, person with role. Without such clarity and resolution others will not be taken in by the most ingenious disguises. Believability thus may condition success as fully as performance capacity. For without maintaining the status and prestige of leadership by behavior which reassures the members of the group, the capacity to lead is seriously compromised. The leader achieves his status in the name of the group. In effect he is a personification of the group's own identity, so that members of the group ultimately come to identify with him and to adopt his perspectives and he theirs. Through this identification, the group becomes sympathetic and loyal to the leader, and the power which he exercises is a reflection of the esteem in which he is held among its members. His behavior thus is a function of group values and expectations, or is consciously made to appear so by the sensitive leader. Credibility is accorded his ideas since as the reflection of the group he tends to be seen as informed and competent and under these terms his view of the world will be accepted. In consequence, he has the capacity to influence more easily those within the group and those who relate to it than any other group member.

While organizational membership can vary between wide extremes, leadership constitutes regular responsibility and in organizational settings is of indefinite tenure. The power inherent in the role is the basis for ensuring the preservation of the position and also of the incumbent in the position. For the leader will typically maintain some elements of control over the very processes of leader choice, the channels of communication, and even the sense of which are the key problems or critical needs facing the organization. As this is the case, the greatest danger to perpetuity of leadership is posed by other potential leaders with variant views rather than by the followers. It is the coming to dominance of a new ideology, manifest in the form of another potential leader who functions formally or informally, which is most threatening. The need felt in most groups is to perpetuate its primary characteristics. Even with revision in leadership, the continuity of the organizational form builds inevitably on the experience and skills generated by the old leadership. The more technical the organizational skills or the more they are viewed to be technically based, the more unlikely a revolutionary metamorphosis in the group's leadership stance.

Perhaps the personal qualities of leadership, the capacities and abilities of the individual, may be differentiated from the organizational and functional responsibilities which are reflected in the pattern of relationships in and through organizations. The human traits and personal skills often ascribed to the leader are more likely than not optimistic expressions of what leaders perhaps should be, rather than what they are. Idealized characteristics have little meaning without fixing these traits within a reference system of particular values. Assessment of leader behavior must be derived within a value system in which appropriate performance is perceptible from inappropriate performance. Again situational factors govern. Carefully patterned authoritarian leadership may be totally unsuited to the unstructured democratic ambience, just as the reverse would be true. The individual who functions effectively in the context where careful planning is possible may have none of the qualities necessary to the decision-making milieu of recurring crisis. The leader who performs well in a cooperative and friendly setting may be incapacitated in a hostile environment. Very frequently, however, situational requisites are not penetrated with sufficient precision by the parties at interest in order to ensure a genuine match between the propensity of the leader and the situation. The matter is even more complex, for the attributes which appear to be sought are based upon perception before the introduction of a potentially crucial element—the leader's own behavior. Even if a situation appears to call for certain capacities, a new leader may, if he is adroit, bring about a changed set of conditions more nearly suitable to his style. This is undoubtedly the optimistic view of many who are drawn into turbulent organizational waters, in which some will flounder, others sink, and some few make it safely.

The normal condition in librarianship is institutions characterized by organizational personalities of stability and durability, with patterns of relationships which are relatively predictable. In such a climate, leaders are selected or select themselves only uncommonly out of a zeal to catalyze a lively tempo of change in organizational and disciplinary commitment. Revised and variable terms of leadership behavior, as prelude to a shift in organizational personality and ultimately organizational contribution, have yet to be recognized as urgent. As this is so, patterns of behavior which are seen as most successful and most appropriate at the lower hierarchical levels are those attuned to the stable and regular dimensions of organizational effort. It is precisely this condition which rewards the lower level bureaucratic functionary for a contribution which both ensures hierarchical succession and incapacitates him for a more dynamic role when he attains a post of leadership responsibility. Moreover, it confuses him about what appears to be the capricious incongruity of organizational and disciplinary expectations.

The way in which the distinctive nature of problems and requirements in different organizations calls for variable leadership is not always recognized. Nor is it generally realized that leadership behavior may be expressed at more than one point in the structure of governance. In organizations with a strong professional orientation it is fully possible to conceive of the leadership function being distributed through the organization. Such patterns tend to be gaining wider acceptability in organizational forms where professional behavior is set off against administrative role, in which a kind of balance and compromise prevails which lends status and credence to each. The crucial issue is in the delineation of areas subject to decision processes where strategic choices are to be made. A measure of administrative as well as leadership acumen is involved in the perception of these areas where alternate options may be possible. To reduce drastically the zone of choice is to reinforce and perpetuate the status quo. To open it wide, however, may be an invitation to engage endlessly in discourse. Leadership is then expressed in the capacity to recognize fruitful areas of choice which had not formerly been perceived. To do so is to bring before the organization and those who deliberate alternatives a realization of their capacity to choose in ways which open the organization to new options. Seen in this way, leadership behavior consists of a range of patterns devolving about questions to be answered within a framework of purpose, a continuous process of stimulating decision efforts to permit the organization to move toward its ultimate objective in spite of prior limits or constraints.

Inevitably, problems arise in organizations for which the customary problem solving methods are not effective and yet decisions must be made. The capacity to function in crisis is a high order of leadership capability. Perhaps then another measure of leadership behavior is expressed in the ability to derive patterns and plans which anticipate potential crises and so serve effectively to ward them off. The drama of crisis management is thereby rendered unnecessary in consequence of a more orderly and rational prior analysis and preparation. Still organizational ends may, in some instances, best be served by the flamboyant and eleventh-hour antics of a leadership style which deliberately provokes such occasions for their colorful and stimulating effects both within the organization and in its wider context. The variability of leadership behavior at different stages of an organization's history may be germane here. The theatrical and imaginative innovator may be organizationally unattractive when strategies have been carefully calculated and formal method prevails. Conversely the organization which places the highest premium on the certainty of its apparatus and the infallibility of its prior design may be consigning itself to bureaucratic mediocrity. To yield to procedural mechanisms as surrogate for extraordinary organizational response, even when scale and complexity of organization calculate greater efficiency under such terms, is to propel the system toward ultimately becoming its own end.

The mores of the time undoubtedly bear significantly upon leadership behavior, and the more egalitarian ethos of modern times contrasts sharply with the authoritarian patterns which prevailed earlier. In some ways, the contemporary leader may be even less secure than many who are his subordinates. Such a leader no longer sees himself as a person of great power, believing that he can do anything he chooses in a world substantially subject to his control. Even with the rewards of economic advantage, recognition, and status, there is no longer unlimited power so that self-perception may be more nearly as another employee or professional who has taken on added burdens, rather than as shaper of destiny. The emergent leader tends to perceive, in a way which others have not, those very issues which the members of the culture feel most strongly about, and he seeks to derive solutions which express his own identity and with which others can also identify. Such leadership will appeal to individuals who are uncomfortable with the existing condition, yet who do not feel disenfranchised, as well as to those who view the existing system as unresponsive to their needs. A cynic might suggest that the rise of new leaders may be seen to occur with the conscious, positive acquiescence and support of the vested interests in a social or disciplinary structure, with the new ideology seen as a way of sustaining intact many of the values which have gone before. The rise of Hitler is often accounted for in precisely this way. In such a sequence, new ideological leadership emerges following the identification of a crisis caused when the normal measures employed by the system to correct conditions are unable to do so, or are seen as unresponsive to significant elements of discontent. The emergent leader, frequently personified by charismatic qualities or at least often romantically idealized succeeds in identifying not only the nature of the problem but the methods or approaches toward solving it. His commitment to pursue his goals is then expressed in ways which appeal widely to the members of the organization, the discipline, or the culture which gives rise to such alternatives.

The conditions which add to the authority of the appeal are reinforced under terms where emergent leadership is authenticated by the position which the individual holds in the existing disciplinary structure. By virtue of the occupancy of a responsible formal post at a high level, greater credence will be paid to the rationality and legitimacy of ideas and perspectives advanced. In addition, those who enjoy formal posts have the capacity to broadcast their postulates more widely and effectively through the media to which they have access. The loftier the placement, the more the charismatic qualities of the leader are reinforced. Charismatic endowment is imputed only to those who already command a following, and without an existing power base, it is more difficult to win an audience. Here is a considerable roadblock in the path of the new messiahs of librarianship. Without power at the point of their columns the barricades of the entrenched remain invulnerable. Moreover, in any social system when the evidence becomes unassailable that a change is necessary, those who hold the positions of power and responsibility identify themselves as effective agents of transition, impute to themselves those capacities of leadership which will lead the discipline forward. This leadership does not seek genuine change but the perpetuation of the existing order with only minor adjustments. Many are then confused between what is preferred by those in the existing system who are its "legitimate" leaders and by those who seek to replace them.

Crucial is the sense of crisis which can be conveyed by a charismatic leader who preaches a break with past traditions. But the traditionalist may also be an eloquent spokesman. Unless past ideology and disciplinary habits are seen to be in jeopardy, the gospel of change agents can be ignored. The traditional holders of power, counseling prudence, patience, and reason, will continue to be followed.

Actions as well as goals account for the success or failure of the charismatic leader. It is a multifaceted role constructed of ideological goals, the capacity to function inside or outside the formal structure of the discipline, and the strategy with which to spread the contagion of the new views. The flexibility of the discipline or organizational structure which he is attempting to influence is perhaps the most crucial consideration of all. Miscalculation, or even a correct reading of the scene which then inhibits, is a strong deterrent to leadership performance. To the extent that an individual sees himself as powerless, to that extent he forecloses upon functioning in imaginative ways. He then rationalizes why he cannot be more and do more, and satisfies himself with the condition of minor functionary subject to circumstances beyond his control.

When leadership in professional disciplines depends upon revised ideology, influence rests upon the appeal of those who proclaim a revised philosophy. Personalities which are potentially charismatic are constantly being produced by the social system but some who have such qualities may be ignored or identified as deviants. Such a trend is most pronounced in librarianship with its small tolerance for diversity or unorthodox ideology. It is possible only to speculate about the number of potential leaders who have already become disenchanted and gravitated to other occupational forms which offer greater promise of creative options. One might consider, too, the many active younger figures who have tied their expectation to the belief that libraries and librarianship can be reoriented to new goals and may simply drop out if nothing can be changed in the period ahead.

In the process of change, the charismatic leader is seen as innovator and spokesman for new ideas which distinguish his philosophy from the views of those who would protect and maintain the status quo. Charismatic leadership may also find expression among those who seek to conserve the system as it has been. Such a figure tends to be more uncommon. (Lawrence Clarke Powell may be the most notable illustration of the latter in recent library history in his eloquent articulation of the primacy of the book.) For the institutions of the system already have in their administrative class those committed to stability, who are safe and trusted figures, who have the power to avoid or minimize attack either from those in the system or those to whom it is responsible. It is the prophet of the new, the different, the unorthodox, who must arise and attract followers behind a fresh ideological banner. Such opportunity changes with times and conditions. The cause of social responsibility in librarianship for example, would have been premature in the 1950s, before the general theme had attained broader circulation in the society. In periods of crisis, the incidence of new leadership is frequent. It is crisis which often inspires charismatic leadership as it conditions the identification of such leadership by others. Charisma is called for by a climate of discontent in a specific social or disciplinary culture. It is built not only upon a plausible political, economic, or social framework oriented to the resolution of this discontent, but it is spawned out of the passion and the language of those who specify how and why their solution will resolve the problem.

Leadership behavior can also be related to the exercise and use of power, both in the context of organizational politics and in personal interactions where the manner of its application is various. The use of rewards by fostering pleasurable interpersonal relationships is commonplace. Its alternative is a kind of coercion which causes psychological distress by inflicting control and influence in ways which are disturbing to the individual. Aggression or avoidance, either form of the disruption of normal relationships, results in frustration and despair. Referent power stems from the way in which one individual identifies with another or with a group. It is the means whereby new entrants are typically socialized to identify with the behavioral patterns of the experienced. In this the leader is model. His behavior becomes the norm, eliciting response from those who would emulate leadership. Thus those subject to this conditioning come to behave in ways which they assume will be accepted or admired. Such is the power which influences social behavior to the perspectives of the leader. In specific disciplines, power frequently is embodied in those recognized for their technical or intellectual prowess. The recognition of the value of such powers is seen in the according of a leadership role which legitimatizes this capacity and its importance through high placement in the formal structure of the organization. Again, personal behavior among those in the process of adjusting to work situations and organizational norms is influenced by perceptions of the nature of the attributes which receive high reward. The leader is once again role model.

The use of coercive power more nearly fits the authoritarian leadership pattern than the democratic, but it is widely employed in bureaucratic forms such as libraries, in spite of its many dysfunctional consequences, for it is seen as a strong controlling device. Yet coercion, more often than not, leads to frustration and compliance as an expedient rather than a commitment. Ultimately, the result can be a sharp deterioration in communication, mounting hostility and suspicion, which gives rise to social relationships to alleviate such concerns, or perhaps reinforces them through cliques and rumors and other mechanisms. The final outcome may heighten personal conflict, reduce morale, and provoke disinterest or displacement of loyalties and commitments.

Leadership behavior calls for the capacity to generate and manipulate ideas, to grasp the implications of cultural and disciplinary phenomena, and to transform them into terms consistent with the organizational capacity to respond. In time of change, the key decisions identify the direction, the timing, and the processes of change more than the means to incremental efficiency. But even those organizations with reputations for being extremely well managed tend to be organized to administer yesterday's ideas. Planning which conceives of alternatives only within a constricted framework limits flexibility.

Change is painful, as it is disruptive, for it assails self-interest and may threaten status as well as emotional and intellectual well-being. Leadership strategy which is incongruent with personal goals of those in the organization rests upon uncertain and chancey ground. But strategy may be seen against short- or long-term perspective. High cost in the short run may be the surest route to ultimate attainment, just as it is possible to deplete organizational resources in order to make a maximum showing in the short term. The measure of effective leadership behavior must be drawn against ultimate organizational contribution not in the results of brief skirmish or more drawn-out battle, but as the outcome of an entire campaign.

No single style of behavior can be effective for all times in all places. Whether problem-oriented or focused on human relations, authoritarian or democratic, incisive decision-maker or methodical, the precise specification will be a function of the meshing of leader capacity with organizational or disciplinary requirements at a particular point in time. To identify his own contribution, a potential leader must be able to diagnose his own behavior and his own personality and value commitments in relation to organizational variables. The organizational factors may be patent or they may be obscured. They may hinge significantly upon the views of those to whom the leader will be responsible or upon the characteristics and strivings of colleagues and followers in the existing framework or upon neither. If incongruity between leader perspectives and organizational expectations is to arise in consequence of the expression of the leadership role, this must be anticipated in the strategic design. Variations in the degree of tolerance between prior expectations and leadership behavior range from the extreme of serious confinement imposed in highly structured mode to the absence of any constraints whatsoever upon style and leader behavior. Yet more than simply leadership behavior is in question. Style and expectation among those who follow may either reinforce or make absurd the contribution of the leader. Docile followers suit authoritarian leaders; others would prefer to spawn creative organizational responses. The capacity to reject or accept leadership or to place constraints on power resides with those who follow. Expectations born of earlier patterns are influential in conditioning attitudes. These can be positive or negative, depending upon the sense of organizational satisfaction with prior leadership. In some instances the leader must either adapt his style to coincide with organizational expectations or change these expectations about his behavior. Since behavior and personality individually and organizationally develop over periods of time, drastic change in any of the parties at interest is, at best, only a limited prospect. This necessitates the calculation of various strategies of persuasion and, if this fails, coercion.

The same may be true with regard to those superordinate to the leader, for the seeds of discord are imbedded in mistaken expectations here as well. Potential strife is averted when what is tolerable and what is intolerable leadership behavior is clearly perceived by both, before the fact. Leadership style and behavior are, in great part, the consequence of disciplinary and organizational history. The objectives of the profession and of the institutions tend here to receive their clearest expression. This may be the central problem of leadership in librarianship. Leader personality and mode of behavior are the reflections of institutional and disciplinary image. The guideposts, the underlying value system, gives credence to and places the highest premium upon stability, custom, and orderliness. Therein is the dilemma of leadership responsibility. An organizational and disciplinary culture which has given little place to innovativeness and imaginative responses is sorely tested to reconstruct its value terms. The mental set of most who aspire to leadership roles has been conditioned during an occupational lifetime. Those who are its clients expect little more from the institution than the sum of its history and the image which it reflects to the culture as a consequence of its traditions. To then tamper with organizational and professional accomplishment through rude shifts, through dramatic variation, calls for leader behavior which the past has seldom cultivated. Moreover, it would be deeply troubling to many who strongly identify with the patterns of tradition. Yet to be adaptive, to chance alternatives, is always a latent possibility. It simply awaits the awakening of an aroused leadership that sees no other recourse.

One further behavioral tendency which frequently may account for leader success must be added to those specified thus far—personal opportunism. To be opportunistic is to conceive that the potential exists for blending individual striving with organizational goals and so to promote personal ambition within the medium of institutional attainment. In the identification of leadership with organizational aspirations, the most powerful rationalization for leadership behavior is found. Administration and leadership are frequently confused. Administration is the occupancy of office. Leadership is the assumption of responsibility for bringing together commitment, understanding, determination, and organizational strategy and the pursuit of goals. Leadership, at its best, moves an organization in such a way that it avoids a total posture of opportunism, yet remains pragmatic enough to escape utopianism. Administration tolerates institutional drift. Leadership behavior implies the responsibility to direct the decision processes toward determined goals. The distinction is often reflected in the difference between organizations only marginally able to sustain themselves and those striving to realize their full potential and contribution to the culture. The task of leadership is to assess imaginatively the environment and the consequences of organizational responses to change. Leadership influences the capacity of the organization to be responsive by finding resources and creating internal mechanisms to implement such programs and such ends. Leadership deals in futures. What the organization has been is seen as prelude to what it can become.

Creative leadership translates concern into reconstruction. It extends the boundaries beyond procedure by arranging for the solution to routine problems so that the organization can go beyond the minimum level and concentrate upon alternate options in order to ensure an organizational future. The coherence of the ongoing effort thus becomes the condition from which to shape a future beyond what the present affords. Leadership thereby addresses the need both for a present adaptive organization with integrity and for shaping the next stage in its evolution.

In a time when human beings in and out of organizations feel impotent, the prime requisite of leadership behavior may be that catalytic quality which stems from commitment founded in optimism, anticipating progress as a counterpart to resignation. It is expressed in genuine efforts to translate such caring into forceful programs in the belief that opinions and values do count, that they can influence the course of events, particularly in the organization where one assumes responsibility. This type of leadership is founded on faith born of high purpose. In contemporary context, such striving tends to liberate the forms of individual expression, reducing constraints upon nonconformity. Leadership becomes the mechanism for enlisting members of the enterprise to join in as it fosters variety and difference; it enhances new groupings and arrangements, all as expressions of the variability and variety of human potential. For one of the conscious ends of such leadership is found in the measure of freedom accorded the individual. The group which honors the freedom of its members holds its goals adaptable, does not irrevocably bind up the future but shapes it from changing perspectives and changing aspirations. This type of leadership calls for a reconstructed sense of what is organizationally rational and legitimate. It rejects the tyranny of hierarchy and ritual. It substitutes, instead, more open forms and procedures, more flexibility, more communication, and it inspires and encourages expression from all those in it who are moved to work toward its goals.

True leadership behavior, because it calls upon uncommon capacity, because it is not precisely susceptible of measurement, perhaps most of all because it is often neither sought by those who would be influenced by it nor understood by those who would practice it, is seldom found. Instead there is displacement. Those who could or should lead simply hold office and are compulsively drawn to those operational areas which can serve as outlet of their purely administrative aspirations. Nor is it that these areas of concern are irrelevant or inappropriate, but only that they are all too seldom perceived in any context of overall disciplinary or institutional contribution of purpose. In libraries, physical-plant enlargement attracts zeal of this nature, as does the building of book collections. Such striving may be part of a whole cultural syndrome which equates achievement with physical reality. For this is an important reason why buildings receive endowments and collections bear the names of their donors. A library building and the book collection are real and tangible things. A building and book collection can be seen, they can be understood, they demonstrate without question the pragmatism of the administrator who was responsible for their presence. The attention of the administrator is transferred from what should be the main concern, the individuals for whom the organization exists, to a view of responsibility identified more nearly with tangible artifacts and physical properties. Psychological values and reassurances clearly flow from such attainment rather than as consequence of client-response efforts which are only so very ephemeral. A new building is forever.

Certain characteristics of librarianship and of library administration tend to constrain leadership. One is a kind of waiting and hoping born of desires and wishes but not translated into forceful action. Passivity thus is reflected in resignation, opportunity is seen as foreclosed, responsibility for engendering significant accomplishment is seen to reside elsewhere. Such a stance puts its hope in the passage of time as the powerful corrective for realizing dreams. Somehow faith will bring progress, even without the participation of those who want it most. But passive waiting turns frequently to hopelessness and despair, to self-deluding fantasy which masks the absence of dedication to the strategy needed to bring a more sanguine condition. Another characteristic of librarianship is the longing to enshrine a leadership figure in whom to impute godlike wisdom and understanding. The more physically and psychologically distant he is placed, the more he is mystically endowed, the more all others can be absolved of responsibility for the organizational destiny. Yet with the current involvement in a number of disciplines by many who have traditionally been voiceless, traditional library leadership is being rejected by greater numbers.

An even more subtle factor affecting the presence or absence of leadership behavior is related to the perception which those who hold positions of responsibility have of their roles and of the image which they reflect to others. A certain self-assurance, confidence, perhaps readiness to behave aggressively whenever necessary, sparks the behavior of a leader sure of himself, sure of his cause, and seen so by others. It is just such a quality which separates the natural winners from the losers, differentiates those who will be humbly accepting from those who will fight for more. An administrative class with such a personality, such a style, becomes a leadership class. And almost as direct consequence of such self-perception and the acting out of such behavior, this becomes the view also held in the mind's eye of those who observe them. But this is hardly the self-perception of most librarians. The stereotype of submission and toleration of marginal conditions persists among the library administrative class, and a static condition is inexorably perpetuated. For it makes the alternative, a genuine leadership stance founded upon promise and bold operations, seem unrealistic, daring, or ridiculous. It is for this reason that different leadership models are so essential and that, in underdeveloped cultures, they must often be sought in other more advanced settings. Only by recognizing what is fit and what is right can one aspire to more than what history has conditioned him to expect. In the absence of an environment of bold library leadership in which those who later come to assume the role might receive direct and indirect perception of what constitutes appropriate performance, the observations drawn from experience fail to prepare them to emulate such a forceful style. Thus potential future library leaders do not even understand the possibilities of alternatives to the routine assumption of the administrative role. The lackluster performance of those who assume roles of leadership potential now does not inspire future leaders to assume greater responsibility for true leadership since they are confident of their own capacity to achieve at a level which seemingly demands no more than what they have witnessed. Leadership style is absorbed only through working and observing in an atmosphere of exemplary performance. Unless those being acculturated to accept later responsibility do perceive differences, it is inordinately difficult for them to understand the demands of leadership, to say nothing of making such a standard their own bench-mark level of aspiration. In the absence of leadership standards at an appropriate level within the library context, or until one has been derived, the cues and models must be sought elsewhere—in the tenacious performance of the city manager, in the visionary aspirations of the college president, in the statesmanlike expression of the academic department head—wherever creative and imaginative leadership is conducted and expressed with zest and self-assurance and wherever such performance is seen to achieve respect and recognition.

PART II

The Real World
of Librarianship

CHAPTER 6

Institutional Administration

U p to this point we have been principally engaged with theory and ideology. While the focus has been upon innovation and change with leadership as the prime catalytic element, libraries have been treated only tangentially, linked to the theoretical arguments as the particular case in point rather than as the precise subject of analysis. Attention turns now to the realities of librarianship, to the patterns and the characteristics of existing disciplinary and institutional practice. The perspectives are drawn from my analysis of empirical data, from the evidence of the field's literature, and as a consequence of personal assessment as a participant observer for many years.

A PROFILE OF LIBRARY LEADERS

The characteristics of the library administrative class which follow are based upon a questionnaire study conducted in 1969. The findings, the methodology, and the statistical details have been reported elsewhere.[1] Essentially the studies sought to ascertain the degree to which the senior administrator in each significant form of library—public, academic, school, and special—is committed to and able to foster change in his organization. The information gathered ranged from social and educational background, career patterns, and value orientations of the library executives to institutional data on the actual change record and structure of the organizations with which they are associated. In all but one instance, the sample was large enough to permit of generalizations beyond the

1. See Mary Lee Bundy and Paul Wasserman, *A Study of the Executive in Library and Information Activity*, a series of reports (see Preface).

respondents to the entire class of administrators of the particular type of library involved.[2]

It would be very difficult, and misleading, to draw a composite profile of the library administrator. The contexts are discrete, and the characteristics of those administratively responsible in the several types of libraries vary significantly enough to defy a homogeneous portrait. Still certain characteristics and certain attitudes transcend institutional differences, and in such instances, generalizations may be drawn across types of library lines in deriving explanations for the ways in which administrative behavior is conditioned in librarianship. The most predominant feature is that library administrators are selected almost exclusively from the ranks of librarianship. This has not always been the case and speaks of the degree to which the discipline has succeeded in furthering the professionalization of its managerial class, thereby coming to be near universally perceived as a field of expertise requiring technical direction. The present Librarian of Congress, L. Quincy Mumford, is the first professional librarian to hold the post. As this is so, those who hold topmost positions in each type of library, drawn as they are from the occupation, strongly identify with its professional norms. Moreover, not only are the library administrators acculturated to the conventional values of the field through institutionalized experience, but for 90 percent or more of those practicing in academic, public or school librarianship, the process builds upon the framework of values imparted to them in consequence of formal library education. It is only in the special library that only six out of ten administrators have had library school preparation. Many professional schools are represented. They are spread regionally; they differ in their concentration on particular specialties and by the rate at which they are hospitable to change. But they have been almost universally characterized by a traditionalism which has seldom put them in the vanguard. The effect which they have had, in contrast for example with advanced forms of prototypal libraries, has seldom been as powerful catalyst

---

2. Based on size of student enrollment and size of population served respectively, both the academic and public library sections of the study were stratified samples. A total of 161 out of 198 academic library administrators returned usable questionnaires (81 percent); 102 out of 144 public library administrators responded (71 percent). The universe for the school library supervisors section consisted of the 150 American school systems having student enrollments of over 25,000 and a position of school library supervisor. All were sent questionnaires and 99 were returned completed (66 percent). From those 427 special libraries or information centers employing ten persons or more, 150 were chosen at random, and 95 questionnaires were returned (64 percent). Due to the wide variety of organizational context and forms of service within the special library and information center group, generalizations here were approached with extreme caution and findings presented as suggestive, awaiting further analysis based on more extensive data.

energizing their students to strike out for change. Instead, they have, and do, offer the academically sanctioned ressurance of the perpetuity of existing forms, customs, and values. Such an educational sequence, founded as it is upon tenets which powerfully reinforce the status quo, could scarcely be expected to mold iconoclasts.

Affiliations with professional and technical societies often determine occupational behavior among those who are members and are loyal to them. American library administrators of academic and public libraries tend to identify with the American Library Association. School library supervisors generally maintain membership in the American Library Association, as part of a joint affiliation with the National Education Association. Special librarians lean toward the Special Libraries Association, but some also belong to the American Society for Information Science or to the American Library Association. To the extent that the American Library Association tends to function as a confederation of administrators rather than as a genuine professional society, its natural propensity is to bolster institutional structure by ballyhooing the exploits and the aspirations of institutions as they are.[3] Such value orientations are reflected in documents which are either idealized versions of what libraries would like to believe of themselves[4] or so vague and all embracing as to be impossible of attainment.[5] In the time-honored manner of the trade association, the prime characteristic of this largest of all organizations in librarianship is of protecting the institutions and promoting their intrinsic societal value as is, only with more resources linked irrevocably to the virtue and the joy of reading. As they conceive of the school library, the National Education Association and the American Library Association speak in chorus for a multimedia approach, and for the extension of libraries to schools without them, never to the questions of an alternative ideology of service and client responsibility. The Special Libraries Association and the American Society for Information Science cluster their zeal around the mechanics of the information process. For the information scientist, it is the system and its refinement which elicits the fiercest striving. But in each case the point of departure is the existing

3. These points are elaborated in Mary Lee Bundy and Paul Wasserman, "Professionalism Reconsidered," *College and Research Libraries*, January 1968, pp. 5–26.
4. As in the case of the Library Bill of Rights. A study of school and public libraries in California found considerable discrepancy between librarians' verbal support of freedom-to-read convictions and actual book-selection behavior with respect to controversial materials. See Marjorie Fiske, *Book Selection and Censorship* (Berkeley: University of California Press, 1959), Chapter V.
5. See, for example, *Minimum Standards for Public Library Systems, 1966* (Chicago: American Library Association, 1967). See also Joseph L. Wheeler, "What Good Are Public Library Standards?," *Library Journal*, February 1970, pp. 455–462.

framework, posing little threat to the values and commitments that have always been the library condition. As these bodies form the predominant professional enclaves, so does the ideology reflected in their conferences, meetings, publications, and institutions foster accepted values. While it is true that the occasional session or contribution may assail the norms by proffering an alternative value stance, such diversions are seen as only temporary aberrations which benignly mirror the tolerance of the organizations for diversity. Like the way in which *Fortune* magazine may occasionally glamorize a corporate or managerial failure in its columns without betraying its unswerving allegiance to capitalistic success, so will ALA grant space and time to dissidents, everlastingly confident that its traditional ideology cannot but be reinforced as the consequence. Thus it may be seen that here too, in the philosophy, the ideals, and the public expressions of their professional organizations, the administrators are reconfirmed in their clinging to conventional perspectives.

Although they are functioning as administrators, the overwhelming majority of library executives perceive of themselves as belonging to the occupation of librarianship. Such a self-identity ought to result in the administrator perceiving the professional librarian as a source of ideas. It does not. For the capacity for expression and implementation of change ideals inheres more in present institutional forms in the administrator perceiving himself as the leader. Moreover, as the larger proportion of library administrators has come to librarianship as a second or later career choice and voices no serious regrets in having made this occupational decision, the orientation of the discipline as it is receives powerful endorsement. The greatest majority, if they were to do it again, indicate that they would make the same career choice. The passion for influencing the field to be otherwise is scarcely visible in such a comfortable mesh of discipline and self.

Some clues to the commonality of the perspectives of library administrators who see the existing organizational and professional norms as congruent with their own aspirations are to be found in the socioeconomic backgrounds which they tend overwhelmingly to share. The composition of the group (perhaps capable of extrapolation beyond the administrator to the entire occupation) identifies it as different from the general population. Library administrators are drawn from families in which the majority of the fathers were of the white-collar class, with professional and managerial occupations predominating, with only minimal representation from blue-collar or service occupations in their lineage. It should not then be at all surprising to find the group intrinsically complacent. For the institutional structure as it is and as it has been, and as it is reflected in the values and norms of libraries, has served them well. If the library system, like the educational system, rests on the ideal of equality, but actually is oriented only to a particular class, they are of that particular class. They are not individuals from a group with a heritage of tension or hostility. Their heritage is congruent with traditional cultural perspectives. The society and the institutions which comprise it are thus seen as intrinsically right, in need of some modest adaptation to be sure, but at core sound and unassailable. Those who went before them have shaped these institutions which contribute to their own comfort, security, and satisfaction. As a consequence, only the most strident and belligerent assaults upon the existing institutional arrangements will be given much attention. It is more appealing and less threatening to think of such expressions as temporary aberrations which in time will pass, with the organizations needing only to weather the times, secure in their essential staying power and indestructibility.

Educational Background

Another widely shared characteristic in the backgrounds of the library administrators is the predominance among them of a humanistic undergraduate preparation. Most pronounced among the academic librarians where roughly two thirds were so oriented, it was only among the special library administrators that a high of 20 percent of their number were prepared in the sciences. A modest representation of social-science background is reflected in the ranks of the public library administrators and, as would be expected, school library supervisors were often found to have taken their undergraduate degrees in education. There may be no direct correlative indicator here to link with change disposition. Yet it is clearly the case that the humanities are comprised of the disciplines most firmly committed to the book. As this is so, it is surely not an accident that those who have received their intellectual acculturation here would see the book collection as the prime value. Libraries as books *and* people perhaps, but books as the enduring thing with the collection as the ultimate, closely followed by the building of the temple where they are enshrined. Another class, differently proportioned as to science or social-science background, would perhaps more nearly reflect alternative priorities wherein system or clients might be seen to transcend the artifacts. As the greatest representation among the administrative class remains humanistically committed as a reflection of its education, as their leanings incline toward history, literature, the arts and language, so does this propensity seem to influence the way in which libraries remain rooted and intransigent. For if a library predominantly conveys a sense of congruence between the books reflective of the humanistic heritage and the perspectives of its administrative class, neither those in it nor those whom it is designed to serve conceive of it as potentially otherwise. If values fail to transcend earlier norms, not only do the collections themselves remain unbalanced and distorted (invariably heavily weighted in terms of the humanistic tastes of the librarians themselves)[6] but the client and service terms and the organizational considerations as well as the technical and systems terms remain unquestioned and unaltered.

Social science research has clearly linked change disposition with youth.[7] The propensity to tamper with things is less compelling in maturity, the passion to remake the world is spent. With age there comes, if not always wisdom, then at least a reconciliation of self with social and institutional environment. The fiery urges to be, to do, to become otherwise, personally and organizationally, if they ever were present, tend long since to have abated. Yet the one common characteristic of library administrators is their age. Fewer than 5 percent of any of the groups was under thirty-five years of age at the time of the study. Approximately half of the administrators were over fifty years of age. The condition may be explained, at least in part, by the fact that library careers have often begun later than those in other comparable fields; many are not drawn to librarianship until after prior career experience in other occupations. But regardless of why this is so, the fact remains that the administrative reins rest in the hands of those of middle age or beyond.

A characteristic of the change-oriented is the disposition to be prepared to shift with opportunity or under terms where the local options appear constraining. Here again the evidence disappointingly correlates with the facts of age, for the mobility potential of the library group is decidedly limited. Only a small number are actively interested in opportunities elsewhere. Virtually half would like to be in their present positions five years hence. Approximately one of every five anticipates retirement within the next five years. Only a small percentage of the library administrators describe themselves in such a way as to be in a position in which they could bring about significant change in their settings—even if they were so disposed. This strong identification with

6. A simple test of this proposition is to roughly compare the size of the reference or circulating book collections on art, flower arrangement, and poetry with those on investments, consumer guides, and astronomy in any public library branch.

7. Over the past several decades, an accelerated interest in the problems of aging and creativity has stimulated multidisciplinary efforts to provide a body of data to support, explain and occasionally question such assertions. See, for example, A. T. Welford and James E. Birren, eds., *Behavior, Aging and the Nervous System* (Springfield, Illinois: Charles C Thomas, 1965) and Harvey C. Lehman, *Age and Achievement* (Princeton, N.J.: Princeton University Press, 1953).

the local situation and the nearness to career end may be seen as power-ful constraints to the role of change agent.

There are some degrees of difference which may help to explain varia-tions, but these are only clues rather than firm evidence. The special library administrators provide the sharpest illustration: here 62 percent of those with formal library education are over fifty years of age, but only 30 percent of those without library education are in this age cate-gory; only 16 percent of library school graduates have had science prep-aration, but 43 percent of those without library education are drawn from the sciences; 50 percent of the library school graduates belong to the American Library Association, but only 8 percent of nonlibrary school graduates belong to the same organization. And even within the same group there is pronounced diversity: 70 percent of governmental li-brarians are over fifty, compared to 38 percent of the industrial li-brarians; 73 percent of the government group are drawn from humanistic backgrounds, as opposed to only 41 percent of the industrial librarians. The technological leanings doubtless explain why individuals are drawn to the special library who would not be to other library forms and also provide at least some explanation for the more pronounced tendency of the special libraries to have adapted their procedural system to advanced forms of technology.[8]

Male-Female Ratio in Leadership Group

Librarianship is a discipline in which the number of females is greater than the number of males and it might be tempting to explain away the lack of interest in change as a reflection of the culturally induced strain of passivity among the female of the species. But only in the school library field, where 80 percent of school library supervisors are women, was the composition of administrative leadership such as to permit this hypothesis. Overwhelmingly, the library administrative group is made up of males, and in the particular sphere in which virtually all the topmost administrative positions are male controlled, academic li-braries gave evidence of being the most passive group of all.

The picture which emerges from the data characterizes a class of middle-aged or older individuals firmly rooted in the values of middle class, humanistically educated America, essentially conservative in out-look on the issues which affect their professional decision-making be-havior. In a society in which traditional values are everywhere in ques-tion, the library administrator stands basically unaffected and fails to

8. See Eugene B. Jackson, "The Use of Data Processing Equipment by Libraries and Information Centers—The Significant Results of the SLA-LTP Survey," *Special Libraries*, May 1967, pp. 317–327.

correlate his institution or his role with the changing panorama. While the rhetoric of the discipline proclaims otherwise, the organizations, conditioned by their administrative classes, perpetuate themselves as passive, book-oriented agencies enlisted in the service of an essentially unchanged select clientele. Unconventional perspectives are little in evidence. Serious question of the present condition is expressed by only a small minority among an administrative group that has attained senior-level roles largely because of its capacity to negotiate within the conventional system of libraries and its values, rather than by assaulting it. While the issues are somewhat different in the various types of libraries, certain characteristic expressions of the library administrators revealed their commitment to reinforcing long-standing values.

ADMINISTRATORS' VIEWS OF SERVICE

The notion of self-help is deeply engrained in library administrators. For the academic and school situation, the implication translates to a view that the user must be equipped to serve himself. Such a perspective supports minimal levels of client service and is incompatible with a striving for more advanced forms of reference and information help. Under terms where the library is less committed to the information-seeking, problem-solving process, in the college or the school, where its zeal is centered in equipping users with their own library skills, the sense of the professional-client relationship is undercut among both the practitioners and their potential clients. Where the service orientation is more pronounced, as in the public library, the commitment tends toward traditional forms of provision which detract from other potential contributions. Recreational reading for patrons is almost consensually seen as a legitimate function. The public library administrator thus continues to foster and encourage dependence upon the library for an abundance of such forms of material at a time when there exist many alternate avenues of access. This type of traditional syndrome among public libraries may be less than responsible. Even in the library setting which puts highest premium upon responsiveness to clients, the special library, more than eight in ten administrators felt that "users need to be helped to help themselves," while more than half agreed with the notion that "users frequently demand services that they should be doing for themselves."[9]

9. The special library administrators in the sample included not only those in corporate and governmental libraries, but other specialized forms such as archives and state libraries. As pointed out earlier, such heterogeneity makes generalization more hazardous than in the case of the academic, public, or school library.

The value commitments of each type of library administrator, except in the instance of the school library supervisor where the multimedia concept is firmly planted, put books in the central place. Only a handful of administrators identified a dedication to the information function or responsibility. And where expressed, such a striving tended to be equated with computerization, rather than with enhanced client services. But there is little uniformity even in the aspirational level administrators hold about the future potential of mechanized information storage and retrieval. Some are deeply suspicious and hostile, others cautious about the anticipated rate of developing economically efficient systems. Perhaps most interesting, and clearly a pervasive tendency, was the sense that while advanced forms of information retrieval might be in the offing, they would be most useful in settings other than the administrators' own. The application of technology to local information-service responsibilities was almost universally discounted, with information retrieval equated in the minds of many with large national systems generating bibliographic products for local consumption. For the overwhelming majority of library administrators, developments in information retrieval are not seen as something in which they have any real stake; no sense of urgency is expressed in the need to further their clients' information access through such present or projected developments; any impetus for such advance rests with others. If there is an information revolution in progress, it transcends the program, the goals, the objectives, and the aspirations of library administrators as a general class.

If the composition of library clienteles which has evolved as a consequence of the traditional orientation remains constant, library administrators do not seem concerned. While it is true that three in every four public library administrators agree that "public libraries should be willing to take on more of a community service function," here just as with the other library administrators, only a minority expressed a top priority of concern for the expansion or redirection of service to unreached clienteles. The prime client of the academic library is the faculty, and as in the elementary and secondary school, the use of the library as it has been used in the past is taken for granted. Nonuse is perceived as a reflection of either media or collection limits, seldom as inadequacy of clientele services. Any expression that alternative services and responsibilities toward clients might condition different expectancies among users so as to broaden the scope of clientele is inaudible. Even in the sacred zone of intellectual freedom, so central to the ideological roots of public librarianship, the tendency to be progressive in the rigorous pursuit of this ideal is powerfully circumscribed among significant proportions of its own administrative class. While slightly over half agree and more than a quarter are neutral or undecided, one in five public library administrators is in disagreement that "the profession needs to take a far more aggressive stance on intellectual freedom than it has in the past."

To the extent that administrators perceive the inadequacies of their organization's performance they are likely to foster the changes which may enhance the organizational contribution. With complacency, or with the rationalization of limitations of performance as circumscribed by factors outside their control, the administrators peer out upon their world through rose-colored glasses. The evidence of the opinion of academic library administrators often equates failure in the academic-library situation with the failure of the larger community. Either it does not make its needs known effectively to the library, or it is not aware of what the library has to offer, or as is most commonly the case, it is failing to provide adequate resources for library operations. Fully two of every three administrators disagree with the statement that "libraries have simply failed to respond to changing times and changing needs," while only one in five agrees. The stark term "failure" may of course elicit highly defensive reactions among respondents who see themselves and their institutions subject to criticism. Yet as self-defensiveness about the organizational condition or about individual performance remains deeply rooted as a characteristic, it is unlikely that the formulation of program alternatives and services will rank very high on the organizational agenda.

Even when greater proportions concede the failure of libraries, as in the instance of the school library supervisors, the explanations are couched in terms of space, fund and personnel limitations, virtually never in the library's service aspirations. Only a handful of public library administrators see the information responsibility of the library as undeveloped, or demonstrate concern over the failure of the institutions to reach unserved elements for whom the conventional library remains irrelevant. Among the public library administrators are those, a small but vociferous group, adamant in their expression that to tamper with traditional program perspectives would risk converting the library into a social-service agency. For some of them, if the public library fails, it does no worse than the general run of public institutions in the present culture, and so does not deserve to be singled out for recrimination.

The threat of competitive agencies, media, and programs is perceived by a majority of the administrators at the conceptual level, for most agree that if the library "does not get with it, other agencies will come along to do their job." But translated into terms of alternatives to running the existing course, the inviolability of the traditional attitudes on library role and contribution remains unswerving.

As value orientations remain intransigent, as defensiveness to charges of failure typically call forth traditional forms of rationalization, the commitments which receive strongest expression are those of maintenance and perpetuation, rather than those of change. Goals are unquestioned and the administrator concentrates his zeal on the means of achieving them. The instrumental measures are thus conceived as degrees of success in securing financial resources, effecting improvements of physical arrangements, attraction of staff. Typifying the underdeveloped state which is not yet ready to calculate alternatives until the threshold of minimal provision and security is provided, so library administrators labor diligently to bring their organizations thus far. The long-term expectation is almost undifferentiable from the short-term—it is seen by virtually all the administrators as simply a better provided-for organization, functioning precisely in the present mode with enhanced resources with which to do it more efficiently. Conspicuous by its absence from the aspirational expression of the library administrators is variability in client-service forms. A few express concern with deriving the means to better meet clientele requirements, presumably assuming that furtherance of present designs will automatically ensure client satisfaction. Even fewer specify the attraction of new clienteles as a priority. Attracting unserved elements remains, for the administrative class, essentially a matter either of improved public relations, or of educating the user to the virtue of the library's offerings. It is not a question of inquiring into the intrinsic nature of the institutional goals and priorities out of which the programs and services receive their impetus.

The shared values of the library administrative class in the conventional wisdom of institutional goals is reflected in the high degree of agreement among them upon the means of their achievement. Salient elements of the consensual developmental strategy includes computer applications, cooperative ventures, and utilization of technicians. Earlier pockets of entrenched resistance to the computer in data processing have seemingly been overcome. Overwhelmingly the administrators feel that the computer offers major advantages for their type of library. Moreover, acceptance is actively reflected in the incidence of present use and in concrete plans for the extension of such use. Regional cooperation is coming to academic libraries almost as fully as public libraries, with two thirds of the administrators of academic libraries engaged in regional or national programs. More than one in three of the special library administrators are also involved, and even though only one in six school library supervisors reported participation, to a degree a school library system may already be seen to function as a kind of miniregional system. Still, doubt persists about the efficacy of external reliance, at least among academic librarians who remain committed to the immediacy of local collection development as central to institutional needs. The apprehension of the public librarian tends to be a function of political autonomy in the face of the inexorable need to group collectively. It is in present and anticipated use of technicians that administrators are in greatest consensus; the use of a nonprofessional category was already heavily relied upon by upwards of two thirds of the administrators included in the survey. In coming to rely more extensively upon such paraprofessionals for a wide range of tasks from which librarians are then freed, the central question remains whether efficiency and economy can be attained without denaturing the capacity for client responsiveness.

The prime thrust of aspirational thinking among administrators is toward changes which improve the capacity of their libraries to carry out their existing programs. If in consequence, the ultimate end is to shift the focus of their libraries to a more responsible client role, this is something which the administrators did not specify. More active or responsive forms of information service, increased concentration upon services to alternative clienteles, were little mentioned. The sense of the administrators' perspectives conjures a future library functioning much like the present model, performing the same role in ways become more efficient and economical in consequence of present and projected trends.

Library administrators, precisely like their counterparts in other institutional settings, experience the frustrations of unrealized aspirations. In this discipline, administrators of every type of library complained of budget limits, lack of qualified staff, other problems of staffing, and limited understanding of library needs among those to whom the library is administratively and politically responsible. In spite of such complaints, however, it is abundantly clear that for the greatest proportion of library administrators there is little serious dissatisfaction with the rate of change in their own libraries. Only in the school library group are there as many as one third not satisfied, with just under 10 percent very satisfied; in the other forms fewer than two in ten were not satisfied, with the majority reasonably satisfied. Such measures do not reflect an administrative class ready to propel their organizations forward, but bespeak more nearly a sense of complacency about the present condition. Another revealing perception of the library administrators is seen in their sense of possible personal strategies which they might pursue. When asked to indicate whether they felt particular forms of behavior were "very appropriate" or "not appropriate" in influencing change in their organizations, responses underscore the essential limits in aggressive styles of administrative behavior which could be expected. While two thirds or more in each group endorse the strategy, "Seize on opportunities as they arise; strike while the iron is hot," an even higher proportion advocate "recognition that lasting change is not made overnight." For administrators engaged in budgetary processes, in jurisdictions characterized by rival claims for the same resources among numerous competitors, it is surprising to find that—except for the public library where more than two of every three administrators sanctioned it—virtually nine of every ten administrators feel it is very advisable "to see the library's needs for support in relation to other needs of the community (or organization)." Not only did more administrators subscribe to the notion of "conducting a careful and methodical program of introducing new developments using caution and restraint" than to "adopt a forceful aggressive approach to effecting change," but significant proportions, ranging from one in three to one in two administrators of the different types of libraries, felt that this latter approach was "not appropriate." But if the intensity of change disposition is of any value as indicator of administrative behavior, the most telling revelation of all is that 76 percent of the academic administrators, 58 percent of the public, 72 percent of the school, and 77 percent of the special library administrators characterize themselves as feeling that "readiness to leave if requests are not met in a reasonable time" is not appropriate behavior.

If the status quo of their libraries is imperfect, library administrators seem most disposed to allow time to heal, with gradual modification seen as the route of choice. In ways characteristic of the human condition, sharpest rebuke is reserved for the limits of others and of other institutions. Rationalization thus safeguards self-perception and so self-respect for the library administrators. When it is not the faulty local political or administrative structure, or the insensitive constituency, or the limited staff—aberrations which are not subject to his control—the more familiar whipping boys are library education and the national professional society. All types of administrators shared a critical view of professional education. The fiercely pragmatic bewail the imbalance between theoretical and practical content; the philosophic deride the paucity of intellectual substance. A number lament the limited options of specializations in such concerns as community, media, or computer. But if the administrators hold negative views of professional education, they are even more sharply critical of the American Library Association. Still for the administrators as a class, there are elements of a hate-love syndrome here. If they do not find personal strivings satisfied, the intrinsic need for a confederation representing the institutional interest with which they are identified cannot be dismissed. While many, but typically the academic and public librarians, critically deplore the scale, cumbersomeness, and leadership which is seen as centering its concern upon holding power instead of genuinely serving members or focusing on issues, others bewail its identity as so inextricably interwoven with public librarianship. The defenders of the American Library Association on the other hand specify its many virtues such as the sparkling legislative record, publications of importance in many spheres, workshops and institutes directed to the needs of the field, and they denounce impatient "Johnny-come-latelies" who want too much too soon.

If there is some considerable disillusion then with library education and with the American Library Association, no alternative is seen worthy of the time and effort to set things right. It is simply that library education and the American Library Association provide convenient twin targets for the venting of chronic dissatisfactions in the field, and that the expression of such lament is so deeply engrained in the personality of the discipline that it is regarded as commonplace. Furthermore such expression, no matter how vituperative or vitriolic, places the spokesman under no compunction whatsoever to go beyond bewailing the condition to do something.

The evidence identified an administrative class that tended to conform, that expressed little antagonism to the present values of the discipline. For the overwhelming majority, advancement in the field was seen as dependent upon ability, not upon knowing the right people. Except for the special library administrator, the greatest number disagreed with the statement that "the leadership of this profession is by and large conservative and largely concerned with protecting the status quo." But if many administrators seem comfortable with and committed to how things are at present, there is a minority, numbering from one in four to almost half, who are disposed to give credence to the need for alternatives to the traditional contribution; they agree that libraries are failing to respond to changing times and needs.

Still, countervailing views, symptomatic of well-entrenched conservatism, are reflected in the widely shared view among one of every three academic administrators who agree that "we will be remembered not for the service we gave, but for the collections we leave behind" while the same proportion of public library administrators felt that "while reaching unserved elements is desirable, most libraries have all they can do to keep up with their present users." What is more, the sentiment that all is not well does not automatically translate into prescription and program for change. For no concrete evidence could be discerned which would correlate disaffection or dissatisfaction with a more aggressive blueprint for change in the respondent's own institution.

LEADERSHIP CHARACTERISTICS AT VARIOUS AGE LEVELS

If the facts do not demonstrate an administrative class in librarianship aggressively bent upon reconstruction and revision, perhaps the emergent leadership might be found to differ in kind or in degree. This question could have been pursued in different ways—either by assessing the perspectives of individuals at secondary levels of administration in the same organizations, or by comparing the attitudes, values, and commitments among the respondents along age lines. For reasons of economy and practicality, the latter course was pursued in an analysis of the attitudinal portions of the questionnaire by dividing the group into three categories—age forty-five and under, forty-five to fifty-four, fifty-five and over.

Among public library administrators, the two younger groups appeared to be less book-oriented and more computer-oriented. More of their number tend to agree that "libraries have simply failed to respond to changing times and changing needs." Still differences here were minor, and it was among the youngest group that the smallest percentage expressed optimism about the potential value to local library developments of improved interlibrary cooperative efforts. Perhaps more telling was that a slightly higher percentage of the youngest group (42 percent) than either the middle (32 percent) or oldest group (35 percent) feel that "while reaching unserved elements may be desirable, most libraries have all they can do to keep up with their present users." Ironically, on the issue of intellectual freedom, the youngest, perhaps reflecting the brashness of youth, and the oldest, with possibly least to lose at their stage of elder statesmen, are in league (58 percent in each age group) that "the profession needs to take a far more aggressive stance on intellectual freedom than it has in the past," while the middle age group agreed at the level of only 42 percent. Using the same yardsticks, the youngest school library supervisors are clearly more heavily oriented to newer media, and more disposed to offer students information they require and less concerned with teaching library skills. But the paramount place of books among the youngest group in which 50 percent agree that "librarians need above all to know books," represents no significant difference from those in the older categories.

Perhaps the most striking difference which distinguishes both the public library and school groups by age differences is the variation in the sexual composition of their numbers. Among the public library administrators, 55 percent of those fifty-five years and over are male, 77 percent in the forty-five to fifty-four bracket, and 88 percent of those forty-four years or younger. Among school library supervisors only 8 percent of those fifty-five or older are men, while 23 percent of those forty-five to fifty-four are men, and of those forty-four or younger, 38 percent are male. The same characteristic is discernible among special library administrators where 44 percent of the older, 60 percent of the middle group, and 74 percent of those in the youngest category are male. In these three spheres of librarianship, the incidence of male ascendancy is growing sharply.

Among the special librarians other distinctive variations emerge. In the ranks of the oldest, two thirds are drawn from humanities backgrounds, but this is true of only one third in each of the other age categories. A larger proportion of the oldest see no advantages in the computer for their type of library. Paralleling the youngest group of public library administrators, the special library group forty-four years and younger agree in greater numbers that libraries have failed to respond to the times, while in a more limited proportion than among the older group they look to interlibrary cooperation as a prime source of local advantage. The academic group compares essentially with the other young groups. But as in the instance of the school librarians, there is scarcely any observable difference in their view of the primacy of the need to know books (49 percent of those forty-four and under, 52 percent in the middle category, 54 percent of those fifty-five and older). Somewhat fewer however were prone to consider service less significant than collection building. Compared to 32 percent of the middle age group of academic librarians and 38 percent of the oldest category, only 21 percent among the forty-four and under agreed that "we will be remembered not for the service we gave but for the collections we leave behind us."

Quite naturally, reflecting the buoyancy of youth, considerably larger proportions of the forty-four and under agreed that "the leadership of the professions is by and large conservative and largely concerned with protecting the status quo." That is all but the school librarians where it was the middle age category which interestingly expressed the highest incidence of criticism of the leadership. Higher proportions among all but the younger public library group (reaching a high of 38 percent among the forty-four-and-under school library supervisors) advocate "willingness to leave if requests are not met in a reasonable time." Overall, however, the evidence of difference in change disposition is limited and contradictory. There is little basis for assuming that the younger elements among those who assume administrative roles in librarianship are in any fundamental or pronounced ways different from their elders, or that with the passing of time, they will not become them and speak as they do.

Perhaps, essentially, the library administrator may be most clearly perceived as not unlike the general class of administrator who succeeds in the bureaucratic milieu. He is a practical man, dealing with pragmatic things such as buildings and procedures, rather than with philosophy or ideology. If the organization must traffic more sensitively in client terms, he has never been indoctrinated to believe that this is so; for the professional and the institutional culture in which he has forged ahead has never made this evident. Moreover, the pattern of managerial decision-making ultimately resides with him in a traditional bureaucratic authority mode. He reports satisfaction with these existing arrangements. Since decisions rest with him, it is here where change is most likely to be inspired when and if it is inspired.

The kinds of concerns expressed by the library administrators who responded to this inquiry forecast the perpetuation of the libraries under their direction essentially unchanged from the way they have been in the past. Thus libraries if they survive appear to be likely to orient to the same interests, in larger physical plants, with increased numbers of technical and professional functionaries, but neither committed to nor significantly restructured in basic philosophy, in the nature of service, or in clientele priorities. While the survey demonstrates that administrators clearly have aspirations for their libraries, they are little disposed to see these libraries as failing to meet the needs of their communities. Aroused concern about present conditions, necessary as prelude to change, is uncommon. There does not appear to be any disposition to alter in fundamental ways the commitments of the library. It is more likely that library services will not so much be redirected as that operational efficiency will be improved and that in consequence this will make possible the encompassing of larger numbers of books and users within the scope of the library jurisdiction. To some extent this will improve service to traditional users. But the focus of change is unlikely to be on user services or upon programs designed to respond in new and other than conventional ways to constituencies. There is even some question, given the evident concern of administrators that regional cooperation will deflect from local collection building, whether cooperative programs will be permitted to make the delivery function of the library more economic and efficient.

The attitudes and perspectives of library administrators are explainable by their backgrounds. There is nothing in the origins, education, or work experience of the library administrator or in his professional orientation and behavior to lead to expectations that he will be either a change agent or of an entrepreneurial cast of mind. For it is highly likely that in making the choice to enter librarianship and library administration, he elected a career which would be less competitive, more secure, and where only limited kinds of risk-taking behavior would be required. Thus it is not surprising to find that the propensity of the administrator is toward a less than aggressive strategy for change and that he is prepared to accept the gradual and evolutionary form of adaptation which so characterizes the library scene. Another salient factor is the age of administrators. It would be unlikely for those who on the average are so far advanced in years to be functioning energetically as change agents.

Essentially our purpose in accumulating the survey data was to gain insight into the disposition of the administrators with regard to change and to test their general awareness of the need for change in their institutions and in their discipline. The perceptions they revealed were a function of their own knowledge base and the access which they have to reality through information both about their organizational impact and about the influence of libraries in the culture. It is clear that no one thinks constantly about those things which are wrong with his organizational and administrative world. In the face of suggested variations, however, values may be revealed which will identify whether an individual is oriented toward change or comfortable in the present condition. The beginning of organizational adaptation is with the perception of the need for reformation.

Yet the characteristics of a failing organization are never obvious to those who cannot genuinely conceive of a situation very much different from what is, when they have no effective mechanism to identify whether something is wrong or needs adaptation. Without such feedback there tends to be less motivation to think about alternatives and to promote them against lethargy or even opposition. For library administrators, as others, tend to see that which they prefer to see, and are influenced largely by stereotypes, oversimplification, personalization of the facts, and an eagerness to retain political equilibrium. It is always likely to be the bureaucratic norm which puts the accent on the side of the positive, bolsters confidence, and so offers reassurance about the existing order.

While the organizational culture fostered under these terms may not be completely one of inaction, if there is no consciousness of different alternatives, everyone can be complacent and satisfied with conditions. Thus those in the organization do what they know they must, and they succeed a little, but perhaps more often they fail. This, however, is not viewed as alarming. It can be perceived differently only by those not identified with the organization and its ritualization of processes, in the lethargy or disinterest of staff, in the limited sensitivity to client terms. What is potentially evident to these others is the manner in which the process and the organizational triviality have overcome the organizational capacity to be creative or responsive, how the organization is ill-equipped to cope with new and uncommon situations, how its capacity to conduct experiment is not encouraged, and the way these dramatic alternatives as feasible options in solving current problems tend to be frowned upon. The capacity to identify the situation thus by administrators who are themselves identified with the established order of things is obviously circumscribed as a function of their very commitment to the status quo. To keep the process going they must disguise their inner qualms and protect the existing order, all of which results in closing off their sense of awareness of alternatives.

When those connected with organizations meet and talk openly and honestly with outsiders, these comparisons inevitably identify organizational limits. Under these terms, however, the response more nearly will be to deprecate these limitations in order to protect personal interests and defend individual contributions. The responsibility to set things right resides with organizational leaders. If they are incapable of devising solutions or of finding the means for having solutions devised, ultimately their tenure may be threatened. If they cannot be their own reformers they must either identify such agents of change or eventually be replaced by others who will. The limits of the aspirations for their organizations among library administrators are doubtless conditioned by the fact that their calculations seldom embrace anything beyond the historic norms. As the mind of the marginal man is fixed upon the calculation of necessities to insure minimal survival requirements, so may the shackles of the mind of those in the managerial ranks of traditional forms of organizations constitute the most powerful of all barriers to change and reconstruction. In this, perhaps library administrators are not alone and isolated. The way things are and have been conspire to abet those who would keep them thus. Thus do locomotive firemen and flight engineers seek to perpetuate their roles even after technology has made them obsolete, and so do countless farmers cling to the land beyond the point when their economic capacity to survive is no longer assured. In part, the very nostalgia for the past receives expression through administrative acts which perpetuate organizational forms which cling to what was, born of the hope as much as the expectation that things will continue to be so.

If one looks for the sources of change in librarianship, the evidence of the study which has been reviewed here demonstrates that the present and emergent administrative class in the field holds very limited promise. Efforts to influence change must be derived in some measure from a questioning of the present system of values in librarianship. It is this value system which explains the attitudes and thus the behavior of librarianship. The administrator is the product of mutually reinforcing social forces—his socioeconomic background, his undergraduate education, his professional preparation, and the practice of librarianship as it has been and as it is. All in combination uphold the administrative view of the continuity of library purpose and of its contribution.

By continuing to support the conventions of the field, the administrator has the weight of the profession on his side. He can afford to ignore the challenges of the environment or fail to perceive them, for his discipline has not offered him any sense of responsibility to act in ways which transcend the traditional. Moreover, clienteles do not militate for a changed role from the institution for which he assumes administrative responsibility. They, just as the traditionalists in the profession, can conceive of libraries as little more than what they have always been and done. The position is bolstered further by a professional education which serves as replacement training center attracting and preparing new entrants for the same long-standing values.

The expressions of client disaffection take many forms. Alternative information systems are derived. Disgruntlement with bureaucratic forms leads to alienation. Still the social and political structure within which libraries exist cannot be expected to chart the way toward a reconstituted and reoriented commitment from libraries. Its power is only to punish the institution which appears to be irrelevant by withholding resources and patronage from the institution. The redefinition, the reassessment of the library's role and contribution, remains thus a professional responsibility, with the main burden in the hands of its leadership. The administrative class in librarianship, as the evidence of the present study has demonstrated, proves to be more a class of officeholders than of leaders. The general causes for this have been discussed, but if leadership for change does not inhere in the ranks of library directors, then its traces must be sought elsewhere and it is to exploring such trails that our attention shall be drawn hereafter.

CHAPTER 7

The Influence of Education and Library Literature

In order to understand the direction of librarianship more clearly, it is necessary to comprehend the full play of forces upon its practice and ideology. Doubtless among the more salient influences upon library leadership are the factors of local political, jurisdictional, financial, and clientele expression. To generalize these phenomena in any but the broad brush strokes which characterize a society at a particular moment, as has been attempted somewhat in the earlier chapters, would be hazardous. Even to treat the discrete areas which appear quite specifically in a national framework to bear upon library leadership is to assume a brash posture. For one thing, the portrait of these phenomena must, in the present context and without hard empirical basis, rely upon personal reflections and analysis. Even more troublesome is the fact that the phenomena deserve far more painstaking and critical review than is feasible within the limits of the present work. Each tangent represents a whole complex sector deserving more sophisticated and penetrating assessment than it has yet received anywhere. The lack of such contribution inevitably triggers precisely the present form of glossy impressionism. Still, to avoid bringing before the camera as many of the elements as make up the scene, even if some are viewed in somewhat blurred form either because of flaws in the lens or because they are in motion, would yield a more faulty picture than to neglect them completely. Herein resides the rationale for the assessments which follow in this and the next chapter.

EDUCATION, EDUCATORS, AND RESEARCH

In other disciplines, the intellectual base is found in professional schools where within the scholarly framework of the university new ideas are inspired and tested, ultimately broadcast to and among the profession through scholarly media and the export of their disciples. In some fields, the center of a particular school of thought or the main catalytic element of new ideology is found in one university. In others, leadership is more diverse, with different centers spawning competitive schools. At an earlier stage in its history one such enclave reigned un-rivaled in librarianship, the Graduate Library School of the University of Chicago. It was here that the keenest minds were drawn together as teachers and students, here that the consequence of their thinking shaped the parameters of the field's thought, and here where the conceptual bases of practice were designed and probed. It was the University of Chicago which spoke with authority in the columns of its prestigious research journal, through its institutes, in the evidence of its doctoral dissertations, and through the performance of a whole generation of academic library administrators who received their intellectual accultura-tion at this fountain. For almost three decades beginning in 1930 the message was clear and unfaltering: librarianship is a scholarly profession deeply rooted in the humanistic and social sciences, and as these roots are discovered and nourished so will its practice flourish.

This voice has long since become softer, its message lost or forgotten as it sought to adapt to new strains, to comprehend the more rigorous methodologies of science. Its commitment to the ultimate viability of professional practice has been attenuated, as a mélange of discordant elements no longer add up to a consensual theme. Its scholarly journal embarrassingly apes the stalest media of humanistic discipline as it re-mains preoccupied with history and tradition in a time when research and intellectual discourse germane to the contemporary world require equal space. Chicago's links with the profession have grown slack or are now misunderstood. Its orientation, adapted in part toward experimental design, appears to bear only a tenuous relationship to overriding policy issues of the field. Its role as leading intellectual force is thus abdicated, rejected, or lost by default. No longer does one central voice speak with authority as intellectual hub of the discipline. Now many different voices are heard to form a discordant chorus, which even in sum add up to a lower decibel level than did the voice of that single powerful institution in librarianship's past.

Intellectual leadership has thus been dispersed. But in partial conse-quence of its earlier history when only one school spoke with authority and the others served more nearly as replacement training centers for libraries, and due to its very pragmatic orientation, library education is still in the process of finding its place in the university. Those of the cast of mind and intellectual perspectives who might have gravitated toward teaching and research roles, correctly assessed practice as the area holding out more alluring incentives. For they perceived how the most influential scholars in library education were not intrinsically of librarianship, but had been recruited from other disciplines in order to help enrich an impoverished pursuit. The faculty and research component of librarianship thus has tended to remain a weaker segment than its administrative coterie. In consequence, library education, cast in the role of ineffectual and underdeveloped sector, was further reinforced in its minor role. Where schools existed they tended to be marginal in terms of resources and scale of faculty, and while lodged in the university they were not of the university. Their faculties, in default of attracting the best minds produced by the graduate centers and in reflection of their deference to practice, worshipped at its shrine by using part-time teachers, retired administrators, and sometimes ineffectual practitioners. That is not to say that effective professional education is handicapped in finding a balance between research and pragmatic components. This could not be the case in any applied profession. It is simply that such a balance was not developed in librarianship.

In such mature disciplines as medicine or law, the academic citadels provide hospitality to scholars and theorists as well as to eminent practitioners, so that learning relies in important part upon the products of research and analysis, as well as upon the lessons of practice. Librarianship is only very slowly, very gradually, gravitating toward the type of intellectual maturity which characterizes the later stages in the process.

> Professional schools, however much nurtured and protected by the university, are sired by a clientele of practitioners. They are elaborations of an apprenticeship system and are close to the grass roots. Their first faculties are chosen for demonstrated success and reputation in the professional field regardless of the usual trappings of academic qualifications. Despite their popularity with students and practitioners, however, these people are considered by the rest of the university community as poor relations, they are forced to defend themselves against charges that they are operating trade schools. Under pressure to attain recognized status as a profession and to achieve academic respectability, they therefore raise the academic standards for faculty members. Gradually this encourages them to think that there are other useful approaches to their subject and reduces their subservience to their immediate clientele. Eventually, at least in the cases of medicine and engineering, the professional school incorporates into its own structure representatives of related basic disciplines and seeks to make fundamental contributions to knowledge.[1]

1. James B. Thompson, "Modern Approaches to Theory in Administration," in Andrew D. Halpin, ed., *Administrative Theory in Education* (Chicago, Ill.: University of Chicago, 1953), p. 38.

For the most part, yet with some important exceptions, the members of the library education community still find themselves isolated from the world of intellectual discourse in the university. They are seen as poor relations precisely because they have yet to identify and to articulate the intellectual basis of their practice and discipline. Constrained thus from finding links with other disciplines which would be reinforcing of the intellectual components of librarianship, they remain segregated, except in political or service activities in which they receive welcome as fellow citizens more readily than as intellectual peers.

The attempts to change are sporadic and variable. The mainstream of library education and the limited research which it conducts continues its course firmly committed to the conventions and traditions of its past, unswervingly oriented to the type of ritualistic indoctrination in rules, procedures, facts, and disciplinary loyalty. If its faculty were disposed to make claims to intellectualism, this would be almost universally disavowed by its students. For the most part, it is seen as pure and simple training for work roles and is recognized as such by students, faculty, and those in practice. The sense that the prime mission of a professional school in a university is to explore and so to discover the intellectual, conceptual underpinning of the discipline is alien. The constraints of time and resources serve as convenient rationalization for centering zeal elsewhere, perhaps reminiscent of the way in which the practitioner enmeshed inextricably in routines thereby explains away his unavailability for more professional pursuits. My observation is that a very large number of those who have been drawn to academic roles in library education are scholars neither by temperament nor intellectual equipment. They are, for the most part, transplanted practitioners. In consequence, there is a considerable disdain of intellectualism among those who might most logically be looked to for intellectual leadership. The more subtly damaging result is that inasmuch as the student who might aspire to scholarship in the field finds his role models among his faculty, seldom in librarianship does he perceive individuals who in their conduct and life style convey the rewards and satisfactions of the intellectual side of the discipline. More nearly than not, when scholarship is engrained in the soul of the faculty member, it is oriented toward tangential concerns or disciplines not intrinsically the stuff of librarianship. Thus scholarly preoccupation may center passionately upon regional history or genealogy, not the issues of librarianship. Another symptom of the limited awareness of the peculiar underdeveloped condition in the discipline is the incongruity of instruction of the basic, usually required courses in such areas as reference and classification, by individuals who have never themselves conducted research or contributed to the scholarly literature on these subjects. The prime requisite for the teaching role tends to be practical experience. The consequence is the perpetuity of what has been and what is, an unquestioned salute to the pragmatic rite and to its limits. The costs of such arrangements are severe. Most significant is the fact that what is, is enshrined rather than questioned. The effect is training but it is not really education.

Those faculty members not drawn from practice are now coming more often from doctoral study in librarianship. With the impetus of the provisions of Title II-B of the Higher Education Act of 1965, this pattern has grown more customary[2] and is resulting in an infusion of different entries into the academic enclaves. But with the remorseless characteristic of the bootstrap effort, the individuals most recently prepared have typically not received effective methodological preparation since they were groomed by those who were themselves unequipped to provide the necessary indoctrination. As this has been the case, the freshly minted PhDs, more nearly than not, have simply soaked up more of the conventional wisdom of library practice and experience in conjunction with only a superficial indoctrination in corollary disciplines. The net effect fails to round out their intellectual perspectives. The culmination of their doctoral work is most often an historical or a bibliographic exercise, or at best a limited assault upon a narrow technical problem, none of which tends to engage the prime issues facing librarianship. It is this sterility which limits the appeal of such work to thoughtful professionals who do not see any value in such a contribution.

As one probes further in attempting to understand the intellectual limits of library education, another pervasive characteristic is that while those who offer instruction may be highly sensitized to the current events in their own discipline, they seem quaintly insulated and isolated from the passions astir in the environment which surrounds the institutions. That is not to say that as citizens they are not aroused and partisan, for many are. But rather that as scholars in library education they do not perceive how the chaos and the challenges of the culture in the cities, in the universities, and in the corporate world, relate to the need for responsiveness and responsibility on the part of libraries. For librarianship is seen fundamentally as a technical pursuit, fixed in an institutional web, little subject to question as to priorities, values, or

2. From 1966 to 1970 the Office of Education awarded 1,941 masters, postmaster and doctoral fellowships. But typifying the fundamental ambiguity and variability in the perspectives of this federal agency which is reflected in the sporadic nature of its support to higher education generally and to library education in particular, by 1971 funds were diverted predominantly to institutes and programs aimed at equalizing employment opportunities in librarianship for minority groups and disadvantaged persons. See *Library Journal*, November 1, 1970, p. 3716.

agenda. Where there is sensitivity, it tends to relate only to suggestions of broadened book collections in order to cover all sides of an issue, or to focus upon technical matters devolving about fair representation in catalogs as they deal with people and ideologies. When library educators do center their attention upon the field, it is invariably within the existing framework, rather than as detached observers perceiving it from the outside. And when they participate in the councils of librarianship, it is as fully as partisans of the existing structure as any in practice. The critical nature of scholarly questioning tends to be absent. The ends of professional effort are seldom in question. Thus does library education abdicate its responsibility for leadership.

Intellectual leadership requires a capacity for self-criticism as prerequisite to the fostering of change. Library education, for the most part, spawns criticism which castigates without the fundamental curiosity and sensitivity which might raise such criticism to a level of abstraction worthy of scholarly discourse. Only in an intellectual wasteland would an observer at the annual meeting of its scholars report the event using gossipy chatter and almost totally avoiding the treatment of any of the intellectual issues which engaged the assemblage. Only in such an ambience would an editor encourage such effort or would the incongruity of this type of expression in the journal go unrecognized by the fraternity for what it is, and also for what it is not, and should be.[3]

Many in librarianship like to think of themselves as intellectuals. But invariably their self-perception is founded not upon substantive commitment to their own discipline, but rather to other fields. It is possible to differentiate the intellectual librarian from the library intellectual. The intellectual librarian uses his intellectual capacity as part of his equipment in his vocational role. It is relevant to the problem-solving processes and to the nature of his contribution. While he sees himself basically as a librarian, his intellectual side is exploited to advance it. The library intellectual, on the other hand, finds his identification in intellectual activities which have no necessary relationship to his library contribution. While he is oriented to the world of the mind, this is a world which is disassociated from his functions as a librarian. There are many library intellectuals but few intellectual librarians. For the intellectual side of librarianship is not taken very seriously by many. The best minds of the discipline gravitate elsewhere. Its academic citadels have themselves denigrated its intellectual pretensions and aspirations by reinforcing effectively the ethos of pragmatism. Still, because professional practice in the field is built upon a model which enforces graduate

3. See Jay E. Daily, "A Happening in College Park," in *Journal of Education for Librarianship*, Spring 1969, pp. 296–300.

study upon those who would be certificated, it must respect intellectual effort at least in a formal sense. But the respect is always accorded to others, sought elsewhere; it is seldom perceived as possible that in its own right, in its own nature, there is a discipline, there is an intellectual underpinning. Highest honors for intellectual achievement, just as among library practitioners who traffic in the ideas of others through the books which are their stock in trade, are placed elsewhere. Just as the Newbery Award book author occupies the highest place of adulation among those who practice children's librarianship, so it does not seem incongruous that the primary speaker at a conference of the scholarly community in librarianship will lecture upon a subject not in the remotest way connected to the intellectual issues of the field.[4]

At its worst, there is a type of profound negativism which implies that the problems of librarianship are basically unsuited to intellectualization —as if there were a fundamental dichotomy between thought and action, between theory and practice. Librarians, like practitioners generally, put greatest emphasis upon action and responsibility for action. It is these capacities which are more valued than contemplation and deep analysis. Nor is such a stance seriously questioned by the tenets of library education. For its values are essentially interchangeable with the practice element of the profession.

Focus on Information Science

If in the mainstream business is conducted as usual, one tributary experiences a swelling flow of traffic. This is in the area variously called information science, documentation, systems analysis, all oriented toward the rationalization of the machinery and processes of library organizations. To capture the essence of this phenomenon while it is so swiftly in motion is to see it, if at all, at a single point in time and from only a single vantage point. A map of the same territory drawn by another, before the region has been fairly staked out and clearly marked off, would doubtless look quite different. Moreover, in such an uncharted zone the symbols used to describe it may only approximate that which is represented. Still, to tell the story of library education without taking account of such development would be to overlook what is perhaps its most lively component.

4. "A polished lecture on the history of the Ohio Valley by Thomas O. Clark, Distinguished Professor of History at Indiana, preceded tours of the remarkable facilities at Indiana University. . . . Though the attendance was thin . . ." Jay E. Daily, "A Symposium at Bloomington," a report on the January 1970 conference of the American Association of Library Schools in *Journal of Education for Librarianship*, Spring 1970, p. 272.

Some traces of the information science field are to be found in the framework of the traditional bastions of library education, some in entirely new centers begun outside the field. Recognition of the need to adapt information and organizations to accommodate new technology is virtually universally shared. The essential problem is whether it is feasible to graft such newer insights and technical skills upon the traditional elements of library education. If this is done, then the question is whether to attempt to equip librarians with new methodological skills or to prepare specialized experts who will gain some library orientation, but concentrate more assiduously on new methods. The problem in essence is whether a new breed is to be fashioned, built upon the old but equipped with new skills, or the territory simply divided between traditional types who would continue to be prepared and a newer type. The consequence of the several viewpoints about the efficacy of alternative routes is that education for librarianship is no longer the discrete and identifiable pattern which it once was.

In many cases the programs remain fundamentally unchanged. In other instances new courses are made available as elective offerings. This is the characteristic of the majority of the traditional programs. Some education offerings, however, give concentrations in information science requiring specialized preparation as a condition of admission at the master's level.[5] In other institutions the main thrust is at the doctoral level.[6] In still other instances, the offerings are in new programs committed to information science, dedicated to generating a new breed of professional and researcher, quite apart from library education as it has been known.[7] In a number of these instances, the concentration of educational concern remains predominantly upon research, with teaching seen only as the proper correlate of such a research commitment.

Where they are more than the occasional courses in the conventional library school, the essential intellectual construct which holds the newer programs together as their integrating rationale is a view of librarianship as a discipline in transition, capable of being shifted in its fundamental nature from a prescientific state founded on rules of thumb and tradition to one with the characteristics of a scientific discipline. Such an argument holds that by bringing mathematics, systems analysis, operations research and analysis to bear upon its problems, logical principles which permit of the rationalization of procedure, built upon unambigu-

5. Some illustrations would be the programs at Drexel University, the University of Pittsburgh, and the University of California, Los Angeles.
6. As is the case at the University of Chicago, Indiana University, and the University of California at Berkeley.
7. Such programs would include those at the Georgia Institute of Technology, Ohio State University, and Lehigh University.

ous cause-effect relationships, will emerge. Ultimately the practice of librarianship would evolve under these terms to become a type of applied engineering, with information handling as the area of application. In order for this to come to pass, a number of conditions are requisite. The capacity of professional students of librarianship to work in the context of the more rigorous methodology of mathematics and systems analysis would have to be guaranteed. The traditional curricular elements would have to give way to courses more amenable to rigorous quantification and precise measurement in their design. And the research necessary to generate many of the themes and lessons which would form the core of the professional content and in the process prepare the next faculty generation would need to be ensured.

Assessment of the actual scene reveals that this process is taking place only in the rare instance within the context of the traditional library educational program. That is to say, recognition of the need for such metamorphosis in the traditional enclaves, even when new leadership perceives this as the logical route, is not generally shared. The effect is for there to be compartmentalization of such concentration within one element of the faculty, leading to a specialty perhaps tied to a specialized research or doctoral sequence, with only very limited implications for the basic professional curriculum which all of the general students pursue. In other instances, and these tend to be at least as common, there is a dissociation of information science education from librarianship, under which terms academic and research programs are begun which have no formal ties either to traditional library education or to the library profession. For want of professional identity, such programs and their faculty and students tend to identify with the technical associations with which many in librarianship and library education are also identified— American Society for Information Science and Special Libraries Association—but for all practical purposes they are outside the mainstream of library education and are not generally perceived by traditional elements within librarianship as forming a component of the field. Such programs are eligible for accreditation by the American Library Association, but no overtures are made to encourage them to identify, and they are impelled by no impulse to do so.

It is too early to tell how these matters will ultimately sort themselves out. A more rigorous applied technology of librarianship, even if its inroads do not universally pervade the professional practitioner community, or the institutions in which it practices, could doubtless influence change in the roles of the librarian and the library. Still the consequence of systematization, of efficiency and economy, is not in any way a correlate of altered objectives, despite the potentially sanguine effects of such modifications. To the extent that the key questions are perceived as value-neutral, subject simply to analytical processes which accept disciplinary commitments, values, and goals as they are—to that extent the solutions will simply further rationalize the institutional processes. Thus while there may be far more powerful technical means in the offing to reinforce the systematization of library processes, the more fundamental choices remain unexposed. In a time when professional zeal is focused upon economy and efficiency, this becomes far more compelling than the value questions. Yet science and engineering are in essence value free. The consequence of an exalted technocracy is the enshrining of the means and the ultimate danger is that the means are the ends. For goals are not factually derived and they are not susceptible of resolution out of the evidence of technique. They are the expression of the professional conscience. As tempting as it might be to abdicate responsibility for both the systematization and the deliberation of the alternatives of organizational attainment to those expert in the engineering and design concerns, it would be folly. For not even the members of the systems community who are most astute about the nature of the problems would seek such responsibility.

> We, as systems engineers know how to use modern technology to achieve a successfully operating advanced library system, provided that the librarian and administrative or executive management of the organization under which the library operates knows what they want to do with their automated library.[8]

In disciplines with strong intellectual components, it is within the academic centers that research and theoretical work are most assiduously prosecuted. But in librarianship the traditions of concept formulation, theory building, or basic study have been uncommon. It is only within recent years that organized effort which transcends the classroom and the work of the independent scholar has been acknowledged to be a formal responsibility, giving rise to centers at institutions like Case Western Reserve University, and the Universities of Illinois, California, Pittsburgh, and Indiana. Here the effort tends normally to cluster around more applied problems, somewhat in the manner of the Bureau of Business Research, a phenomenon of the state university which centers its effort predominantly in the pragmatic problems of the regional business community. More fundamental work into the underlying relationships,

8. David P. Waite, "Developing a Library Automation Program," in *Wilson Library Bulletin*, September 1968, p. 52.

theories, and scientific principles is most often accorded hospitality at centers outside the mainstream of library education: such programs as Ohio State University, Lehigh University, and Georgia Institute of Technology. Because of the tenuous relationship between these programs and library education, the influence of their research is lessened. With the heightened societal concern about libraries and information problems of recent years, in some measure as the consequence of the default of sophistication, capacity, or interest among the educational community in librarianship, much of the work which might have been done in the universities has been carried out in research, development, and consulting organizations which have come into prominence. A more typical loose division of responsibility could have found the research commitment for applied study centered in the proprietary organizations and for more basic work in the universities. But given the limits of research sophistication in library education, the capacity to carry out research has, for the most part, been concentrated in the traditional areas of bibliography and history. The orientation of scholarship has seldom been found in fundamental issues of contemporary significance. The pattern has been for such problems to be explored more nearly in the leading libraries, governmental programs, underlying disciplines, and more recently, in research and development companies rather than in library education. Even with the significant financial stimulus of federal doctoral support to PhD students in recent years,[9] the type of research and even the quantity of research fostered under the banner of library education is one of the least consequential elements of the research in library and information science.[10]

It is not at all surprising, and in fact in keeping with the continuing perception of the marginality of library research in the university, that the President's National Advisory Commission on Libraries proposed to establish a research and development institute as a component of the recommended permanent National Commission on Libraries and Information Science,[11] in order to ensure appropriate prosecution of research upon library problems. It is interesting to note how this recommendation

9. Through 1971–1972, the Office of Education awarded 812 doctoral fellowships.
10. See Paul Wasserman, ed., *LIST 1971: Library and Information Science Today* (New York: Science Associates/International, Inc., 1971). According to the listings in this "international registry for research and innovation" some 150–175 of the 820 research projects and programs described emanate from the library schools.
11. "Recommendation (3): Establishment of a Federal Institute of Library and Information Science as a principal center for basic and applied research in all relevant areas. . . . The models that were prominent in the Commission's thinking were the National Institutes of Health and the National Laboratories of the Atomic Energy Commission." *Library Services for the Nation's Needs: The Report of the National Advisory Commission on Libraries,* July 1, 1968.

was fully supported by the American Library Association.[12] Personified here is the basic suspicion of the discipline of its own capacity to derive and construct the means of pursuing research in its own interest and by its own scholarly element in the universities (which is characteristic of other professional disciplines), without the intervention of the same kind of federal system which is seen to assure adequate support for the functioning of public libraries. But provision of support for library activities and the conduct of research are two very different concepts. Another measure of the field's limited confidence in its intellectual community to function effectively without props is the way in which contractual developments for education in librarianship in developing nations are arranged, not with individual professional schools as is commonplace in such disciplines as public administration, business administration, law, medicine, or agriculture, but with the American Library Association. The rationalization, of course, is that the schools are not strong enough to negotiate or to sustain such relationships unaided; only the American Library Association which can draw from many sources is. The effect is to reinforce, in the psyches of both the professional school community and the profession itself, the notion that such aspirations are beyond the limits of the individual educational programs—this is the business of the national society. Thus is inadequacy perpetuated.

If intellectual leadership is being reflected in the changing nature of library education, its influence is scarcely perceptible. The only novel work in progress related to the curricular concerns of professional education for librarianship appears to be limited to the efforts of the Education Committee of the American Society for Information Science. Its attempts to design a model sequence for the preparation of personnel equipped at the master's level to function as middle-range systems analysts, is fashioned after the successful earlier efforts of the Association for Computing Machinery in deriving model curricula for computer science.[13] The modest degree of variation and experimentation in curricular adaptation at the traditional schools at the most resembles a game of

---

12. See the statement by Roger H. McDonough, then president of the American Library Association. *Hearings before the Select Subcommittee on Education of the House Committee on Education and Labor.* H.R. 8839, April 17, 1969.
13. See Jack Belzer, ed., "Information Science Education Curriculum Development and Evaluation Conference," Proceedings of the Curriculum Committee, Special Interest Group (ASIS), on Education in Information Science, in *American Documentation,* October 1969, pp. 327–376. Also, Jack Belzer, "Education in Information Science," in *Journal of the American Society for Information Science,* July–August 1970, pp. 269–273. In September 1970 the committee conducted a "Delphi Method" Workshop aimed at approaching a consensual base for optimum information science curricula. Data was generated by questionnaires returned from forty-four schools with library science and/or information science sequences.

musical chairs, with the cast of characters, or faculty and students, fundamentally unchanged. New labels for old, regroupings, model terminology, yield only a new vintage of the same wine being poured into a different generation of bottles. Some of the methodological variations are pure and simple devices for translating the tired old anti-intellectual rituals into more complicated technical arrangements for accomplishing ends no less suspect.[14] It may be easy to perceive the essence of such simplistic charades when high-powered and costly equipment is employed to manipulate low-level intelligence—although the agencies which support such efforts continue to be enchanted with any attempt to link library education to computers. But the more esoteric projects, perhaps often characterized by the same intrinsic incongruities, are far less transparent in a discipline which is prone to offer its highest tribute to that which it least comprehends.

Perhaps the essential lethargy and entrenched traditionalism of library education finds clearest expression in the structure and programs of its formal organization, the Association of American Library Schools. Membership is open only to schools which have once passed and continue to qualify under the accreditation rituals enforced not by the schools themselves but rather by a committee of the American Library Association. As an organ of the American Library Association, the perspectives of those who accredit are thus drawn from the traditional sources, unleavened by the point of view of any elements which might be represented if hospitality in such deliberative processes were also afforded to those drawn from education, research, administration, and practice in information sciences. To encourage such revised views would be to invite American Society for Information Science or Special Libraries Association representation into a process that has been carefully guarded by the ALA. But the effect of the very nomenclature of the association, embracing as it does librarianship and only librarianship when it calls itself the Association of American Library Schools, is to repel the newer programs from seeking entry and, in consequence, to inhibit the present membership from dealing with any but the conventional issues seen from the same old vantage point.

14. As may be the case with the Office of Education-funded project designed to acquaint library science master's students with a "wide spectrum of representative reference materials and to learn how to use them in meeting the informational needs of library patrons. . . ." To accomplish these objectives, 167 reference work annotations and 850 questions dealing with these tools were compiled and organized into a linear program. See Thomas P. Slavens, *The Development and Testing of Materials for Computer-Assisted Instruction in the Education of Reference Librarians*, Final Report (Ann Arbor: School of Library Science, University of Michigan, 1970). ERIC, Ed 039–902.

RESEARCH

Virtually inseparable from education, as salient element of a discipline's intellectual thrust, is the research component. Just as at core the educational sequence is seen fundamentally as training for operational roles, research in librarianship is viewed largely as the gathering of facts to support political decisions in individual situations. The intrinsic resistance, symptomatic of the entrenched professional preference for its own tradition, relates perhaps to a view that research may threaten the existing order. If pragmatic librarianship rests on certain assumptions and if the consequence of research may be to cast doubt about these very tenets, here is where risk lies. To encourage, to support, or to believe in research is to tolerate ambiguity—the possibility that there may be other viable alternatives, that existing practice is not divinely inspired. The net effect is a profession which is not only uncomfortable with the idea of research, but fundamentally hostile to it. Its most pronounced syndrome is to equate consulting with research and thus to see its problems as reconcilable in consequence of outside agents addressing specific problems where all that is lacking is the data necessary to arrive at conclusions which match *a priori* convictions. Coupled with this operational view and a reinforcing element in its perpetuation is the manner in which research is treated in the professional curriculum. When a formal course is offered at the master's level, even though there may be a salute to the various social-science methodologies and approaches, it is the bibliographic component which takes precedence. The requisite sophisticated perception of the research process is seldom attained. In part this may be so because the raw material needed to illustrate such effort is commonly drawn from the work of other disciplines, concretely demonstrating that research in librarianship is rare. In part, it is in consequence of the fact that library faculties simply do not conduct very much research, so that the classroom remains unrelated to the world of scholarly inquiry. Nor is the message lost on doctoral students. If the field does not honor research, then the doctoral effort is seen as a combination of entry rite and terminal sequence, seldom as orientation to scholarly life style. In tacit conspiracy with a faculty which is itself uncomfortable with the research role, the student's route to doctoral success is seen as more formal coursework intrinsically undifferentiable from the professional master's content, formalistic requirements of language and tools (although these may not be correlated with research task), and the prosecution of a study which is manageable, comparable enough to the work which has gone before it in the same program so as not to be seen as threatening. Added to this is the necessity for the just-right blend of personality characteristics needed to play successfully the schizoid role of both deferential student and junior colleague.

If the community of library education and practice does not take library research seriously, then neither does the culture which surrounds it. And if the field itself neither supports nor rewards its performance, then neither do those who support the discipline. Thus there is merely reinforced the pragmatic and simplistic view that everyone knows what libraries are for—the only problem is to improve their performance through increased resource allocation. In consequence, research is simply not taken very seriously. While it may be conceded, of course, that to maintain a link with the university it is necessary to assume the correct academic and public relations posture, wherein lip service is paid to the importance and virtues of research to the progress of the field, few are beguiled into believing such mythology. It is one of those insiders' jokes to which virtually all but the most naive in the discipline are privy. The most tragic testimony is that when the cognoscenti in library education or practice are faced with an ambitious or energetic potential scholar, their counsel to such a person would invariably be to pursue doctoral study in some other discipline.

In casting about for explanation for the low ebb of intellectualism in the discipline, perhaps an important clue can be found in the somewhat naive, yet basically cynical, way in which research is viewed within the field as simply another resource to be administered and bureaucratized. The most recent formal expression is contained in the *Aconda Report* (Activities Committee on New Directions for ALA):

> Expand the Office of Research and Development to permit the employment of staff having special competence in the area of research, thus enabling ALA to take an active role of leadership in the development of research in Library Science. . . . Make long-range studies of the feasibility of further expanding the Office of Research and Development to include staff to actually perform some of the research at ALA headquarters.[15]

The statements here do not solely reflect past policy of the American Library Association, but are expressed as part of what its formulators must perceive as a progressive and aspirational design for the future. Nor have these proposals elicited any widespread negative response either from those in practice where this issue tends to be less significant than other aspects of the same report, or from the library education

15. "ACONDA Summary of Major Recommendations," 4e (1) and (4), in *American Libraries*, July–August 1970, p. 685.

community where it is more difficult to find so charitable an explanation for the acceptance or indifference to the recommendations. Essentially what is proposed is that the American Library Association take a firmer role, engage a staff with full-time responsibility to stimulate, coordinate, evaluate, and administer research activities. This would give the association "a voice of authority in communicating with funding agencies and researchers." In the words of the report, ". . . there would be an organization capable of speaking for the entire profession in the area of library research." Thus funding agencies would have only one place to go to determine which research problems were most crucial to the profession.

It is as if the limits of the field's capacity to grapple with its fundamental problems could be resolved if only one more office were established, one more officialdom authorized, one more layer of bureaucracy invented to insinuate itself into an impoverished sphere in order to divert politically, in still another way, attention to the substantive problems. For the climate of research, the substance of research, is unmentioned; it is only the process, as if all that is needed to ensure good works of the mind is the existence of functionaries who will oversee and inspire. Once more there is the simple assumption that in a discipline so bereft of research talent, none but the ineffectual or corrupt would have the audacity to assume such a role for reasons genuinely related to the research culture of the field rather than for the power, prestige, and influence inherent in such a position. It is as if research in the field was a process susceptible to central planning and monitoring, as if research expertise were widespread and ready to be exploited, as if the intrinsic problem of research were not a lack of understanding, capacity, hospitable climate, but simply the lack of a central secretariat to administer and coordinate. Which competent and self-respecting researcher, in a discipline where such human resources are exceedingly scarce, could take such an office seriously as anything but competitor for the same limited resources?

No matter what virtues may lie in organization, they almost invariably lack the power to surprise or affect us remarkably by carrying individuals beyond the normal limits of their awareness. Only the individual researcher can do this, and the individual researcher is simply not susceptible of being organized.

To design a new function, to establish a new functionary, somehow is expected to make the future right for research in librarianship, and incidentally for association planning.[16] The attendant confusion is ex-

16. From previous citation, Item 4e (3): "Establish a permanent Committee on Planning to provide the thorough planning necessary to achieve the long-range goals of the Association."

tended when under such terms some unsophisticated individual is identified for the role. Given the already existing limited understanding of research in the field, reinforced by the formal designation of the individual as its responsible agent by the powerful national association, such an incumbent would be oblivious to his own inadequacies. The irony is complete when such a functionary is taken seriously as a powerful official simply by virtue of his official position, even among those who can perceive the gross incongruities of the entire business. But the greatest numbers in the field, in its officialdom, and in the external bodies to which such a figure relates, would find it not at all out of keeping with what they expect to find in librarianship. For if the office invests the individual with authority, it is thus possible for such functionaries to be taken seriously in spite of themselves.

If an active intellectual opponent in librarianship exists, it is in the sector which perceives the problems of librarianship and information handling as intrinsically systems problems, amenable of solution as a function of rationalizing and computerizing the flow of work, standardization of process, developing evaluative methods for assessment of operations. Such work is being prosecuted in different settings, almost exclusively under terms of external financing, and would include the MIT INTREX Project,[17] the efforts of the national libraries,[18] the automation projects in the University of Chicago, Stanford University, and Columbia University, among others.[19] The most interesting advances

17. Generally considered to be one of the most ambitious library research projects in progress, Project INTREX (*Information Transfer Experiments*) has been engaged since 1965 in a program of experiments and equipment development relevant to the design of future research library systems. Particularly interested in testing techniques for a decentralized full-text access system using a computer-stored "augmented" catalog, the project is establishing a model engineering library at the Massachusetts Institute of Technology. See Carl F. J. Overhage and R. Joyce Harman, eds., *INTREX, Report of a Planning Conference on Information Transfer Experiments, September 3, 1965* (Cambridge, Mass.: MIT Press, 1965). Also, the semiannual activity reports published in September and March of each year.

18. In addition to the well-publicized MARC and MEDLARS programs, the U.S. National Libraries Task Force on Automation and Other Cooperative Services coordinates the relevant activities of the three national libraries and represents an attempt to apply a systems approach to the establishment of an automated network of library services. It is working toward the development of a national data bank of machine-readable cataloging information, a similar facility with respect to the location of serials, and general compatability in the practices of the three libraries. See Samuel Lazerow, "The U.S. National Libraries Task Force" in *Special Libraries*, November 1968, pp. 698–703. Also the Association of Research Libraries, *Minutes of the 75th Meeting*, January 17–18, 1970 (Princeton, N.J.: Association of Research Libraries, 1970), pp. 123–124.

19. See Herman H. Fussler, "The University of Chicago Automation Project, a Summary," pp. 10–18; Charles Payne and Kennie Hecht, "The University of Chicago Book Processing System," pp. 134–143; Paul J. Fasana, "Automation Efforts at the Columbia University Libraries, a Summary," pp. 19–41; Edwin B. Parker, "Develop-

are detailed in the *Annual Review of Information Science and Technology*, perhaps the most significant effort to assess the state-of-the-art, with a workmanlike and expertly edited blend of contributions from information scientists, computer persons, library automation experts, the occasional behavioral scientist, and library educators who seek to straddle between librarianship and information science. Yet as we have suggested, the influence of such work has not yet altered the educational process for librarianship in any fundamental way. The limits are those of faculty competence, student recruitment, and selection which imposes no admissions standards which call for prior study in mathematics and logic and a typical pattern of recalcitrance to change the safe and familiar course. Even as a new division is spawned in the American Library Association (the Information Science and Automation Division), and the *Journal of Library Automation* is begun, the general outlook and intellectual stance of the discipline remain fundamentally unaffected. The analytic, problem-solving, scientific-management approach to library problems is inspired and refined in consequence of the educational and professional involvement of only a minor segment of its members. Infinitely more zeal is centered in media concerns. For there is a sizable element of library education and practice, perhaps most notably those committed to school libraries, which is sensitive to the advances in educational technology. But the laudatory sense of need to shift from singular devotion to one artifact, the book, to other powerful audio and visual learning devices, appears less to be inspired by the desire to master intellectually the new spheres than merely to broaden the library inventory to embrace new forms. Moreover, even in this instance, it is only after a virtually new occupational group has emerged with responsibility for such instruments that librarianship has finally perceived the threat. The prospect of librarianship anticipating technological advances, participating at an early stage in the experimental and testing process of new instruments so as to exploit them for use with their clienteles, appears exceedingly remote given its deep tradition as essentially bureaucratic rather than experimental culture. For even when the invention is the design of one of its own, as was the case with Fremont Rider and micro-

---

ing a Campus-Based Information Retrieval System (Stanford University)," pp. 213–230; Allen B. Veaner, "Stanford University Library Project SPIRES/BALLOTS (Stanford Public Information Retrieval System and Bibliographic Automation of Large Libraries Using Time-Sharing), a Summary," pp. 42–49. All in *Stanford Conference on Collaborative Library Systems Development Proceedings*. October 4–5, 1968 (Stanford, California: Stanford University Library, 1969), ERIC, ED 131–281. See also the yearly volumes of the ASIS *Annual Review of Information Science and Technology* (Chicago: Encyclopaedia Britannica, 1968–1970). (The first two volumes—1966 and 1967—were published by Interscience in New York.)

form, the impetus for and the ultimate reinforcement of its use in libraries has come from external sponsorship.[20]

Perhaps it has been in consequence of the fashionable predictions which have been made about the eminence into which libraries would be transformed from traditional lines to automated alternatives which have dulled the sensitivities of those in the field to the need for intellectually assaulting the problems themselves. So long as projects such as the MIT effort were in progress, matters were in good hands. But the more significant lesson which is beginning to be learned is that the most fundamental problems of data-processing application to library procedures are organizational and economic rather than technical. Moreover, beyond the purely routine housekeeping applications of record keeping, circulation statistics, and the like, the nagging and least soluble elements of information retrieval are intellectual and not machine problems. Thus the picture is changed only grudgingly. Electronic equipment is being adapted to library procedures, particularly in larger installations where inventory and circulation problems are of such size as to warrant such procedures. But outside of the costly laboratory and experimental efforts, mentioned before, exploitation of computers to library purposes remains in the sphere of procedure. Indeed voices making the greatest claims for the automation of information-retrieval capacity have lately been reduced to a whisper.

It has simply not been in the tradition of librarianship to expect to inspire intellectual leadership. Among the better minds are those represented in the Association of Research Libraries.[21] But here the pattern of leadership centers in organizational and political processes. It is a strategic body, based upon a shared ideology—that of the advancement of the great research libraries and their collections. In this it links itself in common cause with scholarship and research in the universities of size and power which its members represent. While it gains the attention of the Congress, is heeded in the councils of the learned societies and foundations, it is more nearly as spokesman for an important political subculture drawn from the intellectual universe than as intellectual fraternity itself. For as its name connotes, it makes no pretenses to be otherwise. It is an administrative confederation of the largest and most

20. An interesting appeal is made for libraries to begin now to test the new video-tape cassette and converter in order to isolate the system best suited to library purposes in "Memo to ALA/LTP," Editorial, *Library Journal*, September 1970, p. 2857.

21. Founded in 1932 by the librarians of forty-three research libraries, ARL membership presently comprises eighty-five institutions including the larger university libraries in the United States and Canada, the three national libraries, and a number of public and special libraries with substantial research collections.

influential institutions, an organizational and political artifact rather than a spokesman for a scholarly community.

Specialized Developments

Outside the mainstream of the primary intellectual movements which bear upon the course of thinking in librarianship there are a number of cults, but it is difficult to discern clearly their followings or their impact on library ideology. Two of these appear important enough to warrant discussion here. One tends to be an American invention. The other was inspired perhaps in the work of Ranganathan but has been cultivated in Britain, with members of the school centered principally in western Europe and with only very limited representation in the United States. The first, the library-college concept,[22] is embodied in a journal now issued at regular intervals—*The Library College Journal*. In its essence, this philosophy heralds the need for a dramatic shift in the collegiate learning experience from the traditional classroom process to library-centered activity. The idea has captured the imagination of a number in librarianship and outside, as the pages of the journal amply testify.[23] As with all such ideals, however, the realistic aspiration is perhaps more nearly for a gradually enlarged role for the library and its content and a teaching role for its professional staff rather than for a totally reconstructed undergraduate sequence.[24] The other cult is expressed through the writings and teachings of the British Classification Group, a relatively small but highly productive association of librarians and bibliographers who are committed to the centrality of classification as the essence of librarianship.[25] Members of the Classification Research Group have de-

22. Modern articulation of the library-college concept has been most intimately associated with the name of Louis Shores, Dean Emeritus of the Library School, Florida State University, who acknowledges his own debt to Carlyle's affirmation "the true university is a collection of books." As recently outlined by Dean Shores, the successful library-college enables the student to *read intelligently* by himself in a discriminating selection of the "generic book"—defined as "the sum total of man's communication possibilities," encompassing all media, formats, levels, and subjects. See Louis Shores, "Library-College USA" in *ALA Bulletin*, December 1969, pp. 1547–1553.

23. Among others, articles by Carl Rogers, Harvie Branscomb, Alvin Eurich, Robert Jordan, Patricia Knapp, Thomas Minder, and the aforementioned Louis Shores.

24. Each quarterly issue of *The Library College Journal* contains a roundup of current experimentation with the library-college concept, "InNOVAtions" by Louis Shores and Janice Fusaro. Among institutions engaged in one or another form of implementation are: The Federal City College, Kendall College, Oklahoma Christian College, Montieth College, Brown University, Dillard University, and Jackson State University.

25. The Classification Research Group was formed in 1951 as an outgrowth of a committee established at the Royal Society's Scientific Information Conference

vised a number of demonstrably successful schemes for the organization of such specialized subject areas as electrical engineering and occupational safety and health. In recent years a major thrust has been toward the formulation of a general classification system particularly amenable to machine retrieval of specific items of information and efforts in this direction have tended to supersede the more traditional library concerns for the organization of materials on shelves and in catalogs. To this extent it seems likely that the work of the CRG, however stimulating and potentially significant, will for some time continue to be viewed as a somewhat arcane and peripheral area of interest by the library field at large.

The intellectual currents of librarianship can be affected in important ways by the work of other disciplines. Particular prototypal information systems shall be treated later. At this point attention is centered upon the means whereby such transfer processes come to pass. In part, the process is facilitated as faculty members drawn from other fields come to play roles in library education and to introduce new methods and insight into the professional sequence. To the extent that the insularity of library education at both the master's and doctoral level is overcome, more and more students may be encouraged to pursue course work in other disciplines, and to the degree that the problems of librarianship come to engage scholars in other disciplines, the consequence of their work may come to enrich the literature and the idea base of the field. These factors have been, and are now, at work. To a degree such efforts are reflected in sum in the information-science movement, the stirrings of the potential emergent discipline arising out of disparate and variable elements, not yet certain who it is, what it is, or if it is. Yet information science represents only a segment—the information process rationalized, systematized, made economic and efficient. It trades in technical problems rather than human need. The correlation of librarianship with changing perspectives in the culture and the conceptualization of new roles and revised contribution is virtually nonexistent. For the scholarly community perceives libraries at best as only efficient and attractive book dispensing agencies. Or when libraries are the research focus, they are

(London) to study and improve upon current methods of subject organization. The aims and accomplishments of the CRG are summarized in D. J. Foskett "The Classification Research Group, 1952–1962" in LIBRI, 12, 2, 1962, pp. 127–138; Classification and Information Control: Papers Representing the World of the Classification Research Group from 1960–1968, Library Association Research Series No. 1 (London: Library Association, 1970). "Bulletins" describing the ongoing work of the CRG appear at irregular intervals in the Journal of Documentation. See also Derek Austin, "Prospects for a New General Classification" in Journal of Librarianship, July 1969, pp. 149–169.

seen as bureaucracies of a peculiar kind, or as processing systems to be charted and rationalized, or as physical collections to manipulate more efficiently. The conjuring of an alternative paradigm for a library, one oriented to client ends, devised in its essence as information problem-solving instrument of its constituency, is unlikely to emerge from any other intellectual community than librarianship's own. Indeed, when others calculate such designs, they inevitably tend to invent them *de novo*, dismissing the library as intransigent or simply ignoring it.[26] If intellectualism is to be the salvation of librarianship, its messiahs must arise out of its own tribe.

THE PROFESSIONAL MEDIA

The ideology and the intellectual base of a discipline are revealed in the pages of its journals and of its books, for the media of a profession serve as a compelling vehicle for conveying swiftly and widely new ideas and insights. In short, they harbor the potential for being a significant form of intellectual leadership. As a variegated and complex structure of subdisciplines and professional groupings, all of which seem compelled to bring forth one or another form of publication, librarianship and information science suffer from no poverty of print, but are virtually inundated by the published record. Moreover, as a discipline influenced by tangential yet powerful forces upon it, such as the fields of publishing, communications, management, and computer technology, the impressive range of literature which engages the concerns of its more thoughtful practitioners embraces a scope sufficiently wide to defy succinct analysis. For this reason, the treatment here concerns the main publications because they are read by and influence so many librarians.

If the patterns of librarianship were to replicate the norms of other elements of the culture, the more limited scholarly media, dealing with serious discourse derived from research or theoretical analysis, could be expected to shape the thinking of the opinion molding intelligentsia although the widest readership would doubtless be enjoyed by the general national periodical press. Librarianship does not appear to fit such a scheme. Given the paucity of genuine scholarly output, the mass circulation media vie with the other forms in attracting the same material to their pages. For if the pages of the scholarly press are seen both as sterile and restricted in level of readership and if the switching mecha-

26. See, for example, Alfred J. Kahn and others, *Neighborhood Information Centers: A Study and Some Proposals* (New York: Columbia University School of Social Work, 1966).

nisms for transferring ideas from the more sophisticated level of abstraction to the general are not operative, the author preference will tend to the mass media. Especially is this likely to be the case in a profession where prestige is seen in terms of popularity, where scholars, theorists, and practitioners are undifferentiated. The pages of the popular media insure the widest recognition and acclaim. To pursue such a course, however, is to subvert the careful intellectual effort which forms the basis for contribution to more rigorous scholarly media for it puts on notice those who aspire to recognition for the quality of their intellectual contributions, that there may be more convenient and less arduous routes to their goal. And in a field which accords no high honor to those who achieve by rigorous scholarly standards, the temptation is made the greater. The dangers to the academic community of librarianship are particularly acute. For if the scholarly literature of the field is denigrated, if the popular general journals of the field are seen as the media of choice, the incentives to pursue the hard work necessary to achieve scholarly publication are sharply reduced. Cynicism about the intellectual nature of the discipline is thus reinforced. Those drawn from other disciplines particularly tend therefore to conclude that their primary intellectual achievement deserves to be addressed to the media of the fields from which they are drawn, with the least common denominator level seen as adequate enough for publication in the library field.

Library Journal, Wilson Library Bulletin, and American Libraries

The most widely read general-purpose magazine of librarianship is the semimonthly *Library Journal*. As an all-purpose journal oriented to the concerns of the entire library community, the articles appeal to the widest possible cross section of interests. The editorial slant is partisan— assuming what has come to be acknowledged as a forthright and unequivocal stand on such issues as intellectual freedom, civil rights, and social responsibility, all in terms of the goals of librarianship, but also transcending the discipline to the zone of professional conscience in all matters of public concern including the Vietnam war. As partisan and as catalyst, this publication has sought to dramatize editorially the issues of the times, given space in its columns to those who would speak, and exerted its influence in provoking debate on matters of public policy as they relate to the responsibilities of librarianship and of libraries. Perhaps the greatest sensitivity is reflected in the issues which affect the public library institution, even though the magazine does publish a separate section, *School Library Journal*.

Yet, a journal which attempts to be timely and topical is not to be confused with a medium of intellectual discourse. *Library Journal* makes no pretense to be this for it is essentially a muckraking function which it performs, as it opens its pages to controversy and sounds its editorial alarms, catalyzing discussion and debate, and perhaps conveying the impression that librarianship is a testing ground for raging liberalism and social action. The detached insider in the field comes away from each issue with an almost wistful sense of the way in which the editorial personnel seem to be striving to shift the drama of librarianship enacted in its pages to the essentially value-neutral real world of librarianship. An aura is conveyed of a kind of ego-aspirational, conscience-heavy prop for the change-committed, forceful, predominantly younger elements of the profession, including its editors, who are somehow hoping through the power of print to spread the contagion of their passions abroad in a discipline too deeply characterized by lethargy and indifference to be infected by even the most fervent appeal. By playing the role of spokesman for discontent with the status quo of traditional practice, of disciplinary power alignments, and of professional and institutional role models, this journal performs as brooding conscience of the profession and gives constant public expression to the field's limits. Yet while the expressions of discontent may serve as preamble to correctives, in a recalcitrant discipline merely to exorcise itself in public print with remorseless consistency is neither to redress its wrong nor necessarily to serve as surrogate in the matter of professional conscience. For the habitual purging of the professional soul is somewhat akin to attending church regularly, accepting there the righteous tenets of the faith and returning undisturbed to a life of sin. To concede one's sins is not to adapt behavior, unless the palliatives recommended are acceptable and congruent with one's capacity to behave differently. But such perception typically requires the devising of formulas too complex for the pages of the popular press, for such formulations are the consequence of conceptualizations more nearly derived from abstract, theoretical, or research efforts yet to be mounted elsewhere. Such contribution far transcends the outer limits of *Library Journal*'s objectives.

The other general, wide-circulation journal is the *Wilson Library Bulletin*. As a monthly, its claims to newsworthiness are modest but its design is more appealing than that of *Library Journal*. In recent years it has focused on particular issues and reported them boldly and colorfully; an example is foreign and comparative librarianship. In doing so it has commissioned specific articles thereby bringing a broad and ambitious subject into rational perspective. Its editorial point of view is the same as that of the *Library Journal*, expressed perhaps in less strident tones, in keeping a readership composed more heavily of librarians from smaller or school libraries, and with a company image (H. W. Wilson Co.) fixed firmly in the bedrock of its traditional library indexes and other aids. Like many library groups which in convention seek celebrities from the academic world or from public life tangentially related to the discipline of librarianship to add luster to their public forums, the *Wilson Library Bulletin* has often drawn from the same inspiration. The overall effect is a more graceful journal, which sometimes penetrates more deeply into special topical themes, somewhat in the style of the symposium in print. But because the content which it attracts is at its best literary but not always substantive, virtually never conceptually or research based, and since its contributors from outside the profession more often than not have not probed the issues of librarianship and therefore generalize about cultural or societal issues, the net effect is of an attractive coffee-table medium for librarianship. A few issues can be skimmed at one sitting in order to gain a swift sense of its content without running the danger of overlooking any significant news or seminal contribution.

Thus while neither *Library Journal* nor *Wilson Library Bulletin* reflects a scholarly base for assaulting the primary issues of the discipline, in consequence of the ideologies of the editors of each of these media in recent years they have brought the controversies of the field before their readership for discussion and consideration. They have even influenced the official publication of the American Library Association, *American Libraries* (formerly known as the *ALA Bulletin*), to shift from its stuffy institutional stance and, in what has clearly become fashionable in the popular national library media, to engage in provocation of debate and dissent. These three journals contend for the same readership; they are competitive and striving for much the same fare in a profession with more outlets for expression in print than the volume of print-worthy expression. Still *American Libraries*, while devoting its columns to discussion of differences in articles and letters to the editor, amusingly enough still remains the voice of the establishment, the formal vehicle of its authority structure, and it juxtaposes angry letters with the latest word from the ALA hierarchy.

If one seeks to identify a role of intellectual leadership in the general media, he is inevitably disappointed. For even if this were the bent of their editors, and there is no reason to believe that this is the case, nor even for such to be their aspiration, their very frequency of issue, their space limits for substantive contribution, their inappropriateness as vehicles for research reporting, and the varied expectations of their large and diversified readership strongly militate against the assumption of such a role.

Special-Interest Publications

Librarianship has a plethora of journals addressed to special constituencies, from those oriented to type of library, *College and Research
Libraries,* to those addressed to form of practice, *Library Resources and
Technical Services,* to those engaged in a particular geographic area,
Pacific Northwest Library Association Journal. To survey them all would
transcend the present purpose, yet it is clear that a probing analysis of
their content, thrust, and rationale by a serious critic of their contributions is long overdue. Like many of the very processes of libraries,
spawned by once-felt need and perpetuated only because of the inexorable necessity to continue what has been once begun, the fresh air of
detached criticism could not but be helpful for the media as for their
readership. Here we treat only those which are of widest interest and
those which might be expected to influence thought across a broader
spectrum than only a particular library form or field of special practice.
That is not to say that seminal contributions cannot be carried in such
specialized media. Indeed, the fragmented nature of this discipline, like
many others, makes the ideal site for such contributions uncertain, although with time the most influential articles transcend the limits of
their original location as they receive acclaim and are read by others
who do not normally see the specialized sources. But if one compares
librarianship with other disciplines, it leads to the expectation that one
will be able to identify the most powerful and generally recognized media
of the intelligentsia known by all as the source of ideas, the scholarly
voice of the profession, the journal where new theory, philosophy, concept, research, and insight tend to find first expression. Such a search in
librarianship will prove unavailing.

What purports to be the prime intellectual medium of the field was
established at the Graduate Library School of the University of Chicago
in a time when the school was in its ascendancy, early in the 1930s. As
the product of the first academic center to concentrate seriously upon
scholarship and research, the *Library Quarterly* was the only journal for
reporting the theories, abstractions, and concepts and the product of
research of the field. With the passage of time and with the remorseless
changes which have been wrought in the Graduate Library School, the
Library Quartely no longer mirrors the current priorities of the discipline. What is most often reflected in its contents is the confusion of the
discipline, in a type of sterile representation of historical analyses, accounts of obscure studies, reports of narrowly focused research, generally lacking the vitality to link its ideas to the key issues of the field. If

one is seeking a sounding board for new ideas, it would not be in this journal. The librarianship described comes through as a somewhat anachronistic carbon copy of a minor humanistic subdiscipline, obscurantist and distracted from the passions of the contemporary scene. Perhaps this indictment is too severe. Perhaps it is simply that the nature of research and scholarly writing in librarianship is only dull, uninspired, and irrelevant to the modern time, so that the editors cannot attract fare which is both intellectual and significant for other than purely academic purposes. Still, such an argument smacks of the same defensive logic of librarians who argue that they are available, people can come to their libraries, it is not their responsibility if libraries are not used more widely. But the tone of the medium, just as the library, is set by what it does, what it seeks, by the image it conveys of self. The image of the *Library Quarterly* is of a stodgy, middle-aged periodical, bound more to tradition than to fresh ideas, more hospitable to painstakingly footnoted theses on obscure aspects of library history than to the problems of modern librarianship. As this is so, those who conduct research and who do generate abstractions and empirical data, when their orientation is to the behavioral or to the information sciences, are unlikely to perceive this as the setting for their contribution. The *Library Quarterly* may see itself as the bastion of scholarship, defending its pages from brash or unresearched ideas, but if it is a journal of ideas, this is very much lost on those who find in its pages only evidence of minor forays into generally inconsequential avenues of concern. Its insularity may be further conditioned by the fact that it is not responsive to any group, but is the province and the expression of a single school in a private university. Thus it seems undaunted, even oblivious to the howling winds of change which have chilled the bones of those who control the scholarly media in many other professional disciplines. Intellectual leadership seems scarcely to be found in its pages.

Library Trends began with the concept of offering in each issue a judgmental analysis by experts on the state-of-the-art in some specific subdiscipline or broad topic germane to the profession, in order to draw into perspective the major topical issues faced by the field. What has come to be the pattern more nearly is a set of bibliographic forays into the literature, in a range of topics stretched so thin as to attract the interest only of those identified with a narrow topic. In some disciplines the medium of the scholarly community itself adheres to a standard of excellence that is unrivaled. But the *Journal of Education for Librarianship*, issued under the auspices of the Association of American Library Schools, is unencumbered by any such intellectual aspiration. Once more there is a convenient explanation at hand—the paucity of thoughtful writing among those engaged in library education. Still what is reflected in the pages of this medium is a steady disrespect for even the semblance of any scholarly potential in education for librarianship. This is seen in frequent publication of the kind of irrelevant, amateurish papers so devoid of substance that they would embarrass any self-respecting discipline. For the effect of many of the issues is exactly that—a sense of embarrassment, even of insult, to those who purport to be seeking an intellectual basis for the discipline and for library education. In foisting such content on its readership, there is inevitably reinforced among all who come to its pages, the notion of how unsophisticated, how lacking in scholarly standards or aspirations the library education community must be to tolerate such material.

Perhaps the limited standard of the intellectual discourse of the field is most dramatically reflected in the level of its book reviews. For a discipline which traffics so intensively in the medium of the book, this is a striking anomaly for librarianship. For with only rare exception, there is virtually no serious review of the literature of librarianship. Reviews, like librarianship itself, tend to the descriptive and normative account of contents. The rigorous, analytic, scholarly assessment of ideas is most uncommon. The prototype is found in the *Library Journal* reviews—brief, all-purpose, oriented to what and whether to buy for a collection—in which many who are well-meaning amateurs advise other well-meaning amateurs about substantive content in fields of which they often have only the most superficial understanding. The same syndrome is found in the reviews of the field's own products, in space too constrained for serious discussion, in choices of individuals to prepare the reviews who often bring to the task little of the scholarly detachment or keenness of analytic perspective which are taken for granted in other disciplines.[27] The flabby nature of the genre is built into the accounts which frequently assess professional ideas scarcely more penetratingly than the binding, the physical format, or the price of the books. It is as if the reviewers are themselves unable to shift from the stance of book selectors to the posture of scholarly critic. In all the American library media, in *Library Journal*'s "New Professional Reading," *College and Research Libraries*, *Library Quarterly*, or in such specialized features as *Wilson Library Bulletin*'s "New Reference Books," or *Reference Quarterly*, the most pervasive feature is the lack of scholarly sensitivity, a glossing over of substance, a type of superficial treatment which conveys a sense that rigorous and critical reviewing is not the business of

27. The serious nature of the problem for the social sciences is advanced in Lawrence E. Riley and Elmer A. Spreitzer, "Book Reviewing in the Social Sciences," *The American Sociologist*, November 1970, pp. 358–363.

librarianship, only of more intellectually based disciplines. Moreover, the reviews themselves and the space for them are so very limited that the tendency is to afford room only to the most traditional form—the monograph—seldom to the research report, the thesis, or the other potential sources of new idea input. The effect is a periodical literature bereft of the serious analytic assessment of new contributions to the idea flow of the discipline. Thus no sense of discrimination, no shared consensus about the need for a standard of quality of intellectual contribution, comes to pervade the psyche of those who practice in the field. It is as if all is the same and a book is a book. The most significant contribution is cast alongside the minor, the ephemeral, and the peripheral, all in testimony to a quality control mechanism far more sensitive to the constraints of space than to the potential of the ideas contained.

It is only as one looks to the margins of the discipline that any of the characteristics of intellectual aspiration can be perceived. Perhaps this striving achieves its strongest expression in the pages of the *Journal of the American Society for Information Science*. Basically a technical medium, its content is strongly biased toward the experimental, the empirical, the theoretical treatment of information systems and services. It has the ring of a journal written by and addressed to those attempting to fashion a new science, or at least a new branch of engineering. This sense is conveyed through its substantive content, its book reviews, and its letters columns. Its contributors are drawn from as many persuasions as can be discerned seeking shelter under the tent of information science —systems personnel, mathematicians, operations researchers, behavioral scientists, as well as librarians. Yet something is lacking here. Precisely in the same way that its formal conferences are long on sobriety and zeal and short on humor or detachment, and just as its ardent spokesmen are infatuated with the rigor of science and seemingly oblivious to the ways in which the science will be employed or for whom, so are the pages of its journal reflective of the same singlemindedness.[28] The effect tends far more nearly toward technology than toward intellectual leadership. All the while they are centering their zeal upon how to, and only seldom dealing with the basic questions of why, when, or whether to, and for whom. Perhaps it is because the underlying problems are not susceptible to the type of analysis with which science is comfortable. For facts and values can be dichotomized,[29] and one can make a professional life

28. A limitation which has recently received expression in an editorial deploring precisely this condition in *Journal of the American Society for Information Science*, July–August 1970, p. 236.
29. A point emphasized in Herbert A. Simon, *Administrative Behavior*, 2nd ed. (New York: The Macmillan Co., 1960), pp. 4–8, 45–60.

without extending beyond the boundaries of the first zone. Yet scientists have been known to conjure with the uses and abuses of their contribution, to engage in public debate in the pages of their own media and in the popular press about the meaning and the values of societal choices. It is not until the responsible technical conscience transcends the limits of its technical output that it assumes a role of intellectual leadership in a professional discipline. Such maturity is yet to be reflected in the pages of the *Journal of the American Society for Information Science*.

The treatment of media here has barely scratched the surface, for there may be some 800 to 1,000 journals of librarianship in the United States alone.[30] Among those which even pretend to more than ephemeral character, virtually all tend to be superficially written, platitudinous, generally limited in insight. At best the periodic media can be seen as somewhat akin to trade literature, written by and for practitioners, a sharing of opinions and experiences, subject to none of the tests to which those who contribute to a more rigorous literature are subject and only occasionally rising to the level of graceful prose so admired by the many within the ranks of librarianship who have literary leanings. It may even be possible to question cynically whether in some of the regional and state journals hospitality is not afforded most typically to those in administrative roles more by virtue of their status than on the basis of whether they have something to say or whether they say it coherently. While the periodicals may be subscribed to widely, for libraries are their own best customers, and possibly even widely read, the intellectual influence which they exert cannot exceed the level of their substantive insight.[31] The periodical press of librarianship may be many things,[32] but

30. At best a rough estimate since serials do not occasion the regular monitoring characteristic of book publishing output. The figure is derived from Mary Adele Springman and Betty Martin Brown, *Directory of Library Periodicals* (Philadelphia: Drexel Press, 1967).

31. In response to the question, "How would you rate the following as sources of professional ideas and stimulation for you?" (Librarians on your staff; other librarians; library meetings; special institutes and conferences; professional library journals and other literature; people outside the library field; literature outside librarianship), professional library journals and other literature were ranked second by academic, public, and school library administrators (topped by "other librarians" in the case of academic and public library respondents and by "special institutes and conferences" by school library supervisors). The administrators of special libraries and information centers ranked "professional library journals and other literature of librarianship and information science" sixth, preceded by "professional meetings, staff professionals, other information professionals, special institutes and conferences, and people outside the information fields." See Mary Lee Bundy and Paul Wasserman, *op. cit.,* Footnote 1, Chapter VI.

32. Modest growth toward the professionalization of library periodicals is detailed in Edward Dudley, "Our International Journals" in *Journal of Librarianship*, July 1970, pp. 205–210.

even by employing the most generous yardstick, it fails to measure up as significant intellectual force within the discipline.

In librarianship the alternate routes, those not formalized in the regular publication stream, may be carrying the more significant messages. Here would be found the mimeographed releases of new groups, concerned, say, with social responsibility, whose ideas move too fast to be jelled into the traditional fare of the journal. And here the emphemeral technical reports provide way stations between research and practice and book form.[33] Here, too, could be classified the testimony and debate of hearings of governmental bodies and commissions which live a half life of obscurity, in spite of the significance of their intelligence, as a consequence of the form which they take,[34] or do not receive general attention until they appear in traditional book form.[35] But the prime misfortune of the periodic medium in librarianship is an almost studied absence of intellectualism. Despite the great number of regular magazines, there is no single review medium of distinction which embraces the field's intellectual concerns. The periodical press, like much of the discipline, tends to be bland and innocuous. The standard is at the level of the least common denominator. Virtually anything is publishable.

STATUS OF PROFESSIONAL BOOK PUBLISHING

Given the fact that the business of librarianship is still buying, storing, and dissemenating books, it is surprising that in their preoccupation with standards of acceptability for publications for their clients librarians have almost totally neglected to apply minimal criteria to their own professional literature. Until very recently, even while its preferred route of entry to practice was via educational preparation in the universities, the sum of its intellectual arsenal has been the actual tools of the trade—the subject and national bibliographies, the codes, the indexes, the schedules

33. One illustration of the latter phenomenon would be the following: Ronald G. Havelock, et al., *Planning for Innovation through Dissemination and Utilization of Knowledge*, A Final Report to the U.S. Department of HEW, Office of Education, Bureau of Research (Ann Arbor: Center for Dissemination and Utilization of Scientific Knowledge, Institute for Social Research, University of Michigan, 1969).

34. One such case which emerged to serve as a powerful influence on the discipline was the celebrated "Weinberg report," *Science, Government and Information*, A Report of the President's Science Advisory Committee (Washington: Government Printing Office, 1963).

35. As, for example, Douglas M. Knight and E. Shipley Nourse, eds., *Libraries at Large: Tradition, Innovation and the National Interest* (New York: R. R. Bowker, 1969), The Resource Book Based on the Materials of the National Advisory Commission on Libraries.

—with only a smattering of textbook perennials distinctly oriented to practice.[36] Thus library literature equates with bibliography, guides, manuals, indexes, and abstracts more nearly than with scholarly books. It follows quite naturally, therefore, that the publishing firms most closely associated with the discipline have been the H. W. Wilson Co. and the R. R. Bowker Co. each long concerned with the development of such tools and each, interestingly enough, founded and inspired by men who are seen as pioneers of both publishing and librarianship.[37] This preoccupation with the working tools of practice, even into the post–World War II era, made it uncommon for anything other than the occasional university-press volume from Chicago or Columbia to treat the intellectual side of the discipline. Until very recently, with the exception of the more limited types of technical publication normally the outgrowth of committee efforts in the American Library Association or the Special Libraries Association, book publishing in the library field tended to be almost synonymous with Wilson and Bowker. There was no identifiable scholarly literature of librarianship.

Unlike other professional and scholarly disciplines with their long-standing tradition of texts and treatises tied loosely to the idea flow of the field and to its classrooms, the limited academic and intellectual marketplace within librarianship, compared with the more lucrative market for those tomes which are more nearly the tools of the librarian's trade, has until quite recently kept any but the specialized reference publishers from manifesting serious interest. Until recently, and perhaps paralleling the way in which computer manufacturers ignored the library market until their basic industrial market appeared saturated and the potential of the alternative market opportunities in librarianship was revealed to them, the textbook and the scholarly market in the discipline, as differentiated from libraries themselves, was very much overlooked. The consequence is that the general publishing industry had few formal or informal ties to the centers where new ideas are spawned. They have not, in their normal ways, tended to inspire, commission, or even have access to the manuscripts and the contributions which grow out of work in librarianship. In part, such a limit may be explained by the differences between library education and other academic fields. Until very recently, the numbers of students engaged in library education were in-

36. Illustrations would be: Joseph Lewis Wheeler and Herbert Goldhor, *Practical Administration of Public Libraries* (New York: Harper & Row, 1962); Margaret Mann, *Introduction to Cataloging and the Classification of Books*, 2nd ed. (Chicago: American Library Association, 1943); and Mary Duncan Carter and Wallace John Bonk, *Building Library Collections*, 3rd ed. (Metuchen, N.J.: Scarecrow Press, 1969).
37. Halsey William Wilson, 1868–1954, and Richard Rogers Bowker, 1848–1933.

significant.[38] And it is the scholarly group which tends most heavily to generate and exploit intellectual products. Even more significant is that progress in academia among faculty members has not conformed to the typical routes for advancement and prestige attainment seen in other fields as formal publication. For in library education the doctorate has more nearly been seen as terminal achievement than as intellectual baptism. Once achieved, the PhD has assured progress for its holder, typically in the practice of library administration. Even when engaged in the teaching of librarianship, the PhD in librarianship has not been subject to the propellants toward publication which exist in other disciplines. Without the sustenance of the marketplace, in the absence of a scholarly tradition, perhaps it is not so ironic to find that in librarianship, a field more sensitive than others to the physical quality of the book, only limited-edition publishers who do not typically afford the same standards to their products have served as the primary agencies of publication.

Scarecrow Press and Shoe String Press have been in the field longest. Each was the creature of the imagination of librarians[39] who could envisage the potential and the need and the capacity of the discipline to prove the economic viability of limited editions produced without many of the normal publishing amenities and at a cost low enough to sustain them in a limited market. Those who held editorial and managerial control of these firms dealt with the art of the possible. Their responsibility was seldom viewed as that of uplifting the caliber of the field's intellectual product, but rather that of satisfying the needs of a small, largely unsophisticated class of readers in a field almost totally unserved by formal book publication.

Book publishing for librarianship appears now to be undergoing a decided metamorphosis. The explanations are to be found in a number of trends. Perhaps the paramount reason may be traced to the broader interest in the field. The inroads of information science may explain why Wiley, primarily a technical publisher, would publish its influential series edited by Becker and Hayes,[40] or the way in which the Massachu-

38. Over the last decade the number of students receiving bachelor's and higher degrees in library science has more than tripled from 1,967 in 1958–1959 (*The Bowker Annual 1969*, Table 15, p. 170) to 7,638 in 1969–1970 (*Earned Degrees Conferred 1969–70—Institutional Data*, by Mary Evans Hooper, Higher Education Surveys Branch, National Center for Educational Statistics, U.S.O.E., H.E.W., p. 408).
39. Ralph R. Shaw and John H. Ottemiller, 1916–1968. With a long career in many facets of librarianship, most recently Ralph Shaw has been Director of Library Activities and Professor, University of Hawaii. Shortly before his death, Ottemiller resigned his position as Associate Librarian, Yale University, to devote full time to the Shoe String Press.
40. The Wiley Information Science Series, Wiley-Interscience, a Division of John Wiley & Sons, New York.

setts Institute of Technology Press has come to discern the intellectual basis of the problems of the field by bringing out a whole group of studies based upon research and analysis of what are fundamentally library problems. The allure of the market for books for library education and librarianship has been sufficient also to attract McGraw-Hill into launching a series devoted to the field,[41] and the attraction of this market appeals to others as well. Included is the relatively young reprint publishing firm, Greenwood Publishing Corporation, which has branched into original publishing for librarianship with its Contributions in Librarianship and Information Science series, to complement their series in sociology, history, and political science. In addition, there are new publishing enterprises committed virtually in their entirety to library texts, studies, and comparable forms of publication.[42] Thus even if the profession itself has not yet perceived of the way in which change is coming, those who assess the field and its potential do not have their vision blurred.

The effect of a recent research history heavily subsidized through federal financing of such effort carried out in research and development firms, among doctoral students, and derived from intensive surveys of library problems of organization and technology, has markedly influenced the greater availability of new publications. Still, these expressions take variable form, as often as not in the ephemeral report broadcast through the Office of Education ERIC System (Educational Resources Information Centers) or the Clearing House for Science and Technology (now the National Technical Information Service) or as a National Science Foundation report. Only much later, if at all, do they find their way into standard book form. Frequently, contributors may be people looking at fundamental library problems, but from the vantage point of some other discipline and they are oriented to the literature of the fields from which they are drawn. And just as their biases and intellectual ambitions lead them to place their articles in the more prestigious journals of their own field rather than in those of librarianship, so do they naturally gravitate toward the university presses and the like—in the absence of the full development within librarianship of what could be conceded to be sophisticated publication vehicles. The only segment of the discipline to receive widespread recognition for its intrinsically intellectual contribution by those outside as well as inside the field is information science.

Just as the publishing interest generally, the primary associations seem now to sense the way that this discipline is poised to receive

41. McGraw-Hill Series in Library Education, McGraw-Hill Book Co., New York.
42. One illustration is Libraries Unlimited, Inc., of Littleton, Colorado, with a full line of library science texts, research reports, and reference works.

stronger intellectual fare than the traditional bibliographic works. This may be less true of the Special Libraries Association than of the other main groups for here the tradition of limiting effort to bibliographic and reference works tends to remain unaffected. In the American Library Association, however, there appears to be an attempt to derive more ambitious designs, using the mechanism of its own publishing machinery to raise the level of intellectual discourse. In the past, American Library Association publishing has simply been a reflection of the values and aspirations of a large proportion of its membership. When not concentrating on standard tools and bibliographies or the reports of committees, publications appeared specifically designed to satisfy the requirements of the marginally professional within librarianship by affording them many forms of self-help material without any pretense to scholarship.

Yet the dilemma of American Library Association publishing is like the dilemma of librarianship when it attempts to use itself as the propellant to advance an academic culture or a public library clientele. If the library chooses to serve as the agent of quality and standards by excising lesser works from its acquisition program by whatever criteria— when the previous norm has been to provide hospitality in the collection to more pedestrian publications—the effect inevitably will be to alienate those who prefer the library to reflect the limited levels of existing tastes and standards rather than to subvert them by influencing a clientele to accept an abnormal new aspirational standard for themselves. This seems to be precisely the position of the American Library Association publications program; the conflict between the need to serve as a reflection of both association affairs and committee activities, and the marginal intellectual perspectives and sophistication of librarianship at the grass roots level. Those concerned with the publishing program must sway not only the control group which monitors their activities, but the general membership of the association as well. Such developments may inevitably be seen as threatening the status quo. For even if the American Library Association is being challenged, it is unlikely that the challenge is seen as one which might be remediated by raising the intellectual level of the association's publications. Even though the overall record of ALA publishing has been oriented to technical rather than intellectual interests, a publishing imprimatur which promises easy access to the built-in market potential of American libraries is not to be lightly dismissed. But the inclusion in its lists of the occasional scholarly study does not intrinsically reorient the potency of its intellectual leadership. Still, in a discipline with such a limited capacity or unwillingness to differentiate qualitatively publishers of its own intellectual products, while ironically highly sensitive to such nuances in other fields of scholarship, an ALA publishing department seriously committed to loftier attainment bears watching.

The American Society for Information Science tends to outpace the other associations in the intellectual quality of its book publications. For one thing its annual conference is geared to provide registrants with published proceedings at the time of the conference. Formal technical papers reflect the basically technical cast of this society. But in a publication program of very modest scale when compared to the American Library Association or even to the Special Libraries Association,[43] the distinctive contribution is the previously mentioned *Annual Review of Information Science and Technology.* Now well established as the most important record of the state-of-the-art in the discipline, this well-edited work provides to the thoughtful student a review of the main elements, with each chapter written by a recognized authority. It has the ring of scholarly authenticity, is comparable to the better regularly published review records issued in other disciplines of greater maturity and standing. But the limits of the periodic medium of ASIS obtain equally as one reviews its modest yet interesting book publishing program. Its intellectual forum centers on means, not ends. Its keenest contributors and the lines of their analysis are sharply focused upon the technical issues as if the more fundamental ethical concerns had been consensually derived, when they have not been. So the tacit consequences of their pages is to reaffirm and reinforce far less than to challenge or to question.

In librarianship then, the hallmarks of a mature intellectual discipline as reflected in its publications are not yet to be found. One effect is that those of the field see little intrinsically to make it comparable to other disciplines with more impressive intellectual arsenals. The classic works are more often than not the work of those of other disciplines.[44] As this is so, intellectualism has neither been expected nor been given a place of prestige. And once more the view of the administrator or the technologist, rather than scholar, as idol of librarianship is reinforced. This is perhaps one of the more subtle consequences of the experience of library education which abundantly demonstrates the pedestrian quality of the

43. The 1970 *Publications ASIS* includes 15 items exclusive of periodicals; *Publications, Special Libraries Association, 1969/70* lists 29 titles plus 6 out-of-print items available from University Microfilms; *Publications 1970, American Library Association* describes 180 ALA imprints alone, as well as materials issued by ALA Divisions.

44. Illustrations would be: Marjorie Fiske, *Book Selection and Censorship* (Berkeley: University of California Press, 1960), and Oliver Garceau, *The Public Library in the Political Process* (New York: Columbia University Press, 1949). Mrs. Fiske is a research psychologist; Dr. Garceau, a political scientist.

field's own publications. Perhaps the best that can be said for the literature of librarianship is that it is like a man asleep for a long time, just being wakened. New organizations are ready to accept his work, larger numbers seem disposed to consider ideas, the only question is whether he will brush off the lethargy of his past and see the need to exercise his imagination and his intellect or whether he will turn over and return to sleep. There may be no one who will bother to awaken him another time.

CHAPTER 8

Governmental, Economic, and Professional Leadership Influences

The course of library development, until the passage of the first Library Services Act in 1956,[1] was little affected by federal efforts, with the exception of the catalog card products of the Library of Congress. But, as the course of education and research has come to be seen more and more as a function in which the whole nation has a stake, libraries have also been seen as one of the strategic elements in the educational process. The effect has been the support of governmental agencies in library efforts. The significant question is whether governmental influence has served to catalyze progress in the discipline, or whether it has simply been to reinforce the status quo. To examine such issues our attention shifts next to the governmental sector.

THE INFLUENCE OF GOVERNMENT

The most central agency relating to the library scene in recent years has been the U.S. Office of Education.[2] The national responsibility in education had been seen from the federal vantage point as only a fact-

1. The Library Services Act of 1956 (P.L. 84–597) authorized grants to the states in the amount of $7.5 million per year for five years for the extension of public library services to sparsely populated rural areas.
2. Principal legislative mandates for library support have been: the Library Services and Construction Act of 1964 (P.L. 89–511, as amended) which extended public library service to urban areas, provided for the construction of public libraries, and authorized support for cooperative programs and specialized services under state library aegis; the Elementary and Secondary Education Act of 1965 (Title II) (P.L. 89–10 as amended) which authorized expenditures for books and materials for school libraries; and the Higher Education Act of 1965 (Title II) (P.L. 89–329 as amended) which concerned library resources for institutions of higher learning, the training of library personnel, and research into various facets of librarianship. The details of these bills and other legislation affecting library development are well summarized in Douglas Knight and E. Shipley Nourse, eds., *Libraries at Large: Tradition, Innovation and the National Interest* (New York: R. R. Bowker, 1969), pp. 548–557.

166

gathering and reporting function. Now the Office of Education has more and more come to be identified with a program of distributing resources to improve the capacity of schools and libraries to respond to contemporary requirements. Beginning with the Library Services Act and on to the Library Services and Construction Act and the Higher Education Act, efforts have centered upon grants administered first through the states for public library support, then later directly to libraries and to library-education programs for the purposes of acquisitions and fellowships, institutes, and research efforts.

To discuss the entire contribution of the federal program, or of even the Office of Education alone, would go beyond the present objective. Here the concern is solely with roughly appraising the leadership influence which has been exercised. There is little question but that public libraries have received strong stimulus through the dollars which have been allocated for their support through the state agencies, but the effect of such increased federal funding upon the public library picture tends to be more uncertain. No standards have evolved, no formal terms of influence have been devised as conditions of support. Moreover, the capacity to generate precisely the right program, to attract imaginative talent in order to provide the stimulus and the leadership for adaptation and so to make judicious choices in the expression of need and support terms to ensure it has been highly variable. This has doubtless been as true of the fellowship programs at the master's and doctoral level as in the provision of support terms for practicing libraries. The limits of a focus for research which would receive encouragement via Office of Education financing serves as an effective constraint against influencing in any appreciable way the nature of libraries or of library education.[3] The limits have been of competent and effective individuals who could identify where and how to allocate resources and make effective use of the new financial support once available. For neither at the point of distribution, nor at the point of receipt, have the criteria been established for translating the federal largesse into precise instruments capable of understanding and review. Moreover, the priorities of need in the field which the Office of Education has seen fit to respond to have been subject to shifting political whim of exceedingly limited stability. In a more

3. Title II-B of the Higher Education Act of 1965 authorized the U.S. Office of Education to establish a Library and Information Science Research Program. Applications for support could be submitted by school districts, colleges, universities, state governments, and other public or private nonprofit agencies for two types of projects: (1) small projects, under $10,000 and administered by USOE regional offices, which were designed to enable exploratory research and pilot studies leading toward more extensive research and demonstration projects; (2) projects in excess of $10,000 requiring approval from USOE Washington staff. During period 1967–1969, ninety-eight projects were funded under the program at a cost of $8,396,258.

sophisticated field, the opportunity to exploit Office of Education resources might have been embraced. But in librarianship, easily as unsophisticated in such terms as those dispensing the funds from the Office of Education, this has not been the case. When the Office of Education moves toward institutes, then librarianship delivers institutes. Further, with the increase in federal funding a kind of reliance upon it has come to be built into the field, so that when resources are reduced the net effect is to upset violently the existing equilibrium. This is as true of fellowships in library education as of financial support to public libraries. There has been little statesmanship within the Office of Education itself. Perhaps it was naive to expect that there might have been. Fundamentally, it has looked to the American Library Association for the political vision out of which would be fashioned required programs. But since the vision of the American Library Association is limited, the inevitable consequence, reflected in the Office of Education program, has been only a limited overall sense of mission or purpose. Moreover, a number of the activities conducted within the Office of Education which relate to libraries have been suspended or separated—as in the instance of research and statistics—so that the library movement never achieved the standing in the agency which might attract influential leadership. Thus there has yet to be a genuine conceptual understanding of the field of librarianship and of its needs within the Office of Education. And in its absence, political opportunism has been inevitable. That is not to say that there have not been several important changes made in librarianship in recent years as a consequence of Office of Education funding in such areas as research and development and through the support of doctoral study among a far larger number than would otherwise have been possible. In addition, a number of government-sponsored institutes on topical themes have brought into focus some legitimate concerns which would not otherwise have seriously engaged librarianship. The entire phenomenon of effective national support terms awaits the more careful critical analysis and review of a scholar of the scene. But it seems clear at least that the gains in librarianship which have accrued as a result of Office of Education funding have been of the slow and steady variety—primarily those administered under the auspices of state library agencies which have aided the more backward library or system to build collections, train and develop staff, and evolve cooperative library service. Doubtless some acquisition programs in libraries have also benefited by the federal largesse and there is no question but that the school library movement received a forward thrust which would not have been possible otherwise. But a sustained sense of priorities, or a dramatic focus upon significant library development, has been faltering. The sands have shifted just as the political climate and at present, and perhaps fortuitously, preoccupation centers upon the city and minorities. Yet there is no underlying rationale, no conceptual frame, only the appropriation of current slogans and a groping for programs which might be popularly understood as the translation of such ideas into actuality. In librarianship, unlike many of the other disciplines represented at the Office of Education, those in the catalytic roles tend seldom to be drawn from the scholarly or leadership vanguard, perhaps because such positions require such a high tolerance for existence within an ever-shifting bureaucracy in which the survival instinct ranks well above the imagination. And perhaps also, because there has yet to be accepted the idea that this agency genuinely holds the potential for serving as a true leadership influence and not merely a political prop for library pump-priming.

The stimulus at the National Science Foundation has been more indirect. Essentially its commitment has not been to libraries but rather to experimental designs oriented to the scientific information requirements of the scholarly and research community. Thus it has encouraged research and development particularly in prototypal automation programs, and experimentation in specialized and unique efforts to make libraries viable in modern terms. It has also supported certain educational programs in information science which reflect a fundamental research cast, in a design to catalyze scholarship in ways which would influence the discipline. In a sense, it has nurtured the avant-garde of librarianship, that element committed more centrally to experiment and change, including such intellectual efforts as the *Annual Review of Information Science and Technology*. Such influence is felt at best in subtle ways. The prime achievement is as unobtrusive catalyst. The measure of impact upon libraries and the significance of such a leadership mode is difficult to evaluate. Moreover, the thrust here has been in the technological sphere, much as the contribution of the American Society for Information Science which has, incidentally, received important support in establishing its identity and furthering its development from the National Science Foundation. There have been successes and failures. But if the effects of National Science Foundation subsidy and leadership were to be measured in terms of how scholarly libraries differ in any way from the way in which they have always functioned or in their priorities, services, and general goals as a result of National Science Foundation influence, such changes would be imperceptible. It may be less that the NSF has failed in offering leadership to librarianship—a role which it has incidentally never accepted or assumed[4]—than that libraries themselves are not

4. In the hearings before a Subcommittee of the Committee on Appropriations, House of Rep., 1968, 90th Congress, 2nd session, NSF testified that although a line item for systems development was increasing from 5.7 to 6.4 million, the increase was not

sensitized to the need for modification. Thus the programs, models, and demonstrations fostered in consequence of National Science Foundation support can generally be seen as unrelated to the needs or the commitment of librarianship.

Perhaps the National Library of Medicine, under the provisions of the Medical Library Assistance Act,[5] has enjoyed the greatest potential for direct leadership. Given the limited scope in the definition of its constituency and with the prime national library in the discipline as its nucleus, its influence has been powerful. Beginning with its MEDLARS[6] effort and with legislative support for evolving an integrated national system of medical libraries and the capacity to design such a scheme in conformity with the regionalization of medical libraries, the effort has gone farther than in any other field of librarianship. Also, by virtue of its delimiting the zone of its application, all research, educational efforts, and building and acquisitions support could exist as component parts of an overall master design. Moreover, lubricated by the federal dollars funneled to all of the program components, the acceptability of the leadership of the National Library of Medicine could be far more tolerable to those in this specialized sphere than to those in contexts more dispersed across the wider spectrum of librarianship. For if such a scheme can be seen as directly reinforcing the aspiration of those who seek to advance medical libraries, all the components mesh—educational program grants, scholarship and research support, subsidies for medical library buildings—to propel the entire discipline forward. And the overall vision and planning, built upon the judicious use of technical experts in each area of development, is one rough master design for the field and its evolving needs. In sum, there tends more nearly to be a viable

---

reflected in the proportion allocated for science library system development, which amount of .5 million was unchanged from the previous year.
5. The Medical Library Assistance Act of 1965 (P.L. 89–291) authorized expenditures over a five-year period for construction of medical libraries, training of medical librarians, research and development in the field, development of a national system of regional medical libraries, support of biomedical publications, and establishment of National Library of Medicine branches where needed. The Medical Library Assistance Extension Act of 1970 (P.L. 91–212) authorized increased appropriations for three more years for several terms in the original legislation.
6. Operational as of January 1964, the MEDLARS (MEDical Literature Analysis and Retrieval System) program involves the preparation of citations for publication in the computer-produced *Index Medicus* (a subject-author index to some 2,300 biomedical journals) and *Current Catalog* (author-title-subject access to publications cataloged by NLM and a number of cooperating institutions). The system permits the assembly of bibliographies on special subjects of wide interest as well as demand searches through the files in response to specific requests. See Charles J. Austin, *MEDLARS 1963–1967* (Washington, D.C.: GPO, 1968); and F. Wilfred Lancaster, "MEDLARS: A Report on the Evaluation of Its Operating Efficiency" in *American Documentation*, April 1969, pp. 119–142.

and plausible program tied to a manageable sphere where differences can be understood, where influences can be measured, and where by virtue of the involvement of recognized leaders from the discipline itself in the councils of planning, widespread support and acquiescence normally follow. The gravest limits have tended to be those of insecurity about the sustenance of the design given a recent history of stop-and-go federal funding, freezes and the like. Such confused terms have not only had a remorseless effect on program capabilities and continuity, but have aggravated what, under the best terms, are the awkward and cumbersome constraints of the federal bureaucracy. One effect is reflected in the exceedingly high rate of turnover among the officials who are responsible for these programs.[7] For the recent federal political and fiscal climate has been rough weather indeed, and the inevitable consequence is to disrupt continuity and to depress expectations of progress in the discipline. Still, the National Library of Medicine appears to offer considerable promise. And the field of medical librarianship, as a discrete and identifiable interlocking system, seems most susceptible of developing into a sophisticated library network. Unhappily, the situation at present is clouded by all of the ambiguities which plague governmental efforts in times of political and fiscal uncertainty.

The Library of Congress

In the context of leadership for libraries, the Library of Congress would seem a natural central force. Yet this has never been seen as its mandate. While it does assume responsibilities which transcend its own limited concerns, such as the present work in developing machine-readable catalog copy,[8] it remains the Congressional library more than the

7. Since the Medical Library Assistance Act of 1965, the associate directors responsible for Extramural Programs at NLM have been Dr. Marjorie Wilson, Mr. David Kefauver, and Dr. Lee L. Langley. The Research, Training and Publications Division also has undergone changes in the supervisory structure and has a new division chief, Dr. Roger Dahlen, and some internal organization changes. There are presently three program officers, each of whom is responsible for research as well as the other functions of the division; formerly only one of the three was responsible for research.
8. Project MARC (Machine-Readable Cataloging) began in 1965 with the development at the Library of Congress of a format for machine readable catalog records which were distributed on tape to a limited number of libraries over the next few years. In 1969 the Library of Congress initiated weekly mailings of the tapes containing LC cataloging information in the MARC II communications format for all English language monographs currently processed at LC. Some sixty-two libraries throughout the country are currently participating. See Henriette Avram, "MARC—The First Two Years" in *Library Resources and Technical Services*, Summer 1968, pp. 245–250; and "MARC Program Research and Development; a Progress Report," in *Journal of Library Automation*, December 1969, pp. 242–265.

national library. The implications of such a self-perception, even when corroborated by such a view by members of the Congress, commit its striving far more exclusively to the solutions of its own problems than to those which engage the entire library community. In part, this may be in consequence of the latent suspicion and fear among many in librarianship of possible domination by any federal body, creating a situation wherein the Library of Congress is reluctant to inflict its leadership influence upon the profession. The same constraints might well be operative even if the Library of Congress were a national library distinct from being a library for Congress. If there is leadership, it is most forcefully reflected in the specialized programs of acquisition linked to the aspirations of the scholarly community.[9] That is of course not to say that many highly significant and commendable programs have not been established by the Library of Congress. To cite one of many would require only the identification of the work of the Division of the Blind, from its inception with braille service in 1931 and recorded books in 1934 to the present activities as a leading force in library services for the visually handicapped. Yet in very recent memory, it has only been in its espousal of the MARC system that the Library of Congress has actually taken a program to the library world and sought to explain, to educate, and then to lead librarianship. This effort, however, can be seen as the traditional contribution of catalog card sets for sale to libraries, updated now that it is magnetic tapes, but still exercising influence in one narrow corner of library practice. While the underlying conceptual posture is seen as supportive of uniform cataloging procedures, doubtless a valuable and viable standardizing influence upon libraries, such efforts tend more nearly to be extrapolations from internal Library of Congress procedures to the rest of the library community, rather than derived from the priorities of the needs of libraries. There is no legislative mandate for the Library of Congress to be or to do otherwise. Still, so circumscribed an influence from a great national library, given its residual prestige and expertise, in a field where leadership voices are scarcely audible, seems a dubious modesty, reflecting perhaps the limits of ideas as much as a political stance. The National Agricultural Library has yet to assert the potential significance which it might have, a consequence perhaps of the

9. Under the terms of Title II-C of the Higher Education Act of 1965, the Library of Congress engaged in a National Program for Acquisitions and Cataloging (NPAC) aimed at procuring and processing for cooperating American libraries all currently published foreign materials of scholarly interest. Hampered by uneven congressional support, NPAC nonetheless managed to make an impressive contribution to research collections in the United States, as well as toward the establishment of bibliographic controls in the less developed countries with which it deals.

generally limited nature of the subject discipline with which it has been engaged.

Other federal agencies which only tangentially relate to the main concerns of librarianship have influenced some information responsibilities. Most notable have been the Commerce Department in its sponsorship of the Clearinghouse for Federal Scientific and Technological Information (now the National Technical Information Service),[10] and NASA.[11] For in fashioning new instruments for the control of the research and development in their fields, they have provided librarianship with access to new classes of information from novel sources and in nontraditional forms. Moreover, with the fostering of formal information systems in discrete subject fields under federal auspices (the Office of Education ERIC system is the most far-reaching illustration),[12] new products and services are being generated which extend the capacity of libraries to develop specialized collections and to be more responsive to clientele requirements with materials which go beyond books, journals, and the standard forms of government documents. The degree of library

---

10. Operated by the Department of Commerce for some twenty years under one or another designation, the Clearinghouse for Federal Scientific and Technical Information has served as a collecting, announcing, and disseminating agency for U.S. government technical report literature and translations of selected foreign materials. Its principal publication, *U.S. Government Research and Development Reports*, annually abstracts approximately 50,000 titles, arranged in subject categories and indexed in the concurrently published *USGRDR Index*. In September 1970, Clearinghouse functions were transferred from the National Bureau of Standards to the newly established National Technical Information Service.

11. Under the terms of the National Aeronautics and Space Act of 1958, the NASA Office of Technology Utilization operates an information system which collects, abstracts, indexes, and disseminates materials relative to worldwide aerospace research and development. The central computer store presently comprises bibliographic records for close to one million documents. Materials are regularly announced in two publications: *Scientific and Technical Aerospace Reports* (STAR) and (under contract with the American Institute of Aeronautics and Astronautics) *International Aerospace Abstracts* (IAA). NASA/SCAN (Selected Current Aerospace Notices) is an SDI system which reports materials in over 180 specialized subject areas. The NASA/RECON (REmote CONsole) service provides instant machine access to the central information store and is available at twenty-six NASA terminals throughout the country.

12. In June 1964 the U.S. Office of Education established the Educational Resources Information Center (ERIC) to serve as a national information system disseminating educational research results and other research and resource materials. The network consists of a coordinating staff in Washington, D.C., and specialized clearinghouses located throughout the country, primarily within universities and professional associations. Each clearinghouse is responsible for acquiring, evaluating, abstracting and indexing pertinent materials within a particular educational area. An abstract index, *Research in Education*, is published monthly as is *Current Index to Journals in Education*, which covers some 500 periodicals in the field.

acceptance of such nonconventional instruments of information control is yet difficult to measure.

The government library system itself could be seen as a potential leadership influence. Yet, as indicated in Chapter 6, its administrative ranks are peopled by a much older and presumably thus less aspiring group than even the norms of librarianship across the board. Prototypal governmental libraries are virtually nonexistent and, as a group, the federal libraries are still seeking to advance beyond the limited stage of development reported in the most recent study devoted to them.[13] One direct consequence is in the establishment of the Federal Library Committee in 1965 by the Library of Congress and the Bureau of the Budget for the purpose of concentrating the intellectual resources present in the federal library and library-related information community[14]: to achieve better utilization of library resources and facilities; to provide more effective planning, development, and operation of federal libraries; to promote an optimum exchange of experience, skill, and resources. The secretariat and a task force—subcommittee—work group operating method seeks to implement these goals. The committee is thus a type of catalytic body for experimentation, research, and coordination. Using the deliberative capacities of agency library representatives, supported in its attempts to conduct research and planning from foundation, Office of Education, and U.S. Army Corps of Engineers grant and contract funds, the committee seeks to upgrade the development and contribution of federal libraries. But it is far from being a leadership influence for librarianship generally.

Committee on Scientific and Technical Information

Another body which, until the recent past, enjoyed the prestige of high bureaucratic placement in the Office of Science and Technology within the Executive Office of the President is COSATI. COSATI (Committee on Scientific and Technical Information) was established in 1962 as part of the Federal Council for Science and Technology which advises the President on relevant federal programs affecting more than one agency. COSATI has been principally concerned with the development and codification of standard practices and procedures among the information-handling activities of federal agencies and with the improvement, extension, and integration of bibliographic services in the scientific and technological fields. Formerly directed by a staff assistant who reported

---

13. Luther H. Evans et al., *Federal Departmental Libraries: A Summary Report of a Survey and a Conference.* Harold Orlans, ed. (Washington, D.C.: Brookings Institution, 1963).
14. Federal Register. Document 65-7080. Saturday, July 3, 1965.

to the Federal Council on Science and Technology and more recently administered by the Director of the Office of Science Information Services of the National Science Foundation, this group is made up of a large number of committees comprised of representatives of government agencies and invited nongovernmental observers, and it centers its activities upon the range of problems crucial to the scientific and technological community in the United States. The priority here is to increase the rationality of the national scientific information systems rather than of libraries. But the concerns come together at frequent points. The influence of its work upon librarianship is only to the degree that those drawn from librarianship may influence its agenda or, in turn, be influenced in their own roles as a result of participation in the affairs of COSATI. There is a COSATI Task Group on Libraries, consisting of both federal and nonfederal librarians and COSATI and the Federal Library Committee share observer status in each other's deliberative bodies. Jointly, COSATI and the Federal Library Committee have sponsored conferences on federal information resources derived from a recognition of a responsibility to interact with the nonfederal sector—the state, local, and private users.[15] But other than through such forums for the exchange of information and discussion, primarily focused upon the needs of research libraries and the shortcomings of federal information resources, COSATI's effects upon librarianship are indirect.

National Commission and Information Science

It was precisely the fact of the widely diffused nature of governmental effort with regard to librarianship which provided the essential rationale for the enactment of legislation authorizing establishment of the permanent National Commission on Libraries and Information Science.[16] A direct outgrowth of the recommendations of the President's National Advisory Commission on Libraries,[17] the present commission is charged with broad advisory, planning, research and development, and evaluative responsibilities relating to the nation's information needs and resources. Essentially, the creation of such a body is the concrete expression of the very limits of the leadership role which government effort has exercised in libraries thus far. Still, the question remains whether the plain-

15. See, for example, *Proceedings of a Conference on Federal Information Resources: Identification, Availability and Use.* Washington, D.C., March 26–27, 1970. Sponsored by the COSATI Task Group on Library Programs and the Federal Library Committee.
16. P. L. 91-345. *An Act to Establish a National Commission on Libraries and Information Science,* July 20, 1970.
17. The report and supporting documents comprise the work of Knight and Nourse (see Footnote 2).

tive appeal for imaginative leadership in influencing the library affairs of the nation through such a mechanism will be an effective force or simply one more political instrument. The steps which led to its creation are a tribute to the political acumen of all who played an advocacy role in its enactment,[18] to the earlier commission and its report and to the many who made the case for establishment of such a vehicle as a separate, independent body so that it could not be coopted into the existing structure of limited response mechanisms. The power and the prestige are fully in evidence, but the nature and the caliber of the commission's efforts will inevitably reflect the stature of those who comprise its membership and, more particularly, those who direct its work. Whether it will exercise leadership remains to be seen.

THE INFLUENCE OF THE PROFIT-MAKING SECTOR

Libraries do not function in isolation. They depend upon outside forces —those which produce products and services for libraries, as well as those which compete for the leisure time of real and potential clienteles. Most salient, perhaps, are the producers of information products for which libraries are a primary outlet, the publishing industry and those elements of the consulting, research, and development business upon which librarianship relies.

It is interesting to note the establishment in 1969 of the Information Industry Association. This is an organization whose membership perceives information as a commodity with a clear value in the marketplace. In line with its desire to further private enterprise, it questions the legitimacy of governmental efforts which establish or perpetuate information systems and programs which it would prefer to be left to the profit sector. This line of argument suggests that the political inspiration which brings into being certain new programs represents simply a latter day manifestation of federal boondoggling, extended to the information sphere. Such at least is the view expressed toward the State Technical Services program,[19] a federal program designed to maximize the transmittal of scientific and technological information from the public to the

18. Among those testifying before the House Education Subcommittee in April 1969 were Roger McDonough, president of ALA; Robert Vosper; and Joseph Becker. Dr. William Dix, then president-elect of ALA, testified before the Senate Education Subcommittee.
19. The State Technical Services Act of 1965 (P. L. 89-182). Objections to the Act from segments of the private sector are summarized in the statements from the National Association of Manufacturers and the National Society for Professional Engineers. See Hearings before the Subcommittee on Commerce and Finance of the Committee on Interstate and Foreign Commerce. HR 3420, June 1, 2, 3, 1965, pp. 109–110, 128–129.

private sector. The fact that it was managed and controlled by nonprofit organizations, such as state universities and state economic and development departments, and contracted much of its work out through nonprofit organizations undoubtedly conditions such perspectives. Yet one wonders whether social or even economic justice is advanced by assaulting new and developmental information designs, impossible of attainment without federal intervention, before they have an opportunity to demonstrate their viability.[20] The same logic might well be addressed against the Agricultural Extension Service by the commercial interests which surround agriculture if the service were being founded today.[21]

There is little question of the disposition of governmental officials to shift the exploitation of governmental information to the commercial sector, even when it has been developed by the governmental agencies themselves. Recent illustrations would include the Current Index to Journals in Education, published by the CCM Information Corp. (a subsidiary of Crowell-Collier & Macmillan, Inc.) from data generated by the ERIC system, the registration statements and supporting documentation from the Securities and Exchange Commission by LEASCO System & Research Corp. and the arrangements for publication of the Bibliography of Agriculture compiled by the National Agricultural Library by the aforementioned CCM Information Corp.

The question of leadership influence arises in consequence of how the interests of libraries, and of their clienteles, may best be served. If such matters are left to a political determination in which the commercial sector is seen as the primary party at interest, information access may be made more costly, thus reinforcing the terms whereby prohibitive pricing restricts intelligence from those who deserve access, especially if the intelligence is derived from government sources and expense.

The disposition of questions which relate to responsibilities in the handling, distribution, and pricing of information are of prime concern to librarianship. Such issues relate directly to their capacity to perform. It is not at all clear that the interests of the private profit-making sector are identical with the aspirations of librarianship. Without sophisticated analysis of where and how library clienteles are best served, librarianship defaults in its responsibilities. Such issues have yet to engage librari-

20. For defense of the program and support for its continuation, see Arthur D. Little, Inc., *Program Evaluation of the Office of State Technical Services* (Cambridge, Mass.: Arthur D. Little, Inc., 1969).
21. Early in this century the Department of Agriculture and the state colleges initiated the employment of trained county agents to aid the nation's farmers in applying the results of scientific advances to their farming practices. The program received legislative sanction in 1914 with the passage of the Cooperative Agriculture Extension Act (Smith-Lever Act) which authorized Federal support on a state-matching-fund basis.

anship, due either to naivete or to a studied posture of avoiding volatile questions. One wonders whether such matters might not more appropriately engage the attention of those who work for the advancement of libraries rather than such public relations activities as National Library Week. If there is no sophisticated advocate concerned with the information consumer in a culture unstructured to protect his interests, the information system will even further gravitate toward designs for those who can best afford to pay. The consequence would be for the informationally rich to get richer still. Conversely, the informationally disadvantaged would be denied once more the access to intelligence which might advance their knowledgeability and thus their lives.

In some ways, one might regard the phenomenon of a profit-making company, instead of government, using government-developed information as an attempt to be informationally responsive by ensuring, through commercial exploitation, the widening of the market for this intelligence. At the same time, however, when the government stands aside, and when one organization becomes the middleman, there is virtually no chance for competition among publishers with the almost inevitable result that the prices for information are higher than if it were distributed by government. This is quite a different matter from those instances when the government contracts with a single organization on the basis of competitive bidding to serve as distributing agency for its publications; the NASA facility operated by a subsidiary of Informatics Corporation would be an illustration. Under the latter terms, the monopoly control is limited to the term of the contract and the pricing policy is derived by the government agency.

Certain of the theoretical advantages which accrue from government effort in its own behalf leave some room for doubt, even when contracts are drawn on the basis of competitive bidding. A case in point may be the documentation system carried out by the National Cash Register Company in selling copies of the ERIC System's microfiche. Under this system reports of research conducted under Office of Education auspices are listed and described in *Research in Education,* and the original documents upon which the abstracts are based are made available from the National Cash Register Company. The attractiveness of such a commercial relationship in the distribution of thousands of documents at relatively low cost is obviously enhanced to the degree that it involves standing orders for comprehensive collections of all of the document output in particular subfields of education. To distribute automatically under such terms is both efficient and lucrative for the contractor. But so would such a process be under government administration. The crucial question is the efficiency of the service which libraries receive when they require and order a specific document. Not surprisingly, the commercial interest is oriented to the profit-making potential and thus to its volume and standing order business. To identify and reproduce a single document is another matter and more at the mercy of the typical bureaucratic syndrome of time lag. One cannot help but speculate as to whether the fact that profitability is not at question in a government established and run enterprise like the National Technical Information Service does not make for more responsiveness to client need than profit-making operations. In such an equation there must also be calculated the relative effectiveness of a distribution machinery which controls most of the standard published output of government, the Government Printing Office, an agency little-known for efficiency in distribution or in broadcasting the availability of its product. Upon these matters the voice of librarianship has been only sporadically heard.

Commercial interests demonstrate a mounting entrepreneurial concern in information products.[22] Such concern translates into new media forms, access to information via nontraditional technological means and, perhaps ultimately, to information utilities themselves. While new and evolving forms remain imprecise, the monitoring and the informed policy formulations with regard to eventual outcomes seem as much the province of librarianship's concern as of those whose interests arise out of entrepreneurial zeal. The profit-making sector views with alarm government subsidization of information developmental efforts in professional and scientific societies. The consequence of such pressure is to increase the apprehension of those in the government who provide the resources which spawn informational efforts as competitive with those of private industry. If the consequence is for government to approach more gingerly the development of informational efforts which might tread on proprietary territorial prerogatives and to defer to the latter out of threat of possible political reprisal, library leadership could be a countervailing force. But if, in fact, librarianship assumes no role, then those whose professional interests may be most affected can be expected to remain oblivious to the importance of such questions.[23]

22. The role and interests of the private sector are vigorously advanced and defended by Herbert S. White, then Vice-President, LEASCO Systems & Research Corp., in "Perspectives on the Use of Information," *Proceedings of a Conference on Federal Information Resources: Identification, Availability and Use* (Washington, D.C.: COSATI, Task Group on Library Programs, 1970).
23. Except for the article in *Library Journal*, May 15, 1970, p. 1803, drawing attention to the program and discussions during the 1970 annual meeting of the Information Industry Association, no other serious attention to these topics has come to the writer's attention in the literature of librarianship in recent years.

Consultants as an Influence

In recent years, libraries, whose growth in scale and complexity has outstripped their capacity to cope with their organizational and technical problems, have turned increasingly toward outside expertise. The consulting phenomenon has become quite pervasive.[24] In reviewing its effects upon librarianship, it is difficult to classify the efforts. Yet in its essential characteristics, two pronounced types may be discriminated— one is the free-lance, part-time professional librarian or library educator, the other is the organization engaged exclusively in consulting work, frequently combined with contract research and development. The consulting firm pursues its role as a business; the part-time library consultant may range from well-meaning amateur to unrivaled authority. The kind of outside expertise needed, and the comparative effectiveness of one type or another, is difficult to gauge.

Individual organizations turn to outsiders for aid for many reasons. Consultants are sometimes employed when local officials know what the solution to a problem is, yet require substantiation from detached experts in order to convince others. Under such terms, consultancy can represent more nearly the political exploitation of outside authority, than analytical perspective. Consulting firms may be somewhat more subject to such compromising pressures than the independent professional, or perhaps sophisticated enough to perceive more clearly what is expected, and may be more prone to exercise political influence in obtaining contracts which result in the delivery of the desired end product. There are also instances in which the use of outside consultants may represent only a cynical administrative ploy to demonstrate that a particular problem is significant enough to warrant outside review, although there is no serious intent or capacity to bring into being any proposed solutions which may be derived. There are no guideposts, no standards, which apply in consulting. The individual consultant who plies his trade as a part-time activity may depend for his reputation upon his years of experience in an administra-

---

24. A total of 2,612 individuals and organizations are indexed in Paul Wasserman, ed., *Consultants and Consulting Organizations* (Ithaca, N.Y.: Graduate School of Business and Public Administration, Cornell University, 1966); and some 4,900 individuals are indexed in Paul Wasserman, ed., *Who's Who in Consulting* (Ithaca, N.Y.: Graduate School of Business and Public Administration, Cornell University, 1968). Even within librarianship itself, there is now a published roster of some 480 active consultants who engage regularly or intermittently in consulting assignments. See John N. Berry, III, ed., *Directory of Library Consultants* (New York: R. R. Bowker, 1969). Moreover, both the SLA and ALA maintain their own rosters of consultants who are available for specific assignments upon request from interested parties.

tive role, for such consultants when they are drawn from practice are almost exclusively principal library administrators. It is not at all uncommon for a consultant to be engaged to review a problem which remains only ineffectually resolved within his own organization. Normally, he will be purveying his conventional wisdom to an organization of lesser scale, but with ambitious designs, so that his authority may be established solely in consequence of his own survival in the larger context. The members of library school faculties tend to be engaged more often for technical assessments. Depending upon the sense in which the problems are seen to require more leisurely review and analysis, and appreciating the constraints which obtain in drawing upon the time and absorbing the costs for practicing library administrators, the academic represents an alternative short of the consulting firm. The individual drawn from the university may have several motives beyond the obvious appeal of the financial incentives. One may be to evangelize some technical dogma. The disciples and missionaries of the LC classification scheme would be one illustration. Moreover, such opportunities provide fresh options for the academic to stay abreast of the pragmatic problems of his discipline and in this way may be seen as reinforcing of the teaching contribution.

Confusion frequently arises between the consulting role and the research role. Often when libraries engage researchers, it is consultants whom they are really seeking. To differentiate the research contribution from the consultative contribution requires perception still uncommon in librarianship. This may be as true for the consumer of the service as for its purveyor. Yet the fact of the matter may be that the expert counselor frequently does yield the best results, or at least the sought for results, with the greatest dispatch and economy. For, not uncommonly, research is a strategic misnomer for engaging expertise to support decisions which have already been formulated. As this is the case, policy makers require substantiating testimony less to understand the nature of the problem than to influence its support by those who assume ultimate control.

The researcher in librarianship may be cast in one of two fundamentally different roles. The first is an authority role. Under these terms, there is deference, not because of what he does and what he learns as a consequence, but rather because he is presumed to be an authority. Another perception of the researcher is as a "hired hand." The sponsor under these terms not only defines the problem, but prescribes the method for its solution. In this way, professional committees design projects, solicit funds, and only then seek individuals competent to conduct the research. This phenomenon illustrates the limited perception of the practicing world which fails to appreciate the need for adequate preparation for the research role and sensitivity to design, both in its formulation and prosecution phases. When this happens, that individual who can be found to demonstrate interest in such an assignment may be far less competent than one who would not accept it without prior involvement in the conception of the design. The more sophisticated researcher who, for whatever reason, prefers to be engaged in such a project, finds himself exploring the means for recasting the research in order to permit him to gather information he may view as more relevant than the instigators of the study did. For often the practical problem requires redefinition, since in its original conception it may not lend itself to mature investigation or analysis. If a project is only broadly defined in the beginning, as is frequently the case, there is opportunity to develop mutual understanding as the program proceeds. Yet, there are formidable barriers and concrete differences between the goals and the values of the organization which may engage the research and the individual himself, which can contribute to the frustrations of such an experience throughout the course of the effort.

Library research is closely tied to accepted and acceptable professional solutions, thus seldom contemplating or testing radical alternatives. Reflecting the pragmatic values of the field, the general nature of the problems studied cluster more nearly around technical issues rather than organization and clientele concerns.

One of the problems of the consultant drawn from library practice or education is that the building expert may know nothing about architecture, the management expert very little about organizational behavior. The most hopeful outcome possible under these terms is the sharing of experience and understanding about the conventional wisdom of the field. To such pronouncements are lent the prestige of the administrator of reputation or the dignity of a university-based affiliation and the authoritative righteousness of the PhD. Moreover, if the solution corresponds with an *a priori* local sense of the problem, all the parties at interest feel satisfied.

The consulting firms which have engaged upon library projects cover a very wide gamut, from the broad management-oriented groups like Cresap McCormick to the one- or two-man office concentrated on specific technical problems like library automation such as R & D Consultants. In between are the research and development firms which carry out special studies (like WESTAT Research Corp.), computer-oriented corporations which develop library tools such as printed book catalogs (LEASCO Systems and Research Corp. would be an illustration), the divisions of large consulting and development organizations which have built up special task groups for concentration upon library efforts (Arthur D. Little, Inc., would be illustrative). Perhaps the most widely known organization is Nelson Associates, an organization which has conducted projects in librarianship in many parts of the country, with particular emphasis upon regional organizational problems. These studies have been carried forth with such frequency, beginning first in New York State, that there is a sharp similarity to the reports, suggesting that the formulas originally derived are seen as viable, with only minor changes necessary to accommodate to the local situation. Of course, in such efforts libraries normally receive what they bargain for —the evidence of the prior work is abundant testimony to what may be expected. In a time when cities are growing more skeptical of the utility of constructing new library buildings, it may be that the pattern followed in San Francisco of engaging an outside consulting organization in order to analyze thoroughly the potential as well as the need against the entire institutional future prospects may come to be more commonplace.[25]

Somewhat different from the consulting effort is the experimental work typically carried out by a firm for a government sponsor. The consequence of such work may more widely affect library attitudes and perspectives than the individual consulting assignment in one organization. For typically, the consulting effort will be addressed to one agency's unique requirements. However, some of the organizations which carry out efforts on behalf of individual institutions or regional jurisdictions have also been active in assignments which focus upon the broader issues of librarianship.[26] The work carried out by organizations like System Development Corporation, Santa Monica, California; Herner & Co., Washington, D.C.; and Charles Bourne & Associates, Menlo Park, California, transcends the boundaries of a single institution. The product of this work, particularly when it is conducted under federal auspices, will result in publication and broad distribution in a way which may come to influence judgments in many more settings than solely the organization which commissioned the original study.

Seen from another perspective and in its relationship to leadership phenomena in librarianship, it is interesting to note the number of imaginative members of the discipline who have gravitated out of library practice and into consulting activity. Such a route is, of course, common in many disciplines, but in librarianship the drain may be more severe. To the extent that library practice fails to sustain the creative interest of

25. *The Urban Central Library* (San Francisco: Arthur D. Little, December 1970).
26. As, for example, a number of the studies commissioned by the National Advisory Commission on Libraries: *Technology and Libraries* (System Development Corporation); *American State Libraries and State Library Agencies* (Nelson Associates, Inc.); and *School Libraries in the United States* (Nelson Associates, Inc.). All in Knight and Nourse (see Footnote 2).

some of its keenest minds—Mortimer Taube, Saul Herner, Eugene Garfield[27] are illustrations—to that extent the availability of innovative and imaginative leadership is reduced. The stimulus of creative talent, even when it is applied to information problems from the outside, exercises its influence upon library affairs. Yet intrinsic to the loss of such expertise to the main stream of librarianship is that intrepreneurially oriented professionals ultimately come to the realization that the capacity of their profession to tolerate such insight is restricted at best. They must devise or identify outside mechanisms for bringing their imaginative designs to bear upon the informational problems which they could not address as practicing professionals. The phenomenon is not limited to consulting. In other instances, such individuals have been drawn into publishing, public administration, university administration, or into other roles beyond the field. Perhaps the ambitions of librarianship are better served when an imaginative leader like Major Owens gravitates from library work with the disadvantaged to assume a central role in the New York City poverty programs as Commissioner of the Community Development Agency, or when an educator of the caliber of Lowell Martin becomes vice-president of a publishing corporation.

The use of outside consultants only seldom involves the point and purpose of the organization. The underlying issues are only uncommonly assessed. As this is so, the options open to the consulting organization are predetermined and it must be seen as enlisted in the service of the agency or the discipline paying for its work, rather than as an unencumbered counseling body committed to exploring and advising on how best to proceed by deliberating all the alternatives to the existing course.

In a way related to the outside consulting phenomenon is the influence which other organizational forms for which libraries serve as the primary market bring to bear. The computer industry is perhaps the most dramatic case in point. Without the participation of hardware and software firms, the advance of automatic processing in libraries would have proceeded more slowly than it has. In some measure, automation progress may be seen as concomitant of the efforts of computer firms to further their own commercial interests. Advancing a market of perhaps limited consequence is understandable when the general computer market seems to be attaining a point of saturation. With their technical assistance, the prototypal designs which are striving to apply technological means to the solution of library problems are commonplace at the beginning of the 1970s. The industry leader, IBM, by counseling in such

27. Each of whom founded his own consulting, research, and development organization based upon satisfying the requirements of the library and information-science community.

experiments, by providing a technical literature built upon prior experience and distributed freely to the library field, and by holding conferences addressed to automation problems in libraries, has doubtless been the most pervasive influence of this type. Moreover, through the contribution of one of its own staff, the late Hans Peter Luhn,[28] new strategies for manipulating and retrieving information have been devised and have come to influence library practice.

Still another related form of influence upon the field is reflected in the way in which organizations which supply services to libraries have adapted their programs so as to improve the capacity of librarianship to devote more of its time and attention to client requirements as a consequence of these services. An organization like Richard Abel provides libraries with the option of acquiring automatically all books in certain subject spheres; other companies, like BroDart and Bowker, offer catalog cards with books and manufactured book catalogs for particular library systems. Such entrepreneurial ventures provide the means for libraries to reduce the complexities of their procedures and lessen their managerial problems, but as a result the zone of decision-making may be sharply reduced in subtle ways. The consequence of receiving books automatically, for example, even with the option to return some of them, is that the area of choice on the part of acquisitions personnel is sharply reduced; while technical performance may become more efficient and economic the net effect may be less than salutary.[29]

It is exceedingly difficult to generalize the significance of the consulting phenomenon for librarianship beyond the point of identifying its pervasiveness. The genuine nature of such contribution, the level of organizational aspiration, the relative naivete or sensitivity of the parties involved, the political and organizational climate for allowing outside perspectives on local problems, and even the motives of the participants are all elements in an exceedingly complex equation. But the endemic nature of the activity may be seen as symptomatic of a larger malaise within librarianship. Here is an institutional form which identifies itself, and is identified by those to whom it is responsible, as very much in need of outside detached analysis, as often lacking in the sophistication to perceive the nature of its problems much less to resolve them. Perhaps

28. Among his pioneering efforts were the devising of the strategies of both KWIC (Keyword in Context) and SDI (Selective Dissemination of Information).
29. See G. Edward Evans, "Book Selection and Book Collection Usage in Academic Libraries," in *The Library Quarterly*, July 1970, pp. 297–308. In a study of circulation records, the author found that librarians (and to a lesser degree faculty) had selected a significantly greater number of titles which had actually been used by patrons than those books which had been purchased by the libraries through blanket-order approval plans.

as a stage in the evolution of an underdeveloped culture, the wisdom of those from more advanced stages of development holds the appeal of yielding guideposts. Still, there is little promise in anticipating leadership which is essentially without the parameters of the institutional form. That institutional form or that discipline which rests its hope for progress upon outside expertise is destined to be disappointed, for it distorts a proper relationship and expects the servant to be the master.

Influence of Other Disciplines

With the increased attention that has been drawn to library and information problems in recent years, the effect has been to attract new insights to the study of its problems through the involvement of different classes of individuals and organizations. Humanistic scholars have, of course, long been identified with libraries. The literature of the field over the years bears witness to their concern with the classic contribution of the library as storehouse of knowledge. But others drawn predominantly from systems analysis and behavioral areas are now coming in increasing numbers to be attracted by the problems of librarianship.[30] Not only are they clustered on the fringes of the field and addressing some of its problems through consulting and research activity,[31] in other university departments directing research upon problems germane to the concerns of the field,[32] but they are being drawn into library organizations themselves[33] and into library education.[34]

As government has come to place a higher value upon information systems and services, as the organizational scale of libraries and information itself has grown, and as support for research and development upon its problems has advanced, new areas susceptible of analysis and problem-solving have come to be seen as appropriate to the expertise of many who have been trained in other disciplines, but possess the unique

30. An example is the article in *Library Journal*, October 15, 1970, by Gerard Salton, a well-known computer scientist engaged in research on information retrieval. See "On the Development of Libraries and Information Centers," pp. 3433–3442.
31. Here might be included such individuals as Lawrence Buckland of Inforonics, Inc.; Monroe Snyder of Operations Research, Inc.; and Don King of Home Testing Institute, a division of Westat Research, Inc.
32. Such individuals as F. F. Liemkuhler at Purdue University, Richard Trueswell at the University of Massachusetts, Manfred Kochen at the University of Michigan, and Norman Baker at Georgia Institute of Technology could be cited.
33. Ben-Ami Lipitz at Yale University, Richard Nance at Southern Methodist University, and Charles Sage at the Iowa University Library System are examples.
34. Among recent faculty members drawn from the outside are Ernest DeProspo from political science at Rutgers University and Jonathan Stanfield, drawn from computer science at the University of Washington. The same phenomenon characterizes the designation of one of the most recent deanships in the field: Thomas H. Mott, Jr., at Rutgers.

methodological capacities needed in newly spawned roles related to libraries. In a time when librarianship and its problems were less consequential, when the information field had not yet attained its present prominence or level of support, such fortuitous developments remained foreclosed. Without question, the influence of all those who are drawn from uncommon backgrounds broadens the capacity of the discipline to assault its most fundamental problems in more imaginative ways than when it could rely upon only those schooled in and so committed to its own conventional wisdom. To a considerable degree we have remarked about these prospects. But another salient factor is the work now very much in progress within particular scholarly disciplines other than librarianship, by those identified more nearly with the disciplines than with information and libraries, upon resolving the information needs of their fields. Such activity tends to underscore two things: first, the significance which is increasingly being accorded to information need in particular scholarly spheres; second, the limits of traditional library service to cope with the expanded intellectual productivity and the more sophisticated forms which information is coming to take in many such fields.

Perhaps the prime catalytic agent which has influenced the enlarged scale of disciplinary efforts to expand and improve, or to devise and implement, particular information systems within the scientific disciplines has been the National Science Foundation. Recognizing the inability of traditional librarianship to deal with the specialized nature of the information requirements of the sciences, and carrying forward its mandate to help assure orderly progress in the sciences, this agency has provided the encouragement and the financial resources necessary for both engendering the earlier research and later for the prototypal systems governing the rationalization of information control in certain of the major scientific disciplines.[35] Thus the avant-garde, the experimentation, and the innovative efforts seen as prelude to the full development of information systems addressed to the needs of scientific disciplines have been enhanced. The none too subtle implication, of course, is that the sensitivity and the sophistication needed to assure such information control patterns more nearly reside with those of the discipline than with those who are concerned primarily with information and its management. And it is not until that point when a final and viable information system is derived that it is then possible for libraries to become an element in the system by acquiring and retaining the file of the information products fashioned out of the work of the scientific group itself.

One effect of this phenomenon has been to draw into the culture of

35. Chemistry, physics, and psychology, among others.

the information discipline many whose primary identification has earlier been with the particular science in which they had been educated.[36] The question of whether this is more a function of the reluctance of librarianship as a professional discipline in its own right to accept the role of designing or evolving an information system for the discrete discipline, or simply a tacit acknowledgement of the superordinance of subject sophistication and understanding over the information side of the problem, may be of only academic concern. Yet the consequence of efforts completely outside the traditional framework of the library field has undoubtedly led to some costly adventures, abortive designs, and solutions which might have been prosecuted with greater dispatch and economy if there had been within the culture of librarianship itself a corps of information designers open to the acceptance of such opportunities and challenges. Still, the fact of the matter is that one consequence of the normal prescribed limits of the library discipline, as represented in the context of its present educational sequence, is that such questions and such problems are almost universally defined as the province of others, except in the most advanced programs such as those of the newer centers for research and education in information science. The assumption of responsibility for fashioning creative responses to the needs of particular constituencies, a responsibility assumed more readily in the early period of library history in the United States when periodical indexes and bibliographic control devices were being invented and put into operation by librarians themselves, no longer obtains. For the pattern of library service which has developed consists, more often than not, in simple direction to the card catalog as the prototype of reference service. That is, librarians normally see responsibility only for providing subject access to book collections. Only when clients of the library request assistance from reference librarians do users receive aid in locating published material, either in book form through a discriminating use of the catalog, or in other forms through the use of abstracting, indexing, or bibliographic services which are provided by outside agencies. It is uncommon indeed to find an American library in which other than in the assignment of subject headings and classification numbers to books, professional librarians seek to anticipate the requirements of their clientele by indexing, abstracting, or otherwise deriving systems of information control for the nonbook form. As this operational syndrome is further and further instilled in the psyche of the discipline, it is not surprising that there is a deep-seated reluctance on the part of virtually all schooled therein to engage in the more inventive tasks of deriving and fashioning new intelligence systems for discrete fields of study.

36. Belver Griffith at Drexel and Charles Bernier at Buffalo are two illustrations.

As the financial support of the National Science Foundation has contributed to creative design by and among scientific societies, other government-inspired information systems are being fashioned. The ERIC System of the Office of Education is perhaps the most widely known such emergent system.[37] Under the terms of this program, subject centers have been established as part of a network for controlling and monitoring the research and development documentation of specific fields. The centers serve as the basic collection and dissemination points, feeding into the national ERIC Center where a regular publication, *Research in Education*, provides abstracts and index access to identify many of the particular publications which have been collected at the centers. The general rationale is seen as an attempt to provide the means at strategic points for capturing the intelligence being generated, for indexing and abstracting it, for preparing state-of-the-art reviews by experts through the availability of specialized collections offering efficient access to the continuing stream of intelligence affecting the subdiscipline. Furthermore, the documents themselves, which are identified through the abstracts and indexes, are made available in photocopies or microforms. For librarianship the dividend out of such programs is found in the indexes, which serve as acquisition guides to the general research literature of the field. Yet in this instance again, the design of a parallel bibliographic system is simply another expression by another broad information constituency, education, of the limits of modern librarianship.

Carrying one stage beyond such designs, and consonant with the representations of the Weinberg Report,[38] is the development of a system of information analysis centers. In such a context the information agent specializes in the particular discipline and is drawn from active research within it in order to play the role of expert in the analysis of the documents of the field. Thus the contribution goes beyond the mere collection of publications and involves the exercise of skilled judgments about which information in those publications is significant, differentiating it

37. At the time of this writing there are nineteen centers in such discrete spheres as linguistics, tests, measurements and evaluation, disadvantaged, and adult education, operating at universities and scientific societies under contract with the Office of Education.
38. ". . . Knowledgeable scientific interpreters who can collect relevant data, review a field, and distill information in a manner that goes to the heart of a technical situation, are more help to the overburdened specialist than is a mere pile of relevant documents. Such knowledgeable scientific middlemen *who themselves contribute to science* are the backbone of the information center; they make an information center a technical institute rather than a technical library." *Science, Government and Information*, A Report of the President's Science Advisory Committee. (Washington: G.P.O., 1963) p. 33.

from the more trivial large mass of publication and literature which in-
undates every field. In such a situation the collecting function is combined with the expert analysis function. This form of activity tends to
be characteristic of the type of responsibility which libraries and librarianship have found repugnant and too costly—in consequence of
the limits of their subject sophistication, or of the limits of their available manpower for such roles. It is avoided even in those most advanced
situations, as in academic libraries, where there are subject bibliographers on the library staff. With uncommon exception, the only discretion in the analysis of information afforded by libraries is in the exercise
of choice in acquisitions. Once this has been done, all of the artifacts
which are collected tend to receive common bibliographic description,
except for certain unusual classes of materials like rare books and documents.

A related phenomenon has been found in community agencies in the
cities, where an information structure is arising in response to the requirements of the poor. Combining the collecting and provision of factual data with the function of serving as referral center to other agencies
and services as well as, often, the assumption of advocacy roles for its
clienteles, such groups seem to be taking on certain information mis-
sions which overlap those of libraries, or at least the potential of
libraries. Virtually every city has such newly invented activities performing in fields of consumer intelligence, legal information, and health and
housing. Here again it is the linking of factual information with a
knowledge of the substantive problems themselves over and above the
published materials which extend the utility of their contribution beyond
the limits which libraries have normally reached. The effect of such developments is thus to sharpen the distinctiveness with which libraries
are identified exclusively with books, rather than with information.

The consequence of the importance of all of the other influences in
the culture which are coming more and more to perceive the links between rational information systems and the destiny of their own disciplines is that it is they, more commonly than librarianship, who are
coming to urge strategies, priorities, and goals in national information
policy.[39] These perspectives arise out of their interests in better information than that which libraries are able to or are prepared to provide, in
education, in science, in social welfare, and in all the other spheres where
there are professionally responsible communities which understand the

39. See, for example, Alfred J. Kahn and others, *Neighborhood Information Centers:
A Study and Some Proposals* (New York: Columbia University School of Social
Work, 1966).

need. The proposals for experimentation are thus brought into being and are influenced by individuals outside the library field.

While such external influences might have provoked a leadership role from librarianship, this has not been perceived as the responsibility of the library. Librarianship has continued to concentrate upon its own limited corner of the universe, upon its conventional prescribed zone of concerns—acquisitions, cataloging, book collection development, reference work. It is the abdication of the semblance of such responsibility for the broad societal information problems which perhaps most disappoints those who hold an aspirational vision of the potential of librarianship.

HOW DO LIBRARIES AND PUBLISHING INFLUENCE EACH OTHER?

Only those aspects of the publishing scene which deal specifically with the intellectual concerns of librarianship itself have been treated thus far. The fact is that since libraries depend almost completely upon externally produced materials and since these materials come from publishing houses, the destiny of librarianship is intertwined with these companies and libraries are inevitably influenced. Whether they exert their influence upon the producers remains more doubtful. For even the level of discourse, which bears upon ways in which the field might enter into strategic decision processes which relate to the range, the scope, the quality, and the substantive content of the works which it acquires, tends to be relatively unsophisticated.[40]

Commercial publishing is a business which is motivated by the profitability of the books it publishes. The decade of the 1960s seen through the mergers, associations, and reorganizations which characterized the affairs of the period is testament to the blurred entrepreneurial vision which saw in the combinations and permutations of electronics, media, and books, a powerful new marketing potential.[41] Yet for all the zeal which has attended such corporate gymnastics, the fact of the matter is

40. Highly uncommon are such discussions as the *Library Journal* editorial, October 1, 1970, p. 3219, which identifies the volume of library purchases of first novels as a factor influencing publishers to chance a greater number of such titles from aspiring new authors.
41. Among the notable mergers and acquisitions between 1962 and 1969: Holt, Rinehart and Winston merged with CBS; RCA acquired Random House; Xerox bought University Microfilms, R. R. Bowker Company, Ginn & Co.; the *New York Times* purchased Microfilming Corp. of America; Bell and Howell purchased Micro Photo and Charles E. Merrill Books, Inc.; ITT acquired Howard Sams.

that in its main lines the publishing industry has been little affected. Traditional forms of publication tend still to form the basis for profitability and the experimental alternatives remain precisely that.[42] But what has not been confused is the way that libraries as a market in consequence of dramatic increases in their number, scale, and local, state and federal support terms have come to represent an even more powerful component of the industry's potential.[43] A subtle measure of the growing importance of the library market is reflected in the way that an increasing number of librarians are being drawn into the editorial and distributive organization of the publishing industry. For sensitivity to this market, to its tastes, to its standards, to its purchasing propensities, is something to reckon with and so no longer is it only the children's literature expert who holds appeal for the industry. As a leadership influence for libraries, publishing leads to the terrain where profit lies. If it can be shown that there is a market, products will follow.[44] To influence for libraries, publishing leads to the terrain where profits lies. If in ways which far transcend the kind of genteel and ritual processes of joint committees of librarians and publishers' representatives which serve as convenient and superficial public relations evidence that mutual problems are under discussion. All the evidence suggests that what is inevitably reflected in the entire range of library-publisher relations is that both mutually reinforce each other in the notion that what they are doing is intrinsically good and important and that the common enterprise is best served simply by convincing more and more people of the essential virtue of their already significant contributions. For it is this which seems most to characterize the mutual backscratching of National Library Week.[45]

Perhaps the principal imbalance in such an equation is that the ultimate consequence for the publishing industry is broadened markets and for librarianship only the more illusory public relations. Moreover, there

42. See Dan Lacy, "The Publishing Industry in Transition" in *Frontiers in Librarianship: Proceedings of the Change Institute 1969*, School of Library and Information Services, University of Maryland, August 10–15, 1969 (Westport, Conn.: Greenwood Publishing Corporation, 1972).
43. As one indication, a comparison of the figures for "Library Book Budgets—Books Only" and "Estimates of Total Sales of All Books" (*The Bowker Annual 1970*, pp. 22 and 28) for the years 1963 and 1968 indicates that in 1963 library book budgets totaled $189,187,000 or 11 percent of sales of $1,673,077,000; in 1968, library book budgets totaled $486,498,680 or 19 percent of sales of $2,568,300,000.
44. Dan Lacy (see Footnote 42).
45. Perhaps librarianship has grown more sophisticated than during the time when public librarians served as "volunteers" and after hours, on their own time (in institutions like the Brooklyn Public Library) acted as unpaid counselors to library patrons on gift-book buying for Christmas.

is something slightly queasy about a relationship in which one of the parties at interest comes to the other in a posture of admiring innocence which the other is not unknown to betray.[46] If the affair, by any other name, is only the classic replaying of the drama of seller assuring buyer of the identity of their interests, then the classic admonition of caveat emptor is sorely neglected by a starry-eyed customer so infatuated with the relationship as to see its own best interests irrevocably served only in a tight linkage with those of the seller. Yet this is precisely the record of librarianship in its unceasing record of congruence with virtually every position the publishing industry has taken in its legislative representations to the United States Congress in recent years.[47]

Perhaps the influence of publishing in fostering the progressive thrust of libraries and of librarianship as a discipline should be sought in areas other than public relations. Interestingly, but not surprisingly, publishers are a stalwart ally in representations for support in every jurisdiction for increased library appropriations, for construction, acquisitions, and for school, public, and academic library development. Still these are all measures which increase the numbers and extend the market. The fundamental striving does not appear to be for a more astute librarianship, but simply for a larger population of library outlets. The consequence of such advances in no way disturbs a relationship with a discipline comprised of well-intentioned amateurs with more resources, more programs, but no greater political or substantive sophistication to play a different role in the relationship. To impute cynical motives to what may be sincere acts is perhaps to condemn the very best intentioned. Yet to play one role precludes the playing of another. And in the drama of benefiting librarianship, the characters cast themselves out of only their own sense of direction. For publishers to seek actively a librarianship which is more astute, more economically sensitized, more politically sophisticated, might shift the comfortable balance which exists. And so it is less than surprising to find that the kinds of encouragement which normally obtain between a supplying industry and the discipline where its products

46. In March 1966, Marvin Scilken, Director of the Orange Public Library (N.J.), testified before a Senate committee on the widespread practice of "library editions" of children's books. Suits were subsequently filed by libraries in New York, Philadelphia, Madison, Wisconsin, and New Jersey. Eighteen publishers were accused of conspiring with wholesalers to fix the price of books by the practice of "net pricing." Recently the New Jersey schools and libraries received $82,000 and over $1,000,000 is being recovered throughout the nation.
47. ALA and AAP (Association of American Publishers)—then ABPC (American Book Publishers Council)—have worked very closely on educational appropriations, book postal rates, import duties on books (the Florence and Beirut agreements), pornography legislation, copyright revision, and "negative option" in standing order purchases.

are exploited, and which represent genuine attempts to advance the practice, are here absent.

Devices widely employed in other fields to uplift professional disciplines are plain for all to see. Typically, the links are with the universities—in research, education, experimentation. Publishing does not enjoy a place of its own in American higher education. That is, there are few academic programs, other than training institutes, which cater specifically to the professional needs of the industry. But professional education for librarianship is lodged in academia. Were publishing to be interested in, or to conceive of any responsibility for, fostering advance or achieving reconstructed perspectives in librarianship, the route is open. Business interests provide endowment through such means as fellowships, grants, research assistance, and the support of university chairs in the subject matter of the discipline. The ultimate effect is a more sophisticated profession in consequence of such subvention. The results must, of course, be perceived as arising from an identity of interest between the benefactor and the field. Indeed when corporate interests support business and technological education and research, the effect is invariably seen as advancing the potential of the industry in which the work is pursued. But any sense that there may be correlation between the intellectual and professional growth of librarianship as a discipline and the welfare and aspirations of publishing is exceedingly difficult to discern.

The only exceptions are to be found among those publishers whose products are seen almost exclusively as the specific tools of librarianship. The H. W. Wilson Company is the prime illustration. This company has fashioned a conscious corporate image of benefactor of librarianship through its careful and democratic distribution of fellowships and its financial support of the ALA whenever such aid has seemed most needed.[48] Certain of the subscription-books publishers have also provided comparable support.[49] In the main, however, the contributions have commonly been in terms of special prizes and awards of modest

48. In 1965, the H. W. Wilson foundation gave $75,000 for six years to finance the new Office for Library Education. In 1969, it supplemented this by $128,400 for three years. It awarded a special grant in-aid in 1967 of $5,400 for an ALA Conference on Manpower. The scholarship program began in 1957 with its 1957–1960 first four-year cycle. It is now in its fourth cycle, 1969–1972. In each cycle every ALA-accredited library school is awarded one $2,000 scholarship, equally divided among the four years, based on a formula for choice. Any graduate school accredited after the order has been decided automatically gets a scholarship following accreditation. At this writing fifty-three schools are eligible.
49. Tangley Oaks Graduate Fellowships up to $3,000 annually are offered by the Tangley Oaks Educational Center (The United Educators, Inc.). The Grolier Society awards $1,000 each year to a librarian who has made an outstanding contribution to the reading of young people.

size and thus have only minor impact, but which succeed in attracting publicity and acclaim for the benefactor in a field honored by such small favors. In short, the publishing industry has seen in librarianship an undiscriminating and accepting market for its good and services, rather than the locale for investing its largesse in order to enhance the promise or the prospects of such a discipline through any grant mechanism relying upon its resources.

Perhaps the publishing industry's sense of librarianship as a docile, accepting, and nondiscriminating market is not unconnected with the field's incapacity to evaluate expertly all the subject spheres which it attempts to cover. The measure of its competence to exercise quality control would tend to be seen as centered more squarely in only the books which serve as problem-solving instruments for librarians themselves. Thus reference books would be their prime area of expertise. Yet even here, the fundamental criticism, the scholarly insight, even in the case of such general sources as encyclopedias, invariably awaits the attention of external examiners when more penetrating analysis is sought than that which is accorded to this decidedly limited portion of the literature in *Subscription Books Bulletin*.[50] It is not surprising, for example, to find the *Encyclopaedia Britannica* subject to discriminating assault by a nonlibrarian rather than by a member of the profession.[51]

The passivity of librarianship vis-à-vis publishing interests is reflected in other ways. One crucial zone is in the exercise of influence over the timeliness of reference books. Since librarians play strategic roles in relation to the information needs of their clienteles, more than any others they might be expected to perceive the adequacy or inadequacy of existing sources. But their voices remain unheard. For librarianship to commission new work or to bring about revisions of outdated material through the offices of its own structure would seem the only logical recourse for a discipline so heavily reliant upon such resources. Yet aside from the occasional committee representation, there is no assertion of what is requisite in any forceful way to either the publishing industry or to its own agent, the American Library Association Publishing Department.[52] For such a belligerent posture is uncommon and untradi-

50. New reference books have been evaluated, compared and, when indicated, recommended for purchase by voluntary committees of librarians since 1930; for example, *Subscription Books Bulletin*, 1930–July 1956 (ALA); *Subscription Books Bulletin*, 1956–1960 (ALA, 1961). In recent years the reviews have been carried in the column "Reference and Subscription Book Reviews" in successive issues of *The Booklist* published semimonthly by ALA.
51. Harvey Einbinder, *The Myth of The Britannica* (New York: Grove Press, 1964).
52. The Reference Service Division's New Reference Tools Committee is charged "to advise on, encourage, and promote the compilation and publication of needed reference tools. . . ." according to the ALA *Organizational Information, 1970–1971*, p. 72.

tional for librarianship which graciously accepts the limits of what is, without perceiving the rights and prerogatives which inhere in its capacity as an influential and powerful decision-making purchasing agent. The situation is somewhat different regarding the reprint industry. This segment of publishing is eagerly responsive to the needs of librarians. But there is a significant difference between responding to a need by merely reproducing existing properties no longer subject to copyright and that of commissioning and engendering new work or new editions.

Yet in the sphere of reprints, too, the essential docility of libraries emerges. Because the economics of reprinting relates profitability to an ensured scale of market, unscrupulous publishers have not been unknown to announce the appearance of reprinted volumes but to fail to publish these works if the number of orders received does not reach the necessary volume. Even when this practice is known to be true, there is no policing by librarianship of its own interests. Aside from bitter feelings among acquisitions librarians, an occasional flurry of letters to editors,[53] no formal means for repressing these unethical practices, by employing such sanctions as blacklisting, has received serious consideration by the profession. Doubtless the root cause of much of the self-denigration lies in the perpetuation of a perception of libraries as marginal customers, rather than as a collectivity having the power and the bargaining leverage to receive recognition as a highly significant market determinant. The fact of the matter is that libraries and librarians are forces to be reckoned with and possess the capacity to influence the ways and the means whereby the products and the services which they employ are made, distributed, and priced. But to be such a force calls for a professional will derived from a renewed self-perception.

One factor limiting the expression of librarianship relative to publishing stems from its lack of sufficient subject expertise to represent the needs of distinctive reading constituencies. Thus academic and technical groups have more often been looked to as authoritative spokesmen. Librarianship has always stood in awe of such well-founded intellectual expertise and interests. Yet librarians far more directly than any other technical group have their finger on the pulse of the general, the broader, reading market. If there is a market-research sector attuned to the tastes, the needs, the aspirations of the reading public, its intelligence may

53. The issue was raised on the editorial page of *Library Journal*, December 1, 1967, p. 4311, when readers were invited to send in information about their experiences with reprint publishers and examples of specific titles that had been ordered and not received. More recently, a letter to the *Library Journal* (November 1, 1970, p. 3701) questions the pricing practices of the reprint houses.

more nearly reside in the collective judgment of school and public librarianship than anywhere else in the society. One of the misfortunes of librarianship is that neither its councils nor its literature accept any responsibility for the expression of such insight. Instead of energetically articulating the hope and the need in ways to effect differences, the traditional stance is to accept what is proffered and to make do. Thus librarianship remains for the most part only the accepting and well-mannered customer of publishing, engaged with it in little more than discrete discourse about societal betterment through reading, the supreme and mutually shared value. And publishing takes no more responsibility for the destiny of librarianship than that of helping to perpetuate it precisely as it is, no better and no worse, but hopefully with increased purchasing power.

THE AMERICAN LIBRARY ASSOCIATION

To assess the role of associations as a leadership influence in librarianship is to attempt to explain an amorphous mélange of intricate components. Still, not to take the association phenomena into consideration would be to neglect a salient factor. The compromise reached here has been to review the largest and the most influential association. The primary place, by virtue of longest history, scale of numbers, and political acceptance of it, is held by the American Library Association.[54] Even if the American Library Association is not fully equipped to serve as spokesman for every type of library interest or on every library-related issue, it is this body which carries the message of librarianship to most of the councils of the culture. Its potential for leadership extends to virtually every question affecting the library world. The hospitality it affords to new ideas and approaches, its instrumental role as political agent of the discipline, the structure of communication through ALA

54. The American Library Association was founded in 1876 and comprised 103 members at the time. As of December 31, 1970, there were 27,038 personal members in ALA (there are duplicate and triplicate division memberships and so the totals far exceed 27,038). This represents a 5,000 drop in membership from the previous year. Income from dues, though, increased 49 percent, or $400,000, as a result of the revision of membership dues. Membership in the fourteen divisions was, in rank order:

12,247	ACRL	7,321	YASD	3,416	ALTA
9,876	AASL	6,872	RSD	2,908	ASP
9,201	PLA	6,796	CSD	2,565	LED
9,072	RTSD	5,081	LAD	1,637	AHIL
		4,842	ISAD	1,196	ASL

(Source: *American Libraries*, April 1971, pp. 418–419).

media, its bearing upon educational patterns in the discipline, are only a sampling of the questions in which the ALA impact may serve to further or to retard the progress of librarianship. It is this association, perhaps more than any other force, which tends to represent a link with the sense of purposive continuity of the entire social system, derived as it is by virtue of its numbers and its representation from such a wide cross section of the discipline and those concerned with it. Perhaps then, the key question is how strongly and well it functions in defining the boundaries, the obligations, and the interests of the discipline against the changing kaleidoscope of the broader culture within which libraries and librarians perform. In a number of the concepts and formulations which follow, the analysis draws upon the work of Corinne Gild.[55]

The American Library Association is understood best if it is considered more nearly as an association of common interests rather than as a technical or professional society. There are no formal membership qualifications. It contrasts with certain other groups which restrict their membership to those who assume professional or technical roles in a discipline and which frequently impose precise requirements—educational credentials, license holding, or years of service are among the common measures employed.[56] The consequence is an exceedingly large membership, having perhaps less identification with a technical profession so much as with the broad general form of the institution in which the work is performed. As this is so, the ALA's tendency for paralleling institutional and hierarchical lines is made more reasonable, and the values inherent in the structure of the organization itself more nearly equate with institutional and hierarchical lines than with the patterns of professional practice. Not surprisingly, its heroes are the successful administrators, both those within the bureaucratic structure of the association itself and those who have achieved success in the institutions where the discipline is practiced.

Like many membership organizations of complexity and scale, the American Library Association is a bureaucratic oligarchy.[57] In the office-

---

55. Corinne Lathrop Gild, *Hidden Hierarchies: The Professions and Government* (New York: Harper & Row, 1966).
56. The Special Libraries Association would be one such body. In August 1970 the association membership voted to amend its by-laws in order to permit a reduction in the number of membership categories, simplify the educational requirements for membership, and delete the requirement that members be currently employed in a special library. See *Special Libraries*, March 1970, pp. 139–140; *Special Libraries*, July/August 1970, pp. 307–308; *Special Libraries*, September 1970, pp. 14a–15a.
57. Max Weber's definition and discussion of bureaucracy as an ideal type implies four central characteristics: rationality in decision-making, impersonality in social relationships, routinization of tasks, and centralization of authority. From *Max Weber: Essays in Sociology*, H. H. Gerth and C. Wright Mills, eds. and trans. (New York: Oxford University Press, 1946). Plato's delineation of the oligarchy as a form

holding ranks of the organization, long tenure characterizes the most powerful positions, while the path to high elective or appointive office is normally through appropriate lower-level service over time. The positions of residual power in the councils of the ALA are occupied by those drawn from the membership who are figures of recognized distinction in the practice of library administration, more nearly than those representative of the practicing professionals or the intellectuals. As is the case in all associations where elected officers are subject to constant turnover, the transient and part-time participation of such elected officials leads the permanent staff to the assumption of strategic roles in decision-making processes and in the formulation of organizational policy. In the ALA, just as in other fields such as education and law, those who occupy positions of power are middle-aged rather than young. The most highly placed elected officers are those who have more control over their own time in consequence of being drawn from the administrative ranks, rather than from the practicing professional group.[58] These councils went unquestioned until recently. This elitist decision structure of those who held power, in the absence of the articulation of clear policies and objectives for the organization, decided where the ALA stood on all the broad issues which were its concern. Just as administrators have had undisputed control over individual libraries, so have those at the pinnacle of the association's affairs managed the destiny of ALA, and thus of American librarianship. The consequence of the strivings of a limited number of disenchanted and disaffected, reflecting the temper of the times in the urge to bring change to librarianship, has just begun to challenge the traditional structure over matters of power as well as abstract principles. Open and express processes of dissent, debate, and overt political action are now established. Still it is interesting to note that by offering hospitality to the expression of counterviews, and even by inviting representation and expressions from such new and threatening quarters, the minority perspectives can be coopted into the ongoing establishment. This may ultimately enhance the capacity of the governing elite to sustain its power through the appearance of a unified association which not only tolerates, but welcomes dissent.[59]

---

of government in which power is misused by a small group of persons remains a useful description for the layman although only cautiously employed by the modern political scientist.

58. Mary Lee Bundy and M. V. Thornton, "Who Runs the American Library Association: Implications for Professional Development," in Mary Lee Bundy and R. Aronson, eds., Social and Political Aspects of Librarianship (Albany: School of Library Science, S.U.N.Y., Albany, 1965, pp. 23–30).

59. ACONDA itself was an example of cooptation. SRRT (Social Responsibilities Round Table), representing the young and not so young dissidents, nominated six members to serve, of which the president of ALA appointed three. SRRT had no

As the upper echelons of the American Library Association have been drawn predominantly from the administrative coterie of librarianship, the organization upholds the conventional values of libraries as they are and as they have always been. To point out the need for dramatic change is to be found mistaken; change is not only inconvenient, there is a significant financial and political stake in conserving the existing situation. Thus the ALA can be seen as impediment to change, not merely in its ritual, but as much in the striving of those who hold power. It is their association, their institution, and their profession. Conflicts over whose institution libraries are and whose interests they should serve can scarcely be tolerated. The disposition is to preserve in the association the same organizational culture as that which exists in individual libraries, with deference to hierarchical authority demanded. It is this stance which frustrates those members who see in the ALA a carbon copy of their own repressing and unimaginative organizations. Yet for most members, this is not the case. Most seem to transfer quite naturally their authority deference from the individual library to the association structure, with no more questioning of the prerogatives and the power of its leadership than of their own institution's administrative class. Under such terms, it may be less than surprising that the governing structure of the association seldom considers the interests of the institution and of the administrative class. It is even more difficult to detect a sensitivity to the concerns of the occupational class of librarians. The ALA, just as the libraries which it reflects, consistently emphasizes the basic financial problems which it faces far more than the substantive issues which make its survival worthwhile.

The ALA functions in a context barren of formal policies. This allows those who hold power to control the organizational destiny. The ALA is not a genuine professional force. The power of its structure is not deployed for the benefit of its members. The ALA represents the in-

---

decision in the choice of the other members the president chose. Alternatives to ALA have been discussed by small groups within both the national SRRT and the local affiliates. In addition, the desire to change the current organization into an "American Librarians Association" have also been vocalized, e.g., by the SRRT Task Force on ALA Reorganization (see SRRT Newsletter, December 1, 1969). As for ACONDA, its First Report, January 1970, recognized that the problem they faced was not one of means but of goals. Robert Sheridan asked "If the Association's primary purpose is library service or service to librarians (or both, if they can survive in one envelope)" (p. 29). ACONDA answered this in its recommendation in the Final Report, June 1970, that "ALA 'continue' to be for both libraries and librarians," and the membership accepted its recommendation. In the council, a resolution that ALA be only a membership-oriented organization was defeated. The "Outline of Alternative Patterns of Organization" Appendix C-6b does not include one which recognizes the different interests of libraries and librarians.

stitution of libraries. Thus it has no professional standards which it believes in enough to mediate between the conflicts arising out of differences between professional, institutional, and community interests. What is required is a mechanism which assures that when an individual needs to do so, he can appeal through his professional association for support from among peers.[60] This is the moral contribution of an association, a contribution which it cannot make when it is dominated by institutional and administrative rather than professional interests. Librarians are seen more nearly as employees rather than as professionals. The ethical standards of the association spell this out quite precisely.[61] But if the professional values of the discipline are not the concern of the ALA, where then are such values to find sustenance? Without the aggressive interposition of a national professional organization into such zones, the atrophy of professional values is sharply abetted. For with all the codes and all the standards and all the other abstract moralizing, the American Library Association has only very recently and very grudgingly, in ways which still provide grounds for suspicion of the real intent, begun a program to aid those attacked on censorship grounds.[62]

60. At the June 1971 meeting in Dallas, the ALA Council approved a new program of action that consolidated intellectual freedom, tenure, academic freedom, due process, fair employment, and ethical questions into one structure, the Staff Committee on Mediation, Arbitration and Inquiry. This committee consists of the executive secretary of the Library Administration Division and the Association of College and Research Libraries, the director of the Office of Intellectual Freedom, and one additional member. All requests for action will be sent to this one committee. If a request for action is sought and an investigation takes place, the four types of sanctions that might occur range from publication of the report to expulsion from ALA. In June 1969 the membership approved a resolution in "support of professional standards for all librarians and the implementation of all such standards by any and all appropriate professional means, including (1) censure and sanctions and (2) accreditation of libraries." The ALA Council passed a similarly phrased resolution in June of 1969, but referred it to the divisions for comment. In June of 1971, after receiving comments from some of the divisions, the council referred it to LAD's board for review, in light of the comments. It should be noted that LAD was not one of those divisions that previously responded, and also that the response was one of generally, "We don't understand it, it is ambiguous." The council did not request a response from LAD by a specific time. So the prognosis is not good at this time for implementation of membership's sentiments.

61. "The librarian should perform his duties with realization of the fact that final jurisdiction over the administration of the library rests in the officially constituted governing authority. This authority may be vested in a designated individual or in a group such as a committee or a board" 1, 4, "Code of Ethics" in *ALA Bulletin*, February 1939, pp. 128–130. However, A Special Committee to Prepare a Code of Ethics was created by the executive board at its 1970 fall meeting to revamp the old code in light of issues and events since 1939.

62. The Freedom to Read Foundation was incorporated in November 1969 as an independent tax-exempt foundation. Though the foundation was a response by ALA to the activists in the association for a defense fund for librarians, these same activists were not convinced of the necessity to establish the foundation outside of

One of the normal expectations from associations is concerned with occupational interests, including such strategic considerations as criteria for entry to the profession. The ALA does its screening more circuitously. Since all who wish to may be members, its discrimination is exercised through the process of accreditation of schools which offer the master's degree.[63] It is only in this indirect way that it monitors the competency of those who practice in libraries. It sets no precise standards for individual libraries,[64] nor does it accredit them.[65] The formulation of measures by which a number of groups intervene to uplift their professional practice is not seen as a societal responsibility of the American Library Association. This remains in the hands of the individual institutional administrator when it is not regulated by the states, as is frequently the case for public and school librarians.

The ALA continues to insist that the problems of both the professional practitioner and the administrator can be accommodated within one society.[66] For, it is reasoned, the imperative issue is to demonstrate a unity in the field, and in its institutions, in order for the entire field to

---

ALA. The reason was in order not to threaten ALA's "tax-exempt status," and hence loss of foundation support. The slogan became "Loss of tax-exempt status," when the possibility was only "change of status." A credibility gap arose when the foundation itself incorporated as a tax-exempt foundation. It was only after much public pressure that the LeRoy C. Merritt Humanitarian Fund was established within the foundation to provide immediate financial assistance to librarians. Another issue was the interlocking relationship between ALA and the foundation board of directors. The constitution provided that a majority of the ALA-appointed members on the board was needed to make decisions. The defense of this mechanism by the director of the Office of Intellectual Freedom, to the effect that this was to prevent a possible takeover of the foundation by "extremists" from the left or right, turned many activists against the foundation as being undemocratic. In June 1970, the council rejected the ACONDA Minority Report on Intellectual Freedom that recommended that ALA not support the foundation. But these and other issues did prompt the council to pass that if the foundation performed unsatisfactorily and if evidenced it would perform better within ALA, then action should be taken to that end.

63. Through its Board of Education for Librarianship (now the Committee on Accreditation), the American Library Association has been accrediting library school programs since 1925. See "Standards for Accreditation" adopted July 15, 1951 (*American Library Association Policies*, ALA, 1965, pp. 45–48).

64. Except for very general statements such as *Minimum Standards for Public Library Systems, 1966* (American Library Association, 1967) and *Standards for School Media Programs* (American Library Association, 1969).

65. There has been sporadic discussion of procedures such as those which obtain in the accreditation of hospitals. See, for example, the article by Harold Roth in *Journal of Education for Librarianship*, Summer 1966.

66. Note however that the California Library Association reorganized in June 1971. It includes as "constituent organizations" a California Society of Librarians and a California Institute of Libraries. Only administrators and institutions are eligible to join the latter. Although administrators are also eligible for the society, they cannot be personal members in both organizations.

receive support from the federal legislature and from the public. Such an argument is no longer universally conceded among teachers even if it still remains the position of the National Education Association, and the pervasiveness of teacher unions, their establishment and flourishing in recent years, offers abundant evidence of the discarding of such a premise by ever growing numbers of teachers.

Yet the cohesiveness of the ALA in the post–World War II era has permitted it to speak with authority in the Congress as the unified voice of American librarianship. The record of federal support for the library movement during this period testifies to its success, if success can be measured in terms of newly won, dramatically significant levels of support for library programs and purposes.[67] The attainment of federal support-dollars during a period in which the national government has come to assume a responsibility for reinforcing state and local education, health, and welfare, does not necessarily equate with progress. Serious critiques of such massive subvention upon the contribution of the field are virtually nonexistent, since those within the ranks who would criticize run the risk of being classed as traitors, while those outside have other areas of concern.[68]

The office of the executive director is the core of the power of the American Library Association. It is this appointed official who remains to influence the councils of the ALA. The executive officer is not only the director of the permanent staff and of the secretariat, but is the one who speaks with authority for the organization. As this is written, the ALA has just identified an appointee to the role of executive director.[69] The unrestrained tenure of the immediate past executive director, covering a period which spans most of the post–World War II era, may explain in part the pattern and the limits of ALA philosophy and policy during a phase in its history when its most notable characteristic may have been its increasing membership scale.

A prime association activity is the dissemination of information

67. By fiscal year 1969 under terms of the Library Services and Construction Act, for public library services and construction alone, financial allocations exceeded 50 million dollars and for college library assistance and library training and research, exceeded 40 million dollars. See *Bowker Annual 1969* (New York: R. R. Bowker Co., 1969), p. 90.

68. One exception is the caustic article by Lowell Martin, "LSA and Library Standards: Two Sides of the Coin," *The Impact of the Library Services Act: Progress and Potential* (Graduate School of Library Science, University of Illinois, 1962, pp. 1–16).

69. "The announcement that Robert Wedgeworth will become executive director of the American Library Association upon the retirement of David Clift this summer has been greeted with general approval . . . "See editorial, *Library Journal*, April 15, 1972, p. 1365.

about new ideas and to contain that which is threatening to the profession. This is what its conferences, meetings, programs, and literature are all about. The overall sense of the ALA emerges as a reassurance of the old values and permanence of libraries. In spite of an Association journal (symptomatically titled after a recent name change *American Libraries*, rather than *American Librarian*), which has opened its columns to controversy, the burden of the evidence suggests a bureaucracy caught up in the procedures which safeguard its time-honored rituals. Dissent is seen as the adolescent stirrings of those who do not truly understand what librarianship really means. The old formulas are sacrosanct, not subject to question.

Perhaps at root, the fundamental problem of the ALA is that it is not and has never been a genuine professional association. For the function of the professional association is to translate into a mechanism of its own the desire for group control, rather than public, client, or employer control, not only over the profession but also over the conditions and the standards of work. The control which the profession seeks is another way of expressing the need for individual freedom derived out of collective security. In this way, the professional practitioners support and encourage the individual and mediate between the individual professional and the organization in which he works. This is not the case in librarianship, has not been the case, nor is there present evidence to suggest that matters are likely to change.

Professional associations also serve as the vehicle for the attainment of prestige for the profession. In efforts to gain status for the profession, the individual is rewarded through his identification with his professional group. In an instance where the striving of the association is addressed to institutional prestige, even this effect is lost. The ALA represents the administrators not the professional practitioners, and thus its identification with institutional goals rather than with those of the practitioner may be seen to be purposeful. At least this is so if one views the world from the vantage point of the library administrator.

The function of exercising control over entrance to work roles, even through the circuitous device of the accreditation of master's degree courses, has not extended upward or downward. In the meanwhile, doctoral work in library education has mushroomed and undergraduate efforts are widely prevalent. In other disciplines where professional practice is influenced by the contribution of corollary functions, the initiative in monitoring the educational preparation of such supportive functionaries has not escaped the attention of the bodies which seek to assure the overall effectiveness of its practice.[70] Moreover, just as the

70. The American Medical Association, for example, accredits schools for medical technologists in conjunction with the American Society of Medical Technologists

association itself is not seen as the hotbed of adaptiveness or creativity, the accreditation effort has resulted in a tendency to perpetuate the existing educational structure rather than to engender a climate supportive of experimentation. The ALA thus exerts subtle control over the very elements of academic curricula which reinforce the appropriateness of the conventional contribution. Practice and education for practice remain mutually reinforcing. In part such a balance affords the mechanism whereby new entrants are chosen who share the ideology and technological values of the existing administrative class thus reducing the threat to the present administrators.

As one looks to the ALA as a leadership force, what is found is a large complex bureaucracy, committed to the institutional ends of librarianship, to public relations and legislative programs. The aspirations of individual professionals are linked with the perpetuation of the existing order. The organization does not perceive the evolution of alternative forms which threaten the authority and the claims of librarianship. In the present period there seem to be arising new interests and new forces within the political structure, unlike the passive membership of the past, which are attempting to differ aggressively, in open dissent, on matters of power and on professional issues. Essentially the question is whether there can and will be a reintegration of interests and perspectives into a newly shaped organizational base; whether there can be consensus in any set of objectives arrived at through realignment of the power structure and a reconstructed sense of professionalism. Given the history and the propensities of those who hold power this is difficult to envision. There may be an effort to co-opt the opposition—that is to say, the conscious bringing into the councils those who represent the interests of the young, the activists, the change committed—based upon the cynical theory that what the "outs" genuinely seek is not a reconstituted structure or revised sense of professional purpose, but personal power. Here the rapprochement takes the form of inviting the newer elements to give voice to their dissatisfaction, to permit their leaders to be drawn ultimately into the elite and thus finally to accept the system and the power structure.[71]

The dissident elements within the ALA may not be satisfied with the

---

and the American Society of Clinical Pathology. This pattern of joint accreditation is followed for such other support occupations as medical assistants, occupational therapists, medical records technicians. They are described in the *Directory of Approved Allied Educational Programs,* American Medical Association, 1971 ed.

71. In some ways, the entire history of the ACONDA process may be so characterized. It is interesting to note that the Social Responsibilities Round Table's constitution and by-laws, called Organization and Action, guards against cooptation by limiting to one the number of ALA "groups" on which a member of its action council or clearinghouse can serve (Section 4(a)5).

trappings of participation, may not find acceptable the grudging allow-
ance of their existence which involves and coerces them, but keeps them
from influencing the association and thus the professional agenda.[72] The
question becomes whether there is then sufficient passion, psychological
and political conviction about the discipline and its potential to break
out of the existing system and derive a new professional organization
and ultimately a reconstituted profession. The new organization could
take the form of a turning away from association effort and embrace
trade unionism. Even while there has been as yet no open disavowal of
ALA as the basis for a heightened tempo of library union activity, such
a turn is possible, particularly in a period when economic conditions
causing retrenchment may occur simultaneously with a disenchantment
about prospects of provoking any true alternative perspectives within
the ALA framework. Professional unions can define and redefine professional boundaries, duties, and responsibilities, and they may be more
amenable to such revision than a national association which functions
largely to reinforce and so to prop up the existing institutions.

Yet, a turn in the ALA's leadership contribution may also come in
consequence of a changing of the guard. More and more complex organizations and societies seem to be turning away from the charismatic and
assertive leader toward the blander bureaucratic personalities who take
their cues from the situation rather than deriving them out of their own
statesmanlike convictions of ideology.[73] The library world does not
appear to mourn the absence of a Carl Milam after throwing off the
yoke of his oppressive style.[74] Interestingly enough, it is one of the
younger group who now pleads for precisely such a form of leadership.[75]
The personality and the image of an organization, and in this the

72. At the failure of a motion to accept an ACONDA minority report recommending
inclusion of the Freedom to Read Foundation within the ALA structure (see note
144), E. J. Josey of the New York State Library and some one hundred sympathizers
"walked out" of the ALA Convention protesting this evidence of the lack of
genuine interest in intellectual freedom on the part of Association members. See
Library Journal, August 1970.
73. James Reston has recently found this phenomenon more in keeping with the
long-term aspirations of the societies which they direct than with the short-term
gains of the more powerful and flamboyant leadership styles of a Charles de Gaulle.
See "The Weakness of Greatness," New York Times, November 13, 1970.
74. Carl Milam served as executive director of the American Library Association,
1920–1948, when he left to become director of the United Nations Library. He accepted nomination for the presidency of the ALA the following year but was soundly
defeated after those opposed to his continued influence on the organization circulated
a petition for other nominees. A generally sympathetic treatment of his tenancy is
contained in Emily Miller Danton, "Mr. ALA—Carl Hastings Milam," ALA Bulletin,
October 1959, pp. 753–762.
75. See Richard B. Moses, "Detroit as Drama or Is the Process the only Payoff?" in
American Libraries, October 1970, pp. 841–842.

American Library Association is no exception, is in many ways reflected in the conduct of its principal governing official. The capacity to mediate and to moderate, forcefully to forge new paths, to perpetuate the conventional power alignments, to engage and further involve new elements in its affairs, may be program contributions furthered or studiously set aside in the next administration. And the capacity of the ALA to function in a leadership role relative to the discipline will undoubtedly be conditioned by such choices.

CHAPTER 9

Prototypal Forms of Librarianship

In further scanning the disciplinary horizon for leadership influences, the most potentially influential phenomena are the actual instances of departure from conventional norms in ways which offer a variable paradigm for library practice. In largest part, the modern dilemma of librarianship is how to transcend the limits of its traditional contribution so as to sustain and advance the institution, the strivings of those in it, and the clients for whom it is intended. The malaise of the field is reflected in the doubt of libraries and of librarians that the traditional roles played remain sufficient. Libraries have been conceived primarily to be collections of resources, gathered in one place, with the materials organized for use by a clientele assumed to be familiar with these resources. Certain of the doubts which now arise relate to such questions as the limits of the collection content, alternatives to the traditional information resources, and whether there should be active intervention of librarians as agents of clienteles for problem-solving purposes. Essentially, the idea of systems (networks) and user orientation (rather than institutional or material orientation) is at issue. The basic problem is that of reconstituting the intellectual framework of the field in order to conjure with options which devolve about potential revisions of the conventional perspectives of the field. For the matter is substantially that of ethics and values and derives from the basic commitments of those who must decide for the library as an institution. However, to specify simply or to idealize in terms of theoretical constructs can never allay the fears and doubts of those for whom the only convincing evidence of possible alternatives arises from demonstration in the real world of practice. It is for this reason that experimental and developmental efforts still hold the greatest promise for inducing the open debate about the value of traditional arrangements and conventions.

The need for a revised paradigm appears to find expression in essentially four discrete areas. The first is represented by efforts to revise the formal arrangement of libraries as systems or networks. This is a fundamental shift from an ideology supportive of the self-sufficient, independent library to one embracing constantly increasing and widening elements of service, cooperation and reciprocal contributions. The second encompasses those devices which attempt to alter the educational design in such a way as to restructure the ingredients of educational preparation for the discipline by shifting the subject content, by experimenting with new modes of teaching and learning, and by evolving through experimentation potential new and emergent work roles for students. The third design centers upon the reconstruction of library activity within an individual setting in such a way as to embrace responsibilities, commitments and clientele responses which vary dramatically from the traditional norms of practice of that institution. The fourth constitutes experimental effort which centers upon new role definitions for the professional function; under its terms the professional practitioner not only assumes a revised relationship vis-à-vis the organizational culture but, even more dramatically, alters the relationship which obtains and the sense in which he is seen by his clients for whom he serves as active agent or advocate.

In no individual instance is there clearly discernible evidence of a fully reconstituted effort which serves incontrovertibly to demonstrate and to convince librarianship that here is a universally acceptable and viable prototype for alternative forms of response. Still it is to the first emergent traces of new designs that it is necessary to turn since it is out of such experimental modes, through demonstration and by example, that the powerful influences for change may hold their greatest inspiration. Such efforts form a crucial element in the leadership structure necessary to beckon and to catalyze others who will follow and thereby ultimately abet the acceptance of different paradigms of the disciplinary contribution. Furthermore, it is clear that the evidence of crisis in conventional library response is written large in the very attempts which the vanguard group mount in order to shape potentially effective alternatives. For this small coterie, the risks of change are seen as less threatening than the tenacious clinging to a structure of practice founded in values which form the basis, at best, for only a shrinking level of professional response.

NEW ORGANIZATIONAL GROUPINGS

To consider regroupings of library forms is to consider a whole range of potential new patterns and relationships. This may represent a more natural evolutionary process than a distinct break with the past. The various arrangements shall be treated separately, not because such designs are mutually exclusive, but rather because it is easier to understand their nature by considering discrete forms as models of different types. Our classification shall cover (a) regroupings by type of library, (b) regroupings by geographic area, (c) regroupings by function, (d) regroupings by subject area, and (e) all encompassing designs.

Reorganization by Type of Library

The classic pattern of regrouping has historically been one of simply evolving a wider span of service for a particular library by organizing its elements on a decentralized basis. The public library branch system and the university system of decentralized departmental libraries are illustrative. The same logic which assumed the organizational and clientele utility of such schemes is inherent in the elaboration of designs to encompass more than the original independently operating single library. Propelled in part by the potential of enhanced support from higher jurisdictional levels once the limits of local service autonomy were transcended, and in part by the twin appeals of managerial economy and extending the collection base to wider numbers of clients, the concept of larger units of service was early advocated by a committee of New York librarians in 1949 and by several subsequent surveys of library development in that state.[1] Although not fully implemented until 1962 with passage of an adequately funded state-aid law, the appeal of the New York model to other regions was apparent. It was to such a design that the earliest federal support terms for libraries were oriented.[2]

As in New York State, from county to a multicounty level, particularly for those geographically dispersed and thinly populated areas, seemed a reasonable progression, with the states serving as prime movers in such

1. A comprehensive review of system development in New York State is contained in Harold S. Hacker, "Implementing Network Plans: Jurisdictional Considerations in the Design of Library Networks," Working Paper D-2, pp. 1–79, *Proceedings of the Conference on Interlibrary Communications and Information Networks*, Airlie House, Warrenton, Virginia, Sept. 28–Oct. 2, 1970, edited by Joseph Becker (Chicago: American Library Association, 1971).
2. Under the terms of the Library Services Act of 1956 (P. L. 84–597) eligibility for federal funds was established upon submission of an acceptable state plan for extension of library services to rural areas. As detailed in early assessments of the legislation, "Every plan includes the goal of larger units of service. Cooperation is the key word in all. . . . Some of the most impressive results of the Library Services Act—brought out in one aspect or another—can be found . . . in the demonstration and development of county and regional library systems and in the initiation and development of cooperative projects." U.S. Office of Education, Library Services Branch, *State Plans Under the LSA* (Washington, D.C.: GPO, 1958), p. 3, and *Supplement 2* (1960), p. 7.

advances. For if the pattern had intrinsic value, why not extend it to wider geographic areas? This direction seemed particularly attractive if the political appeal of these regroupings could be translated into terms of economy, efficiency, and the extension of library service to unserved elements. The basic problem inherent in such designs in many instances was that of relinquishment of local autonomy to the larger jurisdiction. The same rationalizations which at an earlier stage were impeding the development of school systems across a wider base obtained here as well.

Although it calls for the banding together of libraries the library program is essentially the same, with aspirations unchanged. The striving on the part of the control bodies is thus not to do something intrinsically different from the historic contribution of the independent library, but only to extend the economic and political base. In its multicounty service patterns, the public library appears to have been stretched to the limits of its potential for regrouping. The next stages in its ambition, as we shall see, call for cooperative regrouping across type of library lines.

Academic libraries have been more recalcitrant to accept regrouping, but the evidence of cooperative and reciprocal patterns appears to be finding more adherents, particularly in face of mounting financial stringency. Nor are such patterns fundamentally new. The Joint University Libraries System at Nashville, Tennessee has served in such a fashion for a number of years.[3] Because academic libraries are part of an educational complex and seldom function independently, different patterns must usually be evolved. Here the several libraries are obliged to remain identified with their own institutions while simultaneously attempting to derive the benefits of cooperative effort. The appeals to library administrators, and perhaps as frequently to those to whom librarians are responsible, relate fundamentally to two issues. The first is the fact that computer technology holds out promise ultimately for being able to effect economies when adapted to the requirements of libraries with similar problems and responsibilities. The second is the ever mounting spiral of acquisition costs and the concomitant realization that comprehensive collections are not realistic. The consequence is a spate of current experiments in order to design types of academic library collectives oriented to the testing of strategies related to collection building and reciprocity as well as to improvements in technical functions.

Involved typically is a mutually shared investment on the part of

3. Comprising the general reference and research collections of adjacent Vanderbilt University, George Peabody College for Teachers, and Scarritt College, the General Division of the Joint University Libraries was established in 1936 and housed in a central building in 1941. More specialized collections of the several institutions are also maintained in other campus locations.

several institutions in developmental efforts, with the expectation that ultimately there may come into being the operational and organizational terms and continuing interdependencies and relationships generated out of such probings. The several forms which such groupings have taken are reflected in such operations as the following: the Ohio College Library Center, chartered by the State of Ohio in 1967 and encompassing the more than fifty institutions of higher learning throughout the state in a program to provide on-line remote access to a computerized central catalog and circulation file and a computerized technical processing center;[4] the Five Associated University Libraries (FAUL), a coalition of public and private institutions in upstate New York initiated in 1967 to facilitate access to member staff and collection resources and devise a cooperative plan of expansion and growth;[5] and the Library Council of the Consortium of Universities of Washington, D.C., one facet of a 1964 agreement among five institutions in a single metropolitan area to explore means of organizational adaptation to advance common academic goals.[6] Varying widely in aspiration and attainment, at the least each operation represents formal commitment on the part of participating members to the desirability of transcending individual institutional capacity in meeting what has heretofore been the traditional library-service responsibility of the independent academic institution's library. Whether or not such compacts and realignments, in the course of their eventual technological and operational upgrading, can ultimately be expected also to generate enlarged perceptions of, and novel responses to, user needs, remains conjectural.

Regrouping by Geographic Area

Having reached the limits of the potential for reorganization of libraries by type of institution into larger units of service, natural progression led to designs for new groupings without restraint as to type of

4. See Frederick G. Kilgour, "A Regional Network—Ohio College Library Center," in *Datamation*, Feb. 1970, pp. 84–87. The circulation system is now operational, as reported in *Library Journal*, Jan. 1, 1971, p. 20.
5. FAUL development, problems, and projections are summarized by its chief administrative officer in Ron Miller, "A Case Study of the Five Associated University Libraries," Working Paper D-5, *Proceedings*, pp. 1–33 (see Footnote 1).
6. The Consortium of Universities of Washington, D.C. was established in 1964 to coordinate relevant universitywide operations and programs of the five metropolitan institutions. The Library Council has initiated daily materials delivery, photocopying, TWX communication, direct interlibrary borrowing privileges for doctoral and master's candidates, and a modest cooperative acquisitions plan. The second edition of a computer-produced *Union List of Serials* was issued in 1970. Since July 1970, the Library Council has retained a full-time director who is particularly concerned with the definition and implementation of special collection areas for the participating institutions.

library. This has been referred to as the "second generation" of regional networking.[7] Under these terms the regrouping cuts across type of library lines and holds the potential for bringing into a reconstituted information system the resources of every kind of library within the geographic area. Once more the idea finds its inspiration in New York State. This prototypal form has come to be known as the Three R's System[8] which superimposes upon the framework of twenty-two public library systems a pattern of access to the research and reference capabilities in academic, public, and special libraries within nine discrete regional areas.

Again, as was the instance of the larger units of public library service, the main propellant is a statewide library development effort with the prime stakes seen in the political strategy of attracting additional support from higher jurisdictional levels in order to demonstrate the viability of providing information service to different clienteles, drawing upon the resources of libraries of all kinds. In this way, the strategy of resource solicitation is escalated upward, built upon a new set of premises which transcend those of library services to individuals through the mechanism of the public library. Moreover, herein resides the promise of enhanced financial support, as a condition of participation and the sharing of resources, by academic and special libraries, neither of which has yet enjoyed the benefits of public largesse to the degree that public libraries have. In a period when organizational cost-consciousness is constantly mounting, the prospect of such external funding holds powerful allure.

In its ideal state, this reconstituted library scheme would represent a breakthrough for information service and skirt the normal type of library constraints which restrict access to materials by virtue of the limits of individual institutional requirements. Thus, members of the public would have potential recourse to the holdings of academic and special libraries and vice versa. The essence of the design is simple and straightforward. But it does not conjure fully with the entrenched private interests of the organizations and agencies who become party to such activities; both their history and their psychology continue to see primary allegiance addressed to those within the confines of the local institution. Perhaps a more fundamental limit of such a design is that the banding together of libraries does not necessarily dictate any greater sophistication about the product or the service of the library system. All that is effectively

7. Hacker, *Proceedings*, pp. 59–63 (see Footnote 1).
8. For Reference, Research Resources. Thus far school library resources have not been incorporated into the program. The most recent evaluation of the Three R's operation within the context of the total state system can be found in *Report of the Commissioner's Committee on Library Development* (New York: State Department of Education, 1970).

changed is the formalities of interinstitutional relationships. Interlibrary loan thus is raised to a higher level of importance but it is still the traffic in books and the interchange of access to them extended. As a practical matter, clients of the academic and the special library have traditionally had full access to public library resources and oftentimes the reverse has been equally true. Whether the chronic recalcitrance of the great academic library, reluctant to make available its resources outside its institutional bounds, is likely to be lessened under these terms, is a matter for conjecture. Moreover, the problems of political survival in even evolving the designs which make such interrelationships possible have called for the highest degree of caution and circumspection in their plotting. Rather than experimental and innovative efforts, the net effect of many such arrangements, as they can be perceived, has been quietly to derive rigid lines of organizational and structural stability in order to ensure that financial support may be drawn from the appropriate jurisdictional levels. The very process of meeting the detailed operating prescription of a state as to formal structure, albeit essential to satisfy statutory requirements, more frequently than not, may effectively foreclose the possibility of bringing into being alternative approaches to the handling of information needs. Seen most pessimistically, such phenomena may represent merely a new political alliance, reinforcing the survival capacity of the traditional structural interests. Thereby, they may be afforded renewed capacity to elicit support from the state and perhaps ultimately from the federal government, as in the instance of the larger units of service concept for the public library at an earlier stage, through the substitution of a refurbished and updated formula. The true question is whether the promise of improved client response is realized through such devices, or if the proferring is simply the most recent political ploy. The political expediency of the design rests in the expectations which it holds out to the general public to open up a whole new system of library and information access. But these expectations are not tied to any new forms of information service, nor to revised types of response to information needs, so much as to the provision of access to books through interinstitutional lending arrangements which have not been formally evolved in the past.

Regrouping by Function

A variation upon the same theme is the scheme of several libraries taking a common approach to a specific technical need or client service. The historic pattern operative at an earlier stage and continuing into the present is reflected in the development of cooperative processing centers.[9] The latter day prototypal counterpart which represents a departure from focus upon technical process to client need, finds expression in those few attempts which seek to provide public services. A notable illustration in the area of reference activity is the BARC Project headquartered at the San Francisco Public Library.[10] Just as are many of the other prototypal and experimental efforts, BARC receives its funding through state support, and while administered under the jurisdiction of the city library, its program groups together a number of the libraries of the region which have banded together to explore nontraditional alternatives to information services. Stemming from such a design, the base of expectations has been adapted,[11] and under the loose mantel of the regional information phenomenon, have come attempts to reorient library service to specialized clienteles in ways only rarely seen as reference phenomena. Thus, working with street groups in slums and using neighborhood personnel as members of the information team, has led to further experiment with novel forms of information service and demonstration. Some of the interesting by-products have included the generation of special bibliographic contributions and the issuing of a regular publication, Synergy, which sets a standard for institutional library media in its interest in

9. One of the more sophisticated recent operations is the New England Library Information Network (NELINET), involving the active participation of the libraries of the State Universities of Connecticut, New Hampshire, Rhode Island, and Vermont, but open to all academic libraries in the area. The processing center utilizes MARC II and RECON tapes and is developing methods for effective regional utilization of a large machine-readable bibliographic data file. Centralized processing operations serving two or more jurisdictions are currently operating in all but four states. See "Centralized Processing: A Directory of Centers," Library Resources and Technical Services, Summer 1970, pp. 355–389.

10. BARC is the acronym for Bay Area Reference Center. See Richard Coenenberg, "Synergizing Reference Service in the San Francisco Bay Area," ALA Bulletin, December 1968, pp. 1379–1384; and Collin Clark, "Four Alarm Reference Service," Library Journal, April 15, 1968, pp. 1594–1595. The Bay Area Reference Center, located in the San Francisco Public Library, began in 1967 with a two-year $750,000 LSCA grant, to provide reference referral service to public libraries in the North Bay Cooperative Library System.

11. Among the alternatives are telefacsimile transmission between libraries in the North Bay and BARC using telephone lines, use of the teletype to transmit and receive reference questions; workshops (on sources of information), using outside subject experts, have attracted librarians outside of BARC, even members of the public. Topics have ranged from contemporary poetry to genealogy, from sensitivity training to contemporary religions. At the latter, a featured speaker was Anton LeVay of the Satanist cult who spoke on witchcraft. Of the reference questions referred to BARC, as many as half are answered by persons or organizations outside of the library. See the "Somebody Asked Us" column in each issue of Synergy, for examples of these questions.

topical issues, its contemporary format and styles, and its aim to provide information of reference value to the region.

Regrouping by Subject

Perhaps the type of regrouping most difficult for libraries to effect is in the area of subject arrangement. Subject contributions have been made by libraries in the past, if the production of the *Bibliography of Agriculture* by the U.S. Department of Agriculture Library, or the *Engineering Index* by the Engineering Societies Library, can be considered representative. But formal organization of libraries into subject-information systems has been almost unknown. The prototypal form of this phenomenon can best be seen in the effort of the National Library of Medicine, using the MEDLARS device as the base but built also upon a pattern of regional medical libraries. The National Library of Medicine support terms have made it possible for a number of libraries around the country to be so designated and to operate as part of the overall National Library of Medicine system. Simultaneously there is energetic experimentation in at least one of the geographic areas in order to work out the design and implementation problems for a subject system within one region. Headquartered at the Upstate Medical Center Library of SUNY-Syracuse, this Biomedical Communications and Information Network[12] is an operational on-line, real-time system employing remote typewriter terminals located in some ten public and private agencies in the East-Mid-Atlantic area. At this stage in the evolution of such devices, the system permits a high degree of man-machine interaction for search of the central computer store of bibliographic information.

Since the cost of designing such a local system is unquestionably high, it is only where a client population is large enough or strategic enough to support the effort that it is likely to be attempted. It is thus not surprising to find the prototypal form in medicine, a field in which all in the culture are seen to have a high stake. Even if it may be more economic to fashion a national network in order to increase the availability of resources, the distance and the problems are of such an order of magnitude that local or regional experimentation may provide effective clues for the engendering of the more comprehensive system at a later stage. While it is true that there is the same cost of design at the national level as at the regional level, and that the conceptualization of the problem is the

12. See Irwin Pizer, "A Regional Medical Library Network," *Bulletin of the Medical Library Association,* April 1969, pp. 101–115; and Willis E. Bridegam and Erich Meyerhoff, "Library Participation in a Biomedical Communication and Information Network," *Bulletin of the Medical Library Association,* April 1970, pp. 103–111.

same, the greatest value of the regional phenomenon may be reflected in its serving precisely as a prototypal version of the larger network. Essentially, it is a matter of at what point in the cycle the system is being developed. For the present it is perhaps more fruitful to subsidize developmental processes at the regional level, as is the case of the medical program, in order to test viability and thus ultimately evolve programs which can effectively function nationally in subject matter areas. Without regional experimentation, it may not be possible to understand client service requirements which tend to be bypassed on the national scene.

Within the area of subject-information grouping, but representing a unique type, is the data archive which builds upon data collections rather than books and is a distinctive trend particularly noticeable in the social sciences. A construct somewhere between archives and libraries, the contemporary phenomenon may be characterized as an effort to extend the utility of social-science data beyond the original collection purposes through making them available for computer analysis by multiple users. Varying widely in the scope of collection and nature of services,[13] from the largely nonmachine-readable holdings of the Human Relations Area Files to the computerized data sets of the Bureau of Labor Statistics, the success of some of these ventures[14] is assuredly due in part to the existence of a technologically sophisticated group of users—the behaviorally oriented political scientists. It is interesting to note here, too, that those who function in the data archive context as "librarians" or center managers appear to be drawn most heavily from the subject disciplines where the data collections are centered, rather than from traditional librarianship. The basic ability to perceive the discipline and to correlate the intelligence drawn from data-based research with the research structure tends to be more essential than information-handling expertise, at least at the earliest stages. Yet because data problems are of less consequence to the research community than to the information-handling community, individuals who play such roles identify with the professional culture of information, forming an important element of the Special Interest Group in the Behavioral and Social Sciences of the American Society for Information Science.[15]

13. A typology of social science data archives along these dimensions is outlined on pp. 12–14 of the generally useful overview edited by Ralph L. Bisco, *Data Bases, Computers and the Social Sciences* (New York: Wiley-Interscience, 1970).

14. Examples of these include the Inter-University Consortium for Political Research headquartered at the University of Michigan and the Roper Public Opinion Research Center at Williams College.

15. The late Ralph Bisco (technical coordinator for the Council of Social Science Data Archives) and Douglas K. Stewart (Chairman, Executive Council, Social Science

All-Encompassing Designs

There do not yet appear to be any existing prototypal forms of national information systems which cover whole ranges of subject fields and clienteles. Elements of such a plan may be discerned in efforts which have no formal library ties, as the Federal Clearinghouse for Science and Technology, now the National Technical Information Service. Another prototypal design transcending national boundaries and oriented to the information requirements of the international scientific community is the UNISIST program which contemplates the establishment of a mechanism to promote compatability and interchange between existing and proposed information storage and retrieval systems in scientific and technological fields throughout the world.[16] While such designs may proliferate, some of the most fundamental questions relating to their efficacy have not yet been resolved.[17] Nor is it clear what, if any, relationship they will bear to libraries and librarians. The closest approximation to such a format is found in the EDUCOM (Interuniversity Communications Council Inc.) program. This interuniversity cooperative venture attempts to bring together, for purposes of discussion and exchange, those who assume administrative responsibility for local information and communication programs. The design is intended to improve the interinstitutional exchange of intelligence and encompasses not only libraries and computer efforts, but transmission forms of every kind and communication devices ranging from technological to behavioral. The organization appears to be as heavily committed to the problems of political relationships as to economic, copyright, computer technology, and the like. As such, it represents a very early stage in the process of bringing into focus some of the mutual interests oriented to

---

Information Center, University of Pittsburgh) served as successive vice-chairmen of the ASIS-SIG-BSS. A strong plea for active integration of archive-library operations is advanced in Jack Dennis, "The Relation of Social Science Data Archives to Libraries and Wider Information Networks," Working Paper B-4, *Proceedings*, pp. 1–16 (see Footnote 1).

16. See *UNISIST: Study Report on the Feasibility of a World Science Information System* (UNESCO Documents Office, 1971). The twenty-two recommendations made in the report were discussed at an intergovernmental conference convened by UNESCO October 4–9, 1971. UNESCO is now in the process of establishing the UNISIST program to stimulate and catalyze the kind of cooperation envisaged by the report.

17. As pointed out in a recent editorial deploring the lack of progress toward bibliographic standardization. See *College and Research Libraries*, Nov. 1970, p. 377.

improving and enhancing programs of information access.[18] Members of the library community have been involved almost from the outset in EDUCOM activities.[19] The influence on the library scene is not yet clear.

With the possible exception of the all-embracing system and the subject regrouping, experience thus far would not suggest any dramatic departures for library programs in consequence of reconstructed organizational arrangements. Perhaps the fundamental limit is that in these regroupings, the basic rationale is not to design experimental modes of service or of operation, as it is to develop acceptability for the present systems. Present acceptability implies consensus among the parties at interest who are identified with existing norms and values, both on the library side of the equation and in the legislative support bodies. A recent critique of such efforts, while addressed primarily to the use of state-aid funds, clearly delineates how patterns are controlled by librarians who build upon prior discussions, surveys, and analyses, all of which accept the underlying assumptions of traditional library practice.[20] The essential incongruity of the situation may be seen in the fact that political support for the advancement of new ideas is necessary, but that support is given only when design considerations reflect the values of existing norms. In consequence, novel aspirational efforts tend to be effectively negated. The final responsibility for the evaluation and the control of adapted programs remains in the hands of just those individuals who have the greatest stake in the perpetuation of the present programs. And as such designs are recognized and identified, other organizations fall into step so as to enjoy the same political opportunities and economic incentives. The utility and the effectiveness of the designs are taken for granted as are the assumptions upon which they are based—that in-

18. Established in 1964 with eight university participants, EDUCOM membership numbered at the time of writing over a hundred universities, colleges, and academic consortia and service organizations. Publications include staff papers and contract research on computer applications of interest to higher education, and *EDUCOM: The Bulletin of the Interuniversity Communications Council*, issued quarterly. The Educational Information Network (EIN) was initiated in 1969 to provide a switching center for the listing (*EIN Software Catalog*) and exchange of relevant computer programs.

19. Such as Joseph Becker, Director of Information Sciences, EDUCOM, 1966–1969, and vice-president, 1969–1970. Members of the board at the time of this writing include: W. Carl Jackson of Pennsylvania State University; Frederick Kilgour of the Ohio College Library Center; Allen Kent, Director of the Interdisciplinary Program in Information Sciences, University of Pittsburgh; and John McGowan, University Librarian, Northwestern University.

20. See Ralph Blasingame, "A Critical Analysis of State Aid Formulas," *Library Trends*, Oct. 1970, pp. 250–259.

creased resources and broadened organizational terms are an improvement over what went before.

REVISING THE EDUCATIONAL DESIGN

The second important category of adaptation results in consequence of experimental or prototypal designs calculated as part of the educational strategy for the discipline. In order to foster and thus to formulate adapted models, the assumptions which have formed the basis for the educational experience of the field require altering. That is to say, a new conceptual framework forms the basis for revising either the substantive content, the cognitive process, or the perspectives and thus the intellectual contribution of those who offer and receive instruction. Our classification here conceives of essentially three different types of modification. The first has to do with experimentation, based upon a change in assumptions about the nature of professional practice, with the educational sequence seen as the test bed for adapting the role of the practitioner to different terms. The second is built upon a commitment to the changed and changing nature of the technological capacity of the institution in which the professional practitioner is to be employed. The third design parallels somewhat the mechanism of interinstitutional sharing, as reflected in library network activity, with the grouping of the formal structure and relationships in education for librarianship coming to transcend the limits of a single institution and a single professional curriculum.

Experimenting with New Professional Roles

The process builds upon a reconstructed paradigm for the professional contribution of the librarian or information worker. One sharply divergent conceptual perspective hypothesizes an inversion from reactive to proactive functionary. Such a design starts with fashioning services and meeting informational needs for a distinctive community or constituency, rather than the usual approach of building a resource base within the context of the formal and conventional institution. The nature of such a revised sense of the professional role, translated into the context of education for librarianship, calls for sharp divergence in many of the traditional elements of the educational process. Such variations are clearly reflected in considering the ingredients of one such prototypal design, the program for the preparation of urban-information specialists at the University of Maryland.[21]

Under the terms of this program, using as its framework an Office-of-Education-funded institute mounted within a library school, but functioning essentially independently, this experiment attempted to invent and to refine the role and the contribution of the information professional in work with informationally deprived clients in the urban context. Its terms of reference accept the need for the revision and reconstruction of the purpose of a new professional class, building upon librarianship, but departing from it in fundamental ways. The potential for such professionals is seen as that of directly contributing to the solution of social, political, and economic problems in the urban culture, by affording active services and generating programs for client groups, using the public library as the base, but transcending it by assuming staff roles in active organizations and agencies as well. Those drawn into the educational program bring to the experience a background in which the inner city is a familiar ambience; the proportions of black to white students is sharply reversed from the patterns which obtain in normal library education. The formal elements of instruction place high premium upon practical experience in the field. New strategies for information activities on behalf of distinctive clienteles, well beyond the normal concerns of the public library, are tested. Students selected differ in very pronounced ways in background and in motivation from traditional library students. The instructional thrust, stemming from a consensual commitment among program faculty and resource personnel, is to employ an educational process out of an adapted theoretical model of the professional role, in order to invent and perfect a new work role, built upon information expertise. The substantive and intellectual design relies heavily upon the application and involvement of outside consultants and experts, with the learning context drawn widely beyond the traditional boundaries of the university to comprehend the city's streets, its agencies public and private, and many who represent areas uncommon to traditional education for information service. For an understanding of the nature of the urban culture, and the correlation between the informational contribution and the political, social, economic, and psychological issues which have a bearing upon the scene, form essential elements in the cognitive experience. Thus the entire program may be seen as a laboratory in

21. See *Educational Program to Prepare Information Specialists to Work with the Informationally Deprived* (School of Library and Information Services, University of Maryland, June 1970).

which students, faculty, outside experts, and urban context, all form ingredients in a design to shape a uniquely different educational sequence. A drastically adapted professional role is its ultimate product.

Given the radically reconstructed and unorthodox orientation of such a design, it is less surprising to find that a whole range of academic, professional, and institutional difficulties would beset the effort.[22] For such a revised paradigm constitutes a threat to the traditional professional posture. The peril to library orthodoxy of the present design is that it posits the thesis that implicit in the professional contribution is an identification which commits the terms of professional practice from institutional loyalty to client need. In view of the nature of the sketchiness of understanding of the information requirements of many of the elements of the culture which have not traditionally been the concern of librarianship, particularly in the rapidly changing urban setting, the obvious conclusion is to call attention to the limits of conventional library instructional patterns, focused as they are upon institution and publications, rather than upon clients and problem-solving.

The Technical Laboratory Experiment

Experimental designs which revise the technological role for librarianship are simply a variation upon the same theme of professional practice. The difference is in the focus upon the technical system, rather than upon the client, but the problem-solving orientation is similar. Founded upon the thesis that librarianship is susceptible to shifting from its craft basis to a more systematic and scientifically derived discipline which fully rationalizes the process of identifying, storing, and retrieving information, such laboratory efforts promise to advance instruction and research by improving the technical sophistication of students in the process of their educational preparation. The Institute for Library Research at the University of California, at both Los Angeles and Berkeley, serves as the sharpest illustration.[23] Under the terms of such designs, library instruction is committed more fully to a logical and mathematical base, with computer application seen as the basis for improving the potential and the capacity of an evolving science of librarianship to be responsive to information needs. Thus machine-readable files, programming languages, and computer-aided instruction form crucial elements in laboratory exercises adapted to indexing, cataloging, and reference activity,

22. The difficulties are thoroughly aired in Mary Lee Bundy, "Crisis in Library Education," *Library Journal*, March 1, 1971, p. 797.
23. See the fourth progress report issued by the Institute: R. M. Hayes and M. E. Maron, *Institute of Library Research Annual Report, July 1969–June 1970* (Los Angeles: University of California, 1970).

thereby familiarizing the student with the possibility of such applications to their future work. As such efforts are identified with the formal instructional program, first at the doctoral level, and over time more fully at the master's level of instruction, the correlation between experimental and laboratory undertakings with their promise of technological breakthroughs becomes more basically a component of the educational orientation and thus the professsional outlook of those who are prepared in such a way. The Syracuse University program employing MARC tapes in library education[24] is an illustration of a similar pattern, as is the Comparative Systems Laboratory which Case Western Reserve University sity has employed in combining teaching and research into the evaluation of information retrieval systems.[25]

Such experiments, such laboratories, conceive the present as a way station along the route to an evolving new and rigorous discipline of librarianship. In its ultimate terms, professional library practice is visualized as a type of engineering practice built upon a body of scientific theories and laws, with information and bibliographic intelligence as the area of application. Efficiency, economy, and systems analysis are all plotted on the terrain as high roads to such a plateau.

A characteristic which both types of revision of the educational design thus far detailed share is their very heavy reliance upon external funding. Because library education has never been seen by the universities as a laboratory-based discipline, the capacity for library education to elicit appropriate support levels without the intervention of federal contributions is limited. Still, without such adaptations little is changed except for the slogans of change. The momentum cannot be maintained simply and solely by imposing conditions of admission for certain of the students which depart from the normal requirements in library education.[26]

24. The Library Education Experimental Project (LEEP) was initiated by Pauline Atherton of the Syracuse University School of Library Science in 1968 with partial support from the U.S. Office of Education. The program provides access to MARC I and MARC II data bases for analytical studies of cataloging practices at the Library of Congress and for retrieval evaluation investigations. See P. A. Atherton and J. A. Tessier, "Teaching with MARC Tapes," *Journal of Library Automation*, March 1970, pp. 24–35.
25. A division of the School of Library Science at Case Western Reserve University since 1955, the Center for Documentation and Communication Research offers a sequence of specialized courses "carried out in a laboratory atmosphere in order to provide a creative environment for the teaching of documentation techniques." The center is equipped with a computer and full range of peripheral devices. Course descriptions are included in *Academic Program* (Cleveland: The Center for Documentation and Communication Research, School of Library Science, Case Western Reserve University).
26. The Graduate School of Library Service at the University of California at Los Angeles offers two degrees: the M.L.S., with fairly standard admissions require-

Moreover, there is a fundamental and perhaps irreconcilable difference between the conceptual basis for the experiments which start from the point of client commitment from those hinged upon rendering the information process more rational and scientific. In their nature, each commits the educational process to the development of a different form of practitioner for, essentially, they are betting on different things. One holds to the notion that the information specialist centers his zeal intrinsically upon determining the nature of client requirements and then the fashioning of information products and services which match such perceived needs. With the other, the information specialist is the expert and he concentrates, therefore, essentially upon the elments of the information process, ever rationalizing, improving, and redesigning the engineering capacity of the system. Yet, both lines of departure represent alternate routes to traditional library educational patterns. It may not be until another and more advanced stage in the evolution of library education and research that these two promising avenues converge to the point where the product of the library-education sequence is equipped for a professional contribution which fully calculates both requisites.

Experiments in Educational Regrouping

Essentially, it has only been specialized institutes and seminars, convened by associations and by educational agencies, which have tended to transcend the formal constraints of regular university programs. One widely followed mode, adapted to the needs of those active in practice, has been the MARC institutes conducted under the auspices of the Information Science and Automation Division of the American Library Association.[27] Such exposures are designed within their concentrated two- or three-day span, to elucidate the technical content and variable potential for applying magnetic tapes of new cataloging data to local institutional requirements. Formal interrelationships between and among library education programs, in ways which might capitalize on resources and capabilities from other institutions, except for summer visiting faculty and the incidental guest lecturer or seminar participant, have simply not yet advanced beyond the level of academic abstraction.[28] For

---

ments; and the Master of Science in Information Science, which is open to persons who hold appropriate B.A. or B.S. degrees in one of the physical or biological sciences, business administration, or mathematics. One foreign language and a background in mathematics through calculus are also required.

27. As, for example, the MARC Institutes which were held in San Francisco and Boston in 1970 and in Los Angeles and New York City in 1971.

28. See Judith A. Tessier, "Network Services for Library Education and Research" Working Paper, *Proceedings* (see Footnote 1).

the same kind of constraints which make it unappealing for library administrators to relinquish their control and responsibility by relying upon external organizations to satisfy local requirements, doubtless condition the provincial perspectives of library education faculties and administrators.

There have been some experimental beginnings. In the area of data processing, for example, a course developed and taught by Hillis Griffin at the University of Illinois has been put on video tape and is available.[29] Modern video procedures, reduced in both complexity and cost, and widely available among higher educational institutions, undoubtedly are tending to catalyze experiments and demonstrations. Such devices have been employed in at least one educational institution in library education as a response to space limitations.[30] Likewise, programmed instruction materials, using scrambled textbooks as exercise manuals in studies in the use of general classification schemes and in certain other subject cataloging and indexing techniques have led to the development of more advanced efforts.[31] A simple variation on the same theme is the use of collections of readings for instructional purposes.[32]

As in higher education generally, attempts to innovate by designs which conflict with local prerogatives run afoul of local conventions and constraints. There is no reasonable technological barrier to the video taping of instructional packages at leader institutions for export to other institutions. Such video lectures (in combination with selected readings) could be supplemented by visits at periodic intervals from the national or regional authorities. Coordinated and administered by such master teachers, courses of this nature would serve to effectively regroup the educational offerings in selected areas of study. Library education, just as other educational forms, resists such patterns. In a discipline subject to serious limits of pedagogic excellence, in a time of pronounced expansion of library education offerings and student numbers at both the graduate and undergraduate level, and when drastic limits are almost universally placed upon increasing the scale of faculty size, such devices may be useful. The acceptance for such a dramatic departure from normal bureaucratic limits in educational institutions would tread heavily

29. See *JOLA Technical Communications*, Information Science and Automation Division, American Library Association, January 1970, Vol. 1, No. 2, p. 8.
30. See John Phillip Immroth, "I'm a Media Freak! The Use of New Media in the Teaching of Library School Courses," *Library Journal*, June 1, 1971, pp. 1935–1936, for description of methods at University of Pittsburgh.
31. J. J. Boll, *Introduction to Cataloging, Volume I: Descriptive Cataloging*, McGraw-Hill Series in Library Education (New York: McGraw-Hill Book Co., 1971).
32. This is the precise intent of the National Cash Register, Microcard Editions, Inc. Series, *Readers in Librarianship and Information Science*.

upon the sensitivities of many in library education, who, like their counterparts in library practice, think of their student groups just as library administrators think of their clienteles, as being unique, different, and requiring a tailor-made product which only they can fashion. At present, even the sharing of intelligence about curricular modification is exceedingly limited, with the only consensual effort being carried out under the auspices of the Education Committee of ASIS in an effort to derive a model curriculum at the master's level for students of information science.[33] For the present, at least, the greatest promise of revision in the educational design resides exclusively in the singular effort at the individual institution.

NEW INSTITUTIONAL RESPONSES

An important element of prototypal interest is the independent and unique library which carries out a program which varies in significant ways from traditional patterns. Taylor has spoken of an "experimenting library" as something quite different from an "experimental library."[34] As an illustration for the discipline, the library which is fashioning an alternative response offers to the field a view of an alternative strategy and contribution and provides evidence of the possibility for such variation. Of course, to some degree every library carries out a program which includes some elements unique to the local situation. But it is the institution which affords, in sum, a radically reoriented outlook upon its commitments and reflects such perspectives in terms of its ongoing program which holds out promise, challenge and opportunity for others which would emulate such a design.

The Hampshire College Library, begun in 1970 as part of a new and experimental independent liberal arts institution, offers a prototypal form of undergraduate library. The unique characteristic of this library is the way in which it is shaping its program in response to its orientation to the client group, rather than to traditional college library concerns—research and faculty. The library effort is being based upon evaluation and assessment of how those for whom libraries are intended do or do not use libraries, exploiting multiple media forms and arranging for the involvement and instruction of users in information access all as

33. Jack Belzer et al., "Curricula in Information Science: Analysis and Development," *Journal of the American Society for Information Science*, Vol. 22, No. 3 (May–June 1971), pp. 193–223.
34. Robert S. Taylor, "Planning a College Library for the 70's," *Educational Record*, Fall 1969, p. 431.

their essence divert library norms and the purposes of information practice from the institution and its aspirations to the client. The particular models selected here are those of the subject bibliographer in the academic setting, the detached or floating librarian acting out a role in response to client need, the reconstituted role of the reference librarian, and the advocate of a distinctive client group.

The Subject Bibliographer

This form has evolved out of the academic library's aspiration to collect the appropriate materials and build suitable book collections for use by distinctive elements in its clientele. Subject expertise is more heavily valued in the role than library knowhow. Subject bibliographers tend to be drawn from the ranks of those committed to a particular discipline or set of disciplines. Thus they are expected to function as sensitive liaison personnel between faculty groups and the academic library. Since they represent the interests of a single scholarly field or a broader sphere such as the social sciences, their responsibility is to reflect that special interest in collection development, and in reviewing the value and relevance of library programs and services.

To the degree that the bibliographer identifies with a precise clientele with whom he forms colleague relationships and from whom he draws his political support, he is often perceived as alien to the commitments of the library. He may even perform outside the normal bureaucratic constraints of the library. In this manner, the subject bibliographer is one level beyond the departmental librarian who, while attempting to build programs and services for clearly defined constituencies, all the while more nearly remains subject to the hierarchical and bureaucratic limits of the library. Moreover, the subject bibliographer usually identifies with those committed to a particular branch of scholarship. Such role identification and role performance tends then to build into the operational system of the library, an advocacy commitment less to the ends of the library than to the goals of the client group. In the library which aspires to maintain a system of uniform response to the several elements of its constituency, such partisanship contains the seeds of internecine discord. Moreover, to the degree that bibliographers are exempt from the ritual requirements of set hours, work schedules, and supervised assignments, and function in the academic pattern of the independent faculty functionaries with whom they consort, they form a cadre intrinsically upsetting to the library's bureaucratic norms.

Increasing numbers of university and research libraries have as their goal the development of depth of subject collections. The capacity of libraries to build such collections is limited without the intervention of the subject bibliographer. Furthermore, in more and more academic institutions, library attention to constituency need is becoming as much a political as a substantive requisite. Still, the ultimate implications of this emergent role, particularly in consequence of the divergence in the responsibilities, commitments, and loyalties implicit in its performance, are still unclear.[37] So long as the phenomenon remains limited, so long as such functionaries are few in number, they may perhaps be seen as aberrations who can be contained, albeit gingerly, within the customary bureaucratic structure. Even so, they demonstrate a prototypal alternative to earlier role models.

The Floating Librarian

This prototypal form represents more nearly a conceptual proposition than a program reality. Its hypothesis suggests that information personnel have active roles to play, particularly in relation to disadvantaged groups in the culture. Such individuals would gravitate toward clear relationships with client organizations for whom they would then negotiate the information structure in order to advance their client's political, economic, and social ends. Essentially, this projected role involves such functionaries with clients and client groups who do not yet themselves understand the nature of their need for professional information support. And it must find support out of a professional discipline which remains fundamentally uncertain about the need to extend the boundaries of its concern beyond its institutional limits. Still, the power of the idea has captured the imagination of many, particularly among activist elements of the field, and spawned serious institute sessions centered upon assessing the viability of the construct and calculating the means for translating the idea into its operational terms.[38]

The New Reference Librarian

By definition, reference librarianship is a reactive role, in consequence of which it bears little influence upon the nature of library responsibility for anticipating problems or for transmitting intelligence about client requirements. The reference desk is where those who seek information

37. The role of the subject bibliographer has received intensive investigation through a grant from the Council on Library Resources. See Eldred Smith, *The Specialist Librarian and the Academic Research Library* (Berkeley, University of California, May 1971).
38. Mary Lee Bundy, "Educating the Floating Librarian." A challenge paper presented for the Congress for Change, June 20–22, 1969. May 1969, 6 leaves, mimeo.

solicit assistance in negotiating the library collection. The reference librarian is the library's agent in aiding such information seekers. The divorce of the problem-solving agent from the constituency and its normal concerns is customarily complete. But it need not be so. In at least one experimental design, at Hamline University, reference librarians are in the field, working directly and closely with students and faculty precisely in order to derive the information services which they believe will assist in problem solving.[39] As the nature of information needs is distilled, the reference librarian is better able to support user requirements and to exploit on their behalf a switching system which correlates information need with on-campus and off-campus information services. What is unique about such a design is the way it adapts the role of the reference librarian from detached bureaucratic functionary to a close and supportive relationship with clients. Seen thus, the client becomes a real human being needing prompt information access, and the reference librarian is recast in the role of sympathetic and client-committed staff member, knowledgeable about problem terms, not by virtue of single question negotiation, but through direct involvement and association with scholars and students. If the impersonal and depersonalized reference function is to yield to an adapted paradigm of client-oriented process, such a reconstruction of role would appear to bear watching as an original design for shifting to higher ground.

The Advocacy Role

Traditional limits of library service have stopped at the point of attempting to match the user and the information sought. Advocacy implies something more. It carries the professional role beyond, and enlists its expertise in the cause of advancing the needs of the client group first by pragmatically resolving their information problems and then extending beyond into other spheres which relate to a range of other requirements of the constituency. One prototypal illustration of such effort is found in Project LEAP, operated as part of the Buffalo and Erie County Public Library System.[40] With the neighborhood library as a base, community services are committed not to the classic library values of books and reading, but more nearly to serve as a mediating agent for the constituency by bringing intelligence, drawn from whatever source

39. See Jack B. King, Herbert F. Johnson and Anne S. Mavor, "What Future, Reference Librarian?" RQ, Spring 1971, pp. 243–247.
40. See "Programs of the Library Education Assistance Project of Buffalo," Study of Library Services for the Disadvantaged in Buffalo, Rochester and Syracuse (New York: New York University, School of Education, 1969), pp. 74–145.

and in whatever form, to bear upon cultural requirements. If client need runs to specialized programs or the counsel of experts, or to the provision of informational or advisory assistance in resolving occupational, social, or economic problems, such problems are conceived to be within the framework of the advocacy responsibility of the librarian. Thus the information role transcends that of simply locating published sources and becomes one of negotiating the information structure in order to permit clientele, individually and collectively, to make their way and improve their condition in consequence of active intervention on their behalf of library personnel. In a complex time when information access forms a powerful and basic element of the urban problem-solving process, those not adequately sensitized or acculturated to the devices for finding the facts tend to be further disadvantaged and left without the means to negotiate the system. Still, the advocacy role carries as a prime condition for its effectiveness, the service of an indigenous functionary whose values and allegiance may be perceived to correspond unswervingly with those of the client group, rather than with the institutional structure. For there is an important and subtle difference between the value-neutral technical expert who brings his superior knowledge to a client group and one who functions as agent of a client group, sharply and unceasingly conscious of their needs and aspirations, since he himself arises from the culture.

In all of the variable role models of prototypal forms which have been characterized, what appears to be emerging and which is yet far from being accepted is a clear shift from institutional identification to client identification. The groping has yet to be fully conceptualized, or even widely and fully articulated. But the new paradigm contains the basis for a wholly reconstructed sense of the intrinsic professional contribution which departs from prior history and experience. The essential question is whether such experimentation and prototypal development can be expanded, elaborated, and further accommodated within the framework of the library profession and of the field's institutional base. If so, it might well become a new and significant added pattern of response to strengthen the discipline and the institution in order to lend it new vitality and momentum. Or if it is contained and remains exceptional, that coterie of involved individuals may disassociate themselves from the present institutional structure and, like the embryo information science, attempt to forge an emergent professional client-oriented discipline divorced and distinct from librarianship.

PART III

Toward Leadership
for Change

CHAPTER 10

The Problems and the Issues

There is still time for choice in librarianship. But it is passing swiftly. The decision to conduct business as usual is a choice against change. In leadership structure, in value commitments, in discharging their responsibility to the culture, libraries and librarianship correspond perhaps with other institutional forms. There is one important difference: other institutions and other disciplines are more frequently seen as essential to the community. Medical service cannot be dismissed, schools must exist to educate the young. Libraries have yet to relate their contribution to the communities in such a way as to seem indispensable. Thus they are vulnerable to reduced levels of support, to being cast in a stockroom or warehouse role, to being superseded by other forms of information service.

Crisis in American organizational and professional affairs relates to the gap between their contribution and human requirements. It is reflected in the way that social responsibility is often abdicated. Those of the institutions, those of the professions, then cloak themselves in the protective armor of their traditions, pledge their loyalty to the system and to themselves. Too often, the cynicism of the disciplinary culture infects those who would have it otherwise, but who perceive that the burden of attempting to reshape their profession is overly costly of self and seems ultimately impossible of achievement. The tasks are seen as too formidable to yield to the efforts of even the most zealous if the constraints of resource availability, misplaced professional ideology, and clientele misunderstanding must all be assaulted. To forcefully face reality as prelude to reconstruction, to identify incompetence, irrelevance, dysfunction, is to seek to shatter the facade of an institutional and disciplinary structure built to weather the stormiest season. All too frequently in fact, the structure is carefully built to protect those who are sheltered by it from those naive enough to attempt such assault. More-

over, the very act of imaginative and responsible leadership is often be-
leaguered on every side, bringing down the wrath of those impatient
with any rate of change as well as of those who cannot bear to tolerate
the slightest deviance from past norms. The organizational and professional system enforces irresponsibility and punishes creativity.

THE NEED FOR NEW PARADIGMS

It is fashionable to criticize what is, to bewail conditions, to sancti-
moniously vilify the status quo, without suggesting alternatives except
perhaps in flimsy abstraction[1] or in rationalization of the current condition as prelude to a more benign future.[2] Not that it is useless to criticize.
Criticism serves to open debate, to admit to a range of options, and to
awaken a partisanship which must defend itself in the open marketplace
of competitive ideas and prescriptions. Perhaps herein resides the basic
rationale for the present essay—to expose reality and shatter the veneer
of innocence which can serve to disguise and obscure the issues. Without
the protective defense of naivete, good manners no longer equate with
integrity, and business as usual no longer serves to reinforce the self-
righteous assumption of equity and justice in the institutional or professional contribution. To be informed of the issues and of the ills of the
existing order is to be forced to contemplate and to choose.[3]

Alternatives imply competitive options, even if still unformed or ideal-
istic. It is only in a climate of expectation that hope overcomes despair.
Yet the change paradigm remains exceedingly complex, for the future
of librarianship must rest upon continuing the stabilized functions of the
past in balance with adaptations born of revised commitments to client

1. Elements of the State of the Union address by President Nixon in January 1971
which characterize the federal bureaucracy as inefficient and suggest that "a sweeping reorganization of the Executive branch is needed if the government is to keep
up with the times and with the needs of the people," without pursuing the details,
illustrate the point.
2. This forms a prime thesis in Charles A. Reich, *The Greening of America* (New
York: Random House, 1970).
3. The condition of librarianship may be, in this regard, not unlike the condition
of many engaged in its practice who are of the female sex. "It is important to
understand that as with any group whose existence is parasitic to its rulers, women
are a dependency class who live on surplus. And their marginal life frequently
renders them conservative, for like all persons in this situation (slaves are a classic
example here) they identify their own survival with the prosperity of those who
control them. The hope of seeking liberating radical solutions of their own seems
too remote for the majority to dare contemplate and remains so until consciousness
on the subject is raised." Kate Millett, *Sexual Politics* (New York: Doubleday &
Co., 1970), p. 38.

need and the use of evolving technology. There is a fundamental dilemma inherent in such a stance, for it redefines the professional commitment, calling for a new institutional and individual self-conception and contribution. This is a matter of values. But the problem of variability of the professional outlook is more difficult in librarianship than in some other spheres since the catalytic effect of consumer attitudes toward their contribution is almost wholly absent. This is to say, clients of libraries expect no more than what libraries have normally provided; they are far sooner likely to express themselves as a political force in matters of social welfare or public education.

The danger, as it is a danger even to the more consumer-sensitive disciplines and institutions, is that the governing policies come to be formulated in ways which reflect the professional concept of what is appropriate for the institution. When such conceptions do not conform to social and political requirements, they no longer serve as justification, since such justification must rest upon congruence with client need. The professional view of what is appropriate is incorrect as a guide for the institutional contribution when it expresses only the commitment and the perceptions of a special occupational group rather than of the constituency of that profession.

If the library profession does not accept responsibility for furthering societal access to information no one will insist that they do, for the society does not cast librarianship in so influential a role. The librarian is seen essentially as a custodian of books. Indeed the client does not tend to see himself as a client. For in a client relationship he is prepared to solicit the services of an expert consultant in whom he has faith. When there is faith in librarianship, it is almost exclusively related to locating a published work or citation, seldom to problem-solving. The difficulty of revised ideology for such a discipline is thus rendered more awkward, since the complacency and limited expectations of the client system simply reinforces the same self-conception by the occupational group. Because of this, the aims of library professionalism cluster about autonomy in its work, in its content, and in its terms, without outside intrusion. Its public stance is equated with its wholesome intentions to uplift the culture, not through precise program, other than the custodial, but simply because it is felt that the occupation can be trusted to uphold the literate tradition. Thus does it maintain its autonomy to perpetuate itself as it has always been, for the profession itself defines the service, orders the priorities, sets the standards. Because the client is not interested enough in the intricacies of the information system, he leaves the problem to the professional. Before he can ever be aroused to press for a better order of libraries and information services, he must first grow more knowledgeable about the critical nature of the information system in the society through a more penetrating analysis of the claims made by libraries and librarianship. This calls for the kind of insider revelations of the real world of librarianship which have served to open public debate on alternatives for public education and for medicine in recent years.

When a profession insists upon faith from its clientele, it wards off independent analysis and protects its own system of institutionalized authority over not only its means, but its ends as well. In this, librarianship is very much like other technical occupations which put their constituencies at their mercy and who permit themselves to be used only in ways which they define and which they prescribe. In this manner the profession and the institution which exist to serve the client expect constantly to receive increased support for its requirements without any attention from the clientele to the structure of its services or to the special view which it has of its own interests. Libraries thus may cost more, but clients need not be any better off.

Both at the individual institutional and at the professional level the basic pattern of authority in librarianship has been hierarchical. The historical trend, particularly in professional organizations, indicates a shift from authority based upon domination toward reliance upon consensus and group control. Future aspirations for broader based professional contribution, in contrast to the employer-employee relationship, call for a recognition that leadership implies initiative at more points in the organization than solely at its apex. If organizations are to perform successfully, organizational skill in eliciting purposeful participation at every level becomes imperative and recognition must be accorded to those who accept such responsibilities. Moreover, emergent leadership can no longer be expected to follow the prescribed aspirations of the past, using new initiative simply to accomplish old ends. The development of future leadership depends upon fostering equilibrium between the conventional terms and the options to develop innovative avenues different from the past. To extend organizational dominance by cooptation of middle-range personnel to the top management perspective is simply to ensure rigidity. Limitless new administrative arrangements are not the ideal solution either.

Too many people in technically aspiring disciplines believe that increased efficiency of process and evermore sophisticated intraorganizational technique is the formula for clientele satisfaction. The beguiling lure of efficiency of work flow does not translate automatically into more effective products or services. Perhaps even more important is the fact that resource allocation in one sphere precludes the application of the same resources to what may be a more critical area of client requirement. That is to say that with the constraints of inelastic resources a choice for one program or activity is a choice against another. At its extreme, that which warms the heart of the disciple of technique may even subvert the institutional goal. One of the very rare instances when a sophisticated user speaks of such matters follows.[4]

> The high school wave crests at term paper time, when whole shelves are denuded by teenies looking through book after book for something to steal that the teacher won't recognize.
>
> At these times it's best to try medium size branches in the neighborhoods. Since the size of a branch's collection depends on its raw circulation figure, any branch which services a neighborhood full of ladies who read lots of best sellers will have a surprisingly comprehensive (and underused) general collection.
>
> The only thing wrong with the branches is their new catalogue system. The old catalogue, self-service system has been phased out of existence by the Grand Designers on the Parkway, who seem to be committed to the theory that the best way to stimulate interest in books is to make them hard to find. The keystone of this system is the book catalogue. A major advantage of the book catalogue system is that it is cheaper (in the long, long run) than catalogue cards and the labor it takes to file them. The major disadvantage is that it's almost worthless; in the branch library, the catalogues of titles only accidentally resembles the collection of books owned by that branch. In the first place, most books in the branch are not in the catalogue, since the catalogue only lists books acquired since 1960. In the second place, most of the books in the catalogue are not in the library, since the catalogue is a list of all the titles acquired by all 39 branches. So the chances of any listed title being in a sizable branch library are about 1 in 8.
>
> If you persist in using the catalogue, you're offered an assortment of inconveniences. If you can't find the title in the book catalogue, all you can do is ask the librarian if it's on her shelf list. It probably isn't. On the other hand if the title is listed, you can choose from or combine a wide variety of wild goose chases: (1) You can get the call number from the catalogue and go directly to the shelf, where the book probably never was nor will be. (2) You can bother the librarian to look through her shelf list for a book probably never listed there. (3) You can ask the librarian to call another librarian

4. *Collegiate Guide to Philadelphia, 1969.* The Collegiate Guide to Greater Philadelphia, 529 S. 27th Street, Philadelphia, Pa., p. 50.

at central to find out which branches own a copy of the book. Then, you can either rush over to another branch (probably to find out that the book has been checked out) or you can order the book sent to your library, a process which will take at least a week, and may take months. If you have the time, however, make full use of the facilities. The librarians are all well informed, and are unfailingly courteous, even (or especially) when you're trying to beat the system.

It is a commonplace that members of a discipline tend to see the nature of their problem as unique and do not recognize the wider commonality of human experience which they share with comparable fields. It is even true that individual institutions place great stress upon presumed differences in clientele and in regional variation in order to rationalize dissimilarity in function from other like institutions. Yet the literature of the professions and of the institutions offers abundant testimony to the comparability of the issues which engage attention across the lines of discrete fields.[5] There are fruitful lessons to be learned from examining experience in other spheres as part of the quest for reconstructed formulae to ensure a better future. For instance, the modern-day American farmer is a professional manager who controls the decision-making process and is engaged in such organizational functions as purchasing, accounting, labor relations, and distribution, in addition to crop management, using administrative tools long a commonplace of the industrial setting. It is just such a paradigm which explains the perspectives of those engineers and systems analysts who see the salvation of libraries in the identification of efficiency measures for handling acquisitions, inventory management, work flow and personnel terms. For it is a fact that without the rationalization of organizational procedures the library remains a type of amateurish enterprise without the potential for maximizing the effects of the resources available for its work. Still the peril in oversubscription to efficiency measures and the yielding of primacy to the engineering mind is that the means may be enshrined, and the enhancement of productivity achieved at sacrifice to the ultimate ends. For it is only after leadership has calculated a strategy of priority in programs and services based less upon process than upon professional ideology, committed less to abstract efficiency than to aspirations for clientele, that technological management and efficiency measures hold

5. One illustration is the way that professionalism receives self-scrutiny and impassioned prose with the same remorseless frequency in the periodical literature of the accountants, the public relations practitioners, and the physical therapists as much as in librarianship.

greatest promise and reward. For it is only then that methods and procedures are susceptible of evaluation. The reverse would be to assign the calculation of a strategy for the future to the masters of the technology, rather than to those for whom client response ranks as the prime concern.

Potential new paradigms call forth alternative value commitments. Up to the present, libraries and librarianship have rested upon an ideological commitment to a distinct institutional form with its own unique characteristics, thereby ensuring and continuing a cultural response predominantly oriented to certain discrete classes of users. It is this value commitment which is now in question. Other cultural elements are now to be perceived as legitimate potential clienteles with as much stake in the organizational contribution as those who have traditionally enjoyed its offerings. A response system committed to the reconstructed purpose of orienting to differential client needs—whether to the less than literate in the city or to the student as learner in the academic milieu rather than to the faculty as researcher—would be fundamentally different from the habitual patterns. The value issue can also be seen as a question of morality. Youthful cynicism and disaffection often has its roots in clear perceptions of imbalance and inequity in an institutional structure which fails to accord its benefits equally and honestly to all. The essential tragedy of institutional forms which are detached and alienated from legitimate clientele aspirations is that an ever widening chasm develops between their efforts and the evolving and emergent social system. The library is not the only responsible agency addressed to human requirements which has yet to comprehend that it is this responsibility which is its basis for existence. Responsiveness must be to human beings not solely to the collection of artifacts, nor to the intermediate effort of acquiring and processing materials. The justification for its very being begins and ends with the requirements of all the people for whom the institution exists.

The adapting of values is difficult. Habits of mind persist doggedly. Without passion among those who would influence modification of perspectives, leadership fails. To the extent that the value orientation of those who hold power to change librarianship refuses to acknowledge revised commitments and responsibilities in ways more genuine than at the slogan level, the mold solidifies and the arteries harden. There are few, outside librarianship, who expect of libraries any more than the perpetuation of a custodial role linked with books.[6] Librarianship must

6. As is illustrated in the following passage drawn from a recent study on information patterns in the culture: "Most data facilities for research are growing up outside conventional library institutions. Readable behavioral science data are

strive for reconstruction of its designs in ways which seek to comprehend and find devices for the achievement of a broadened purpose. The values of librarianship have in the past centered around technical issues, while the given characteristics of its traditional orientation have remained unquestioned. Moral indignation is aroused only about issues like the FBI seeking records of borrowers of books on bombs, or when an ostensibly pornographic work is questioned by a civil authority. Perhaps these issues conveniently serve to disguise the reality of institutional ideology. It is easy enough to resort to outraged public expression about encroachments upon prerogatives, although the fact of the matter is that the library itself is not above reproach for the limited ways in which it is responsive to legitimate needs for information and services from constituencies for whom prose in questionable taste is scarcely a burning issue. There is no professional outrage over the irrelevance of the institution to large classes of clients and potential clients for whom its efforts hold little meaning and for whom it is therefore socially or politically irresponsible.

The spurious and the more genuine value issues may easily be confused. Censorship serves as a case in point. The public library, and perhaps the school and certain college libraries, are institutional forms which public morality equates with the mores of an earlier time. Forms not forbidden in one social setting, a drugstore for example, are contemplated with righteous indignation in another, the library. This gives rise to an anachronistic and spurious issue as the battleground for the library and its partisans, it serves to deflect attention from the more central question of the library's responsibility to foster a climate and render full access to information in all the ways which it holds the resources to achieve. For the genuine issue in the culture is not whether individuals have free access to suggestive prose, but whether they have access to the intelligence to aid them to improve their social, political, and economic condition. While the librarian and the public censor engage in diversionary combat over issues which have long since lost their meaning, the more basic questions go unquestioned and unanswered; the institution clings to defense mechanisms against enemies who have now become ghosts, dangerous only in the unreal world of librarians and their protagonists living out the bad dreams of another time.

---

understandably greeted with indifference, if not with horror, by research librarians. At this formative stage, conventional libraries appear overwhelmed by information revolutions on other fronts. The differentiation between 'book libraries' and 'data libraries' is likely to persist for some time and may even harden permanently." *Communications Systems and Resources in the Behavioral Sciences,* Publication 1575 (Washington, D.C.: National Academy of Sciences, 1967).

PROBLEMS IN ACCEPTING CHANGE

Even when there is a disposition toward change conditioned by external or internal strivings, the matter of change may be impeded by one or more of the crucial elements of the process: the delineation of the strategy for innovation; the actions of the lower structure as influence in furthering the adaptive decisions which make change possible; and the acceptance of the innovative ideology through the value system and the culture of the individual institution or the professional discipline. The formidability of the barriers to change acceptance even while the pace of development in recent years may have accelerated is reflected dramatically in a somewhat comparable context, education; a period of roughly half a century was required before the kindergarten was completely accepted in school systems.[7]

The process of planned change finds no core principles in the behavioral literature, and the availability of information to support and facilitate innovation offers no assurance of the adoption of alternatives.[8] Furthermore, the process of change is seldom achieved in a smooth and orderly sequence, especially in the case of goal orientation. The human and organizational world, unlike the laboratory, does not progress from logical point to logical point in which precise verification of data or causal phenomena define, unambiguously, relationships and sequential stages. Furthermore, the limits of acceptance are powerfully conditioned by the perceived advantages of the change to those who are charged with its implementation. The greater the degree to which adaptation is seen to be compatible with the values and the normal outlooks and patterns of the culture, the less disruptive of behavior norms, the greater the propensity for acceptability. Still the precise strategy of change introduction may be against the grain of the cultural patterns, not only in ways which fulfill existing or felt needs among those who must accept the change, but which may also be viewed as affecting their economic and prestige potential.

7. See Paul R. Mort and Francis G. Cornell, *American Schools in Transition* (New York: Bureau of Publications, Teachers College, Columbia University, 1941).
8. Havelock makes the telling point that "the technology information program undertaken by the National Aeronautics and Space Administration has been very well financed and elegantly organized, but so far, evaluation studies lead to one conclusion: pitiful." R. G. Havelock, "Dissemination and Translation Roles in Education and Other Fields," *Knowledge Production and Utilization in Administration* (Portland, Ore.: UCEA and Center for the Advanced Study of Educational Administration, 1968).

In many ways, librarianship may be seen to parallel education, and it is even possible to paraphrase for this discipline a set of constraints which McClelland has ascribed as problems in educational change:[9] (1) The diffusiveness of the goals of libraries and of librarianship. As the goals of libraries are multiple and as they are exceedingly vague, so they defy the precision necessary to specify behavioral outcomes in any but transaction records. A primary change impediment is the limit of accepting greater specificity of goals, for the absence of such precise formulations may serve the organizational and disciplinary purpose as insulation to the measurement and the evaluation of its contribution.[10] (2) As a direct consequence of the limits of goal specification, the kind of evaluative assessment and feedback needed in the monitoring of change is absent. Since the expected outcomes from library programs as they bear upon clientele need and satisfaction remain vague, it is only the procedural elements of the process which are subject to scrutiny. It is thus no accident that automation efforts behind the scenes are perceived so widely as the likeliest avenue of innovative potential. (3) The lack of a tradition of inculcating new entrants into the profession with the kind of questioning, critical stance of the institutional and disciplinary framework which spawns innovative commitment. With the educational emphasis upon training, the student does not develop the habits of mind which make for an orientation to experiment and improvisation. The very ritualistic reliance upon authority in the form of formal codes, procedures, even published facts in reference books, is all inhibiting rather than facilitating of originality and openness to novel alternatives. (4) The risks attendant to adaptation and innovation, as they are perceived, both to library administrators and to librarians. As a service agency politically and dependently linked to external environmental elements regardless of type of library and specific context, the library is seen to be highly vulnerable. This vulnerability conditions conservatism and convention rather than innovation and change, since adaptation may jeopardize the existing balance among constituencies and interests with whom library administrators and library staff alike must interrelate. Moreover, the existing system typically reflects a condition that the values and experience of the library group finds as comforting and as comfortable as those upon whom they depend for support. (5) The managerial and financial problems of change introduction. To do something new requires

9. See William A. McClelland, *The Process of Effecting Change*, Professional Paper 32–68 (Alexandria, Va.: George Washington University, Human Resources Research Office, October 1968), pp. 8–19.
10. This point is further elaborated in Paul Wasserman, Chapter II, "Barriers to Objective Formulation," "Toward a Methodology for the Formulation of Objectives in Public Libraries." Dissertation, University of Michigan, 1960.

the application of expertise and resources. Bureaucracy normally impedes shifts in personnel and financial deployment from traditional areas to new zones of application. Existing constituencies only most reluctantly tolerate containment of activities conventionally afforded. Often the organization can neither spare nor find the expertise for innovative efforts. The working agent of change implementation and the funds to hire him and implement his program must be drawn from the outside. This explains in part why it is that the new and most affluent libraries are very often the site for innovative activities.

RECRUITING NEW LEADERSHIP

The burden of the arguments of this volume specify how difficult it is for change to be brought about and how the existing order is inhibiting. If there is to be change, if new paradigms and models are to be derived and espoused and enacted, the prime problem is where and whether and how much the discipline has of the human beings who are committed to work for and who have the ability to influence change in librarianship. If they are not present in sufficient number in key roles now, how can their numbers be made to grow, or is this an impossible quest? The hope for new types receives some encouragement in the forces which are seen everywhere to be shattering earlier stereotypes of anticipated behavior. As little as ten years ago, college students were docile, silent people, sent to universities in order to achieve and to receive their passports to respectability and mediocrity. Today, many appear to be making demands for an education which they will find more honest and meaningful. Welfare mothers, formerly subservient to a welfare system, demand their human rights and the capacity to shape decisions which affect their lives. Clergymen of every denomination are refusing to accept the will of their hierarchical authorities. Black people speak out for rights and opportunities long denied them. The voices of complacency, apathy, and repression are being replaced by cries for justice and an end to unresponsive organizations and institutions. It is a time of ferment. Professional and intellectual groups of conscience and responsibility have begun to examine their professional souls and their social conscience. As institutions are being challenged, a relatively small number of librarians have begun to share in the expression of dissatisfaction and alienation. It is out of such movements that a more sensitive and equitable and imaginative leadership class may ultimately emerge. For while the majority remain quiescent, some of their number are assuredly disposed to follow a new banner in their organizational and disciplinary roles. But I have considerable and serious doubt about the availability of those who would assume leadership roles, doubt about existing professional capabilities, doubt about the sufficiency of the requisite numbers of leaders.

The earlier analysis has identified that while leadership in librarianship is very much needed, it is seldom to be found in the institutions, the professional associations, nor among the intelligentsia. The present institutional administrative class, with a median age well into the fifties,[11] can only be characterized as reinforcing of the status quo.[12] Aspirations for a new leadership thrust from emergent or dissident elements in librarianship or among its intellectuals appear limited. The emergent leaders in the institutional settings seem characterized by a sameness with their predecessors by whom they tend to be coopted to the establishment structure which reinforces its own values by seeking replacements in its own image. The dissidents tend to be more aroused about specific ideological differences with organizational and associational policy than with pragmatically striving for roles of institutional and disciplinary influence and power so as to redirect the field. The intellectuals, when they are not attempting to prop up and to reinforce a sagging institutional structure,[13] tend to cluster busily around the technology, perceiving the problems of libraries as the equivalent of their processes. Innovation equates with changing the means rather than the ends of organizational attainment, and the greatest frequency of such attempts centers in technical rather than service variations.[14]

If the present leadership ranks are thin and the assumption correct that the potential replacements now in the field appear unlikely to achieve dramatically different leadership, the chances for change hinge upon the quality of individuals being drawn to the field now and in the future. Assessment of present entry routes to the field and of those who travel them would then seem to be germane. The stereotypal percep-

11. In addition to the evidence of Chapter 6, see, for example, Henry T. Drennan, "Public Library Goals in the Decade of the 1970's," Bowker Annual, 1970 (New York: R. R. Bowker Co., 1970), pp. 14–22, wherein the median age of public library directors in 1969 is identified as fifty-seven and that of directors of state library agencies as fifty-six.
12. The case is amply documented for the large public library scene in Ruth Kay Maloney, "The 'Average' Director of a Large Public Library," Library Journal, February 1, 1971, p. 443.
13. As may be the case in Lowell Martin, Library Response to Urban Change: A Study of the Chicago Public Library (Chicago: American Library Association, 1969).
14. See, for example, Sidney Forman, "Innovative Practices in College Libraries," College and Research Libraries, November 1968, pp. 486–492. Here the category of administrative practice which was seen as most heavily engaging the concerns of college librarians was the adoption of Library of Congress classification, presumably a change from the Dewey system. A full 43 percent of responding institutions report this as a change.

tion of libraries and of librarians doubtless serves as a powerful propellant to those who select the field and as a deterrent for others. In its crudest terms, librarianship may essentially be seen by many of those at the point of career choice as a dominantly female field centered upon routinized processes, administered by males with leadership and innovative avenues imperceptible. Age at the time of career choice has normally been higher by a good deal than in comparative fields,[15] restricting the career time-span to a shorter period and thereby lessening ambition and aspirations. For appreciable numbers librarianship is a second or third career choice. This combination of factors presents the picture of a fundamentally passive field where tradition and preconditioned expectations about the cultural role of libraries fail in the main to excite the enthusiasm of any but those for whom such expectations are consonant with their own limited leadership aspirations. When there is passion and zeal, and such traits are not totally absent among new recruits, they tend invariably to center upon the transcendent cultural values of books and reading or upon a particular client group (children are doubtless the most frequent) or upon the two in combination. But the sense of ultimately aspiring to a role of leadership in order to affect the destiny of a single institution or of the discipline is virtually nonexistent. Ambition is modest and quite commonly highly circumscribed.

Extracts from written comments of two students themselves, students who may be representative of relatively large numbers of new entrants, illustrate something of the problem:

When I started taking courses a couple of years ago, it was done with some half formed idea of preparing myself to do something with the next 20 years of my life when my children are grown, other than bridge parties and club luncheons and volunteer work. As I have always felt at home in libraries, enjoyed reading, books and discussions, and have a tendency toward order instead of chaos, librarianship seemed to offer a worthwhile goal.

But is it? I'm not so sure. Perhaps this is because at this juncture the obvious needs of libraries are *not* for the type of personalities who have generally been attracted to librarianship. Those of us in the over 30 category have been particularly jolted by some of the demands that seem to be called for. Those of us who hold the traditional middle class view of libraries as quiet depositories of books and periodicals where one goes to seek information or recreation, find the concept of libraries as *active* disseminators of information

15. See, for example, Alice I. Bryan, *The Public Librarian; A Report of the Public Library Inquiry* (New York: Columbia University Press, 1952), pp. 116–120.

not only hard to accept, but rather repugnant—Madison Avenue-ish. Our exposure to learning has been linear and we tend to feel this is the way *it is* and *ought* to be.

The fundamental question that remains in my mind is whether *I* can adapt—or whether I even *want* to. I kind of like traditional libraries—at least the good ones and much prefer the book oriented system.

Another student puts it this way:

Over 30 and female, I come out of the humanities, a generalist, a people-oriented, rather than a machine-oriented creature. I see myself replicated dozens of times over. In the literature, I am the drop-out from "teaching," the mother whose nest is growing empty. And the soap opera question arises: Can I find happiness as a librarian?

I feel that the answer is affirmative, but it may very well be that this interim here is the last time that people such as myself will make adequate librarians at the same time they fulfill career and personality needs. Hackneyed though the phrase is, libraries are going through a period of transition. No longer will the traditional middle class, book oriented library for middle class, white patrons be the model in the period of societal and technological change. As libraries change, they must demand librarians who are subject specialists, who possess different backgrounds, and who demonstrate different capacities.

Despite this rather gloomy picture, the librarian whose qualifications are not as dazzling as the paragon of the future can serve as a transitional figure. If we bring to the profession a modicum of practical wisdom, a healthy intellectual curiosity, a revulsion toward ritualizing the routines, and an awareness that the profession is in a state of flux and will demand flexibility and growth from all those who want a career rather than a job, then we can operate as librarians with a sense of accomplishment—for a while.

Such perspectives are not the stuff from which leaders are made. If in other disciplines students are coming to question the conventional functioning of societal institutions and traditional roles, evidence that the faculties of librarianship are any more committed to deep and critical analysis than their students simply does not exist. For the most part, faculty as well as students are attracted to the stability and the conventions of the institutions and of the discipline. Even to yield such self-scrutiny of personality and potential contribution against the backdrop of a culture in a time of change, as is reflected in the comments above, calls for a faculty which identifies the legitimacy of questions about the changing needs of the institutions for which they are preparing people for career roles. New entrants receive the reassurance of the library efforts which they have observed and observe as they are students. They receive, too, the reassurance of faculties who protect and insulate the students and the libraries by failing to question and by perpetuating formal course work which identifies the responsibilities of the field and of those who will administer the organization's efforts as ritualistic and technical problems rather than those of leadership responsibility.

A key element of the problem is the sources and types of individuals who are recruited to the field, if in fact the traditional means do not yield the requisite leaders. For the most part, recruitment of librarians has been from a thin stratum of relatively high-status social classes, individuals from backgrounds in the humanities with relatively little influx of representatives of lower status and more socially representative elements. Yet without involvement from those who are not entirely comfortable with the going institutional contribution, the prospects of leadership oriented to new ends is lessened. Part of the problem is related to the class structure within libraries which is so heavily oriented to educational development. Thus, unlike the military, the transition from enlisted to officer status depends almost exclusively upon education, and educational options are often foreclosed. Those who enter in the sub-professional ranks are destined to remain there. It is for this reason primarily, that groups not earlier represented among the professional group, notably blacks, when they are encouraged to choose librarianship are invited only when their educational credentials are fully equivalent. The process of their educational acculturation and even of their selection for professional study assures that only those whose orientation is congruent with the going educated middle-class values will be accepted. As the path to entry is effectively blocked for those of variable persuasions —individuals with different styles of life, social and political perspectives, and alternative value assumptions—those recruited remain predominantly committed to the existing order. The mold is broken only to the extent that the normal constraints upon entry are adapted in such a way as to credit other experiences and qualities than the ones which form the conventional basis for choice in library education. This is somewhat in the way that the military acknowledges that leadership is also advanced by admitting into officer candidate school those who have demonstrated their potential in ways other than the traditional formal academic preparation. To restrict the recruitment and educational process to only those who precisely match the conventional formula is to perpetuate what has been.

In these times there are important factors at work which hold considerable potential for the furtherance of librarianship. In one sense the economic situation, reflecting a time of greater adversity than almost any other in recent memory, represents an opportunity. As options are foreclosed and as the vocational marketplace becomes constricted, some of the competitive disciplines and occupations which have seemed brighter than librarianship may have lost some of their luster. Some of the more enterprising may cast about for alternative avenues of opportunity which offer the promise of rewarding careers; they may even sense the untapped potential and the inherent promise of librarianship. Certainly in a time when economic determinants loom larger, the prospect of a worthwhile, socially meaningful career in a stable discipline holds appeal. For this is doubtless what happened in the 1930s and served as the condition which attracted many of the best who later came to lead librarianship during the 1950s and 1960s.

Another important lure is that which librarianship offers for socially useful life work. As libraries are seen as or depicted as potentially linked to human aspirations, they hold promise for those who seek meaningful life roles. The sort of human being who is attracted to movements like the Peace Corps may come to understand why and how a career in libraries offers more opportunity to enhance the human condition than those settings which are committed exclusively to profit-making motivations. To the degree that libraries and librarianship come to be perceived in their identification with human aspirations rather than bureaucratic ritual, such human beings can be appealed to and may find the encouragement to choose librarianship. This combination of a more limited basis for alternative opportunity choices at a time when many young people are electing vocations committed more to human ends, offers the promise of appeal to larger numbers who may come to librarianship not because they are unfit or unsuited for the earlier vocational choices which they have made and thus gravitate to librarianship as a safe harbor, but because they may sense that the opportunity structure of librarianship may be greater.

Librarianship has long labored under the misapprehension that individuals who pursue study in other disciplines to the doctorate are somehow valuable and viable in educational roles in librarianship. This may be part of the syndrome of self-effacement which identifies always the intrinsic intellectual content of any discipline but its own. But the central question is not the formal value of advanced study in another context, but rather the ways in which such variable expertise can assist the field to transcend its conventional limits and thus be reoriented to client terms. During the last decade the premium has been upon methodological sophistication, against the expectation that those who could advance the systematic and procedural concerns of libraries, using the tools of mathematics, operations research, and computer technology, are most effectively equipped to accomplish this. While there is, of course, high value in such expertise, many of the fundamental problems of libraries go well beyond questions of efficiency and economy. In the behavioral realm, individuals prepared in such social-science disciplines as sociology, psychology, and occasionally political science have been seen as attractive recruits for educational roles. The limit of their contribution, however, has been that of accepting and reinforcing the existing structure of librarianship in a way similar to those oriented to technical problems by rationalizing the present condition without posing fundamental questions about the institution or the discipline. The strategic element which has been lacking has been a reconstructed ideological base for librarianship which might transform it from what it is and what it has been—an institution concentrated upon collections and procedures—to a client system.

The most ideal recruits to library education for such a purpose are those few young intellectuals being prepared in the behavioral disciplines who, while their numbers are not very great, are gifted and imaginative enough to dedicate their careers to the exploitation of the discipline for the purposes of human beings. When such young scholars are drawn from the behavioral sciences, they bring to the profession not only the sought for methodological sophistication, but, more importantly, a sensitivity to what the system is all about and the motivation to use their technical knowledge to improve the capacity of the professional structure to be culturally responsive. With law and medicine as prototypes, this could perhaps lead to the development of expertise in building advocacy roles into library structure and arrangements; such attempts would parallel those in which lawyers seek to change laws and public health persons seek to change the structure of public health institutions in order to ensure a more equitable and humane application of their legalistic and scientific preparation.

Such recruits dissatisfied with the static nature and dehumanized academic process, like the freshly minted attorneys who shun Wall Street law firms for what they perceive as more socially purposeful roles, could be drawn to library education if they would see libraries as adaptable institutions and professional practice as potentially relevant to advancing the cause of man.

The same links which have been forged with Purdue University, for example, where doctoral students carry out research on the operations-research types of library problems and then become potential faculty members in library education, could be forged with sociology, psychology, political science, to what might be an even more significant ultimate effect. For if it is true that many committed young scholars today reject as barren the self-regenerating academic culture and choose to apply their insights to those problems and those settings where their efforts can bear upon changing the structure, such liaisons hold high promise. Success in such recruitment would require library educators to accept the need to appeal to those who could assist in the analysis and research process which would revise the ideological framework of the discipline. This is a far different matter from seeking to remain academically fashionable by adding to faculties token representatives of exotic disciplines who do little more than offer broad survey courses in the areas of their prior preparation. Young and committed scholars would form natural alliances with the growing number of people in the field who are disillusioned by the limits of libraries and of librarianship. Thus they might well aid in articulating the conceptual terms to give focus and impetus to the forces which seek to reconstitute the institution and the practice.

Obviously the fundamental problem in recruitment of potential leaders for a discipline is the appeal of the field as it is perceived by those making occupational choices. The ideal device then is to influence favorably the external view of the occupation and of those who practice it. Until the practice of librarians and other professional functionaries is seen to be professionalized and client committed, to promise more to those who are being courted smacks of the same fraudulent lures which characterize so much of contemporary advertising. Still in a time and in a culture when many coming to adulthood seek out avenues of opportunity in which they may help to make the world a better place, if the educational setting and if the institution can at least be seen as potentially flexible the matter is dramatically improved. Then the imaginative, ambitious, and dedicated young people can perhaps be shown the promise and the power of information as a force in the lives of many. If some hospitality to change effort is seen as genuine, such an appeal might be heeded by those who cast about seeking opportunity and hope even where the obstacles are great. Such an appeal is fundamentally different from one which simply seeks replacements who are essentially interchangeable with those who went before them. Put in its negative sense, the appeal may be stated as that of seeking new life and new insight from those sorely needed to set aright an institutional form which has gravitated away from where it should be going. The appeal becomes one of searching out potential leaders who would dedicate their energies and their career lifetimes to the reconstruction of a faltering institution and a faltering professional discipline. Such a perspective of the need for new entrants and the high degree of reliance which must be placed upon them to better the discipline calls for a different awareness of library realities than that which is now the general condition. The need to be and become otherwise is not yet being imposed by the culture. Librarianship itself still controls its destiny.

There may be lessons to be learned in the successes of other occupations steeped in orthodoxy. Police work may be one such parallel. For some time now one individual, a college graduate drawn to police work within the New York City Police Force, Sergeant David Durk, has conducted a one-man campaign to influence college graduates to choose careers as policemen in cities on the East coast. Sergeant Durk has actively recruited a surprising number of graduates of prestigious Ivy League schools so that in recent months about 175 graduates of well known northeastern colleges and universities have taken examinations and more than fifty are now members of the Washington, D.C., police force.[16] This one man with seven years of police experience, and intrigued with the potential for social good which inheres in the role of the police officer, has received a large share of the credit for bringing considerable numbers of effectively prepared college graduates to work for municipal police departments.

Perhaps his primary task was in the dramatization of the appeal of police work. Normally police work has been most attractive to lower middle-class individuals without formal educational preparation. To attract those with further preparation and with intelligence and imagination, and to keep them motivated to stay, requires the constant attraction of challenge and opportunity within the context of the occupation. A passive and irrelevant occupation which affords little promise to advance and to influence the institution in meaningful ways, holds little appeal for those with conviction and ambition. As Sergeant Durk has put it, "If you're a cop, you're the Man. That's what 'power to the people' really means. It's immediate, and it's now."[17]

Analogies with librarianship may be spurious in the respect that in police work the occupation does not call for formal educational accul-

16. In the valedictory address of the Washington, D.C., Police Academy graduating class in February 1971, Officer Joseph B. Green, a Yale man, used the occasion to urge the graduating class to "meet pressure and criticism from 'outside groups' with dialogue and reason—not bitter passiveness." Moreover, Officer Green "accused one 'law enforcement official' of faulty police professionalism by turning his back on public criticism." *Washington Post*, February 13, 1971, pp. B1, B4.
17. See *Washington Post*, July 11, 1970, pp. B1, B3.

turation but rather for a kind of in-service training. There is no inter-mediate long-standing process wherein the recruit intellectualizes the institution's contribution and learns the law of institutional logic rather than honing his own social purpose. Then, too, in his assignment, the policeman is a detached person out in the culture negotiating the social system on his own and the bureaucracy is more distant from him while he relates closely to the constituency through constant interaction. Moreover, in librarianship professionals are seldom perceived as being free agents with zones of activity subject to their own discrimination. They are more nearly viewed by their organizational culture, by library education, and by those who view them in day-to-day performance as employees, carrying out the mandate of institutional administrations rather than guided by their own sense of client need. An important dif-ference between police recruiting and library recruiting is the fact that in librarianship there is a formal educational experience between the re-cruitment and the assumption of the occupational role. The danger is that if the educational experience does not measure up to the perspectives which are being offered to new recruits for an appealing and intel-lectually satisfying work role, they will be disgruntled even before acceptance of their first occupational assignments. More than one highly promising and imaginative student of librarianship has been known to withdraw in consequence of the limits and embarrassments of library education.

Thus for recruitment efforts in librarianship to achieve some measure of success in genuinely appealing to nontraditional recruits two factors are involved. The first calls for an educational experience which clearly identifies with a new and revised work role and provides reinforcement for students who are drawn to librarianship because of it. Beyond this, it calls for the availability of occupational opportunities for these same individuals necessitating a cadre of employers who are willing to hire graduates with such perspectives to work within the context of their organizations. Without either element, recruitment devices are destined to remain at the level of sterile and dishonest rhetoric.

The appeal of the field must be articulated as affording dramatic op-portunities for those who would explore alternatives to the present staid institutional form—whether to the young committed to a more equitable society wherein information is perceived as a propellant for change when adroitly provided to those individuals and groups who seek change; whether to the zealous blacks who would exploit the potential of information to advance the cause and the equipment of their race; whether to the partisan of the student in the academic culture who identifies these clients as informationally disadvantaged. The problem, of course, extends beyond the recruits. Without the capacity and the influence of library school faculties who will conceive of the need to consider alternatives and to challenge the existing values of the profession, there will simply be frustration. The organizations where they might be engaged must also be genuinely supportive and accommodative of individuals drawn to meet a problem rather than to sustain an insitutional form. How to engender such a climate remains the prime unresolved question.

There is an even more subtle problem in the recruitment of leadership. This is a softness of the discipline which allows the attainment of success in the practice of the discipline and in its administration without the level of effort and contribution which characterizes more competitive or demanding professions. Academic rank in library education seldom conforms to the more rigorous standards which obtain in other disciplines. In the administrative role, there is widespread tolerance of mediocrity with the unspoken but clear understanding that in this field uncommon performance is scarcely anticipated or required. These conditions powerfully deter genuine leadership performance or leadership aspirations.

Some who have been drawn to the occupation of librarianship are more intelligent than those by whom they are surrounded. The point here is that some library recruits are so endowed with energy, imagination and commitment to their occupational role that they quickly outdistance their peers. In such a company, those of outstanding ability and ambition stand out in sharp relief. In some instances this serves as deterrent for those who are exceptionally endowed for they will readily and easily, without the hardening and abrasive effect of keen competition, gravitate toward posts of power and responsibility. In such an occupational culture, the effect is frequently to keep the potential giants from reaching the full range of their capacity. Their success is so readily assured that they don't have to develop the more disciplined habits of mind and work which are a commonplace in other disciplines and thus more normally a prelude to the assumption of leadership responsibility. It will only be out of the dramatic adaptation of recruitment strategy which successfully attracts larger numbers of the exceptionally competent and committed that the flabbiness of the present condition may yield to a more demanding regimen of achievement for those who aspire to lead librarianship.

In recruitment, as in every other manifestation of librarianship, value issues often separate institutional from professional ideals. If the central contribution of the discipline is organizational rather than professional, new librarians are selected as replacement parts and are sought and encouraged to the degree that they are seen to correspond with such an occupational role. It is only in recent months that the literature has begun to identify the incongruity between the overbearing weight of institutional constraints upon the capacity for professional performance and to offer tentative alternatives.[18] Still, to revise organizational terms in order to advance the potential of professionalism without an infusion of new entrants for whom such revised terms hold higher promise, is to offer new ground rules for players who may not be at all prone to express themselves professionally any differently from the customary ways. Unless the cycle can be broken, a passive profession reflects this image to those who make occupational choices even when alternate options are open. The task essentially is to devise thrusts and measures for new entrants which discourage the preponderantly passive types and afford new forms of incentives and hospitality for those of a more active strain.[19]

The problems would be far simpler if the leadership needed were a single type, but the forms of leadership are too many and too complex for such simple resolution. One form of leadership uncommonly found is the entrepreneurial. In an institutionally based discipline, all the instincts, the conventions, and the cultural dictates relentlessly avoid risk. A library leader reflects an ideological mandate to react rather than to act. To do otherwise calls for acceptance and assumption of a different value framework. There are alternative models to be found. One such, at the other extreme, is the city manager for whom, unlike the library administrator, tenure of office is at best uncertain and subject to continuing review. This is a totally different pattern from that which obtains in bureaucratic structures where incumbents almost without exception enjoy unlimited tenure. But for the library administrator to behave as if his performance were subject to the same scrutiny as the city manager— or even a superintendent of schools—is not likely to come about until the social, cultural, and political expectations about his performance identify his leadership as one powerful key to the efficacy of a client system. Before that comes to pass, librarians themselves must reconstruct

18. See, for example, the following publications which document recent Cornell University administrative and professional thinking: Cornell University Libraries, *Report of the Committee on Continuing Education and Professional Growth* (Ithaca, N.Y.: Cornell University, August 8, 1969); and David Kaser, "Modernizing the University Library Structure," *College and Research Libraries*, July 1970, pp. 227–231.
19. This matter is detailed at length in Stanley J. Segal, *Personality and Ability Patterns of Librarians*, Final Report submitted to the U.S. Office of Education under Contract No. OEC 1–7–071084–5017, October 1970. This study is one of the technical reports included as part of the study, *A Program of Research into the Identification of Manpower Requirements, the Educational Preparation and the Utilization of Manpower in the Library and Information Profession.*

the public sense of their contribution. And until that time, only the grossest malfeasance, ineffectiveness, or political insensitivity are likely to serve as a basis for the dismissal of library administrators.

The nature of his responsibility is seldom seen as urgent by the library administrator or those who engage him. Unlike the city manager who by virtue of the ideology of his discipline must constantly prove himself in the face of pressure and conflict, the pattern of library leadership sees the process as a piecemeal or gradual adaptation. Radical reform, that is, significant adaptation or modification of ongoing arrangements, is highly uncommon. Library leadership essentially sees itself in a sellers' market with monopoly control. Librarians are costly, budgets are tight, users are many, and they have no other options. The organization's own purposes can thus transcend those of its constituency. Institutional inertia is reassured by the complacency and acceptance of unaroused and undemanding real or potential client groups.

An Agenda for Leaders
for Changing Librarianship

The emphasis of this work has been an attempt to characterize the intrinsic difficulties and complexities of the problems of change propulsion through leadership. Different styles of leadership performance, alternate stages of individual institutional development, variability of political framework, wide ranges in the sensitivity of clientele aspirations, the temper and the temperature of professionalism, all these and more form strategic elements in a multivariate equation which powerfully resists a neat balance. Such a scene defies the prescription of simple-minded homilies to set things right, and such a prescription would surely vitiate the logic of what has gone before. The problems are fundamental, they are long-standing, they are part of the political and historical structure of the discipline. To offer pat solutions would be naive, cynical, and misleading.

Librarianship may be only a minor field in contemporary society. It may very well be that libraries are what they are because the culture has perceived them as negligible. Those who have been drawn to the field have been content to identify with an organizational form and a service effort which has only very slight impact upon its culture. To be so viewed by its clients and by those who ply its craft is to limit the options and to reinforce the marginal nature of the institution and the profession. Aspiration to redirect the field from what it has been can be a powerful lever for change. The underlying rationale is found in the fact that the information requirements of modern times are both significant and complex and that the profession which comes closest to having the historic mandate and responsibility for responding to this need is librarianship. When the relationship between societal information requirements and the design of librarianship is accepted more fully by the profession and perceived by its constituencies, the capacity of the field to change is powerfully enhanced. It is in this light that the representations which follow are made.

PROFESSIONALISM

The culture of librarianship tends to be responsible only to itself. That is to say that the structure of its work, its commitments, and its loyalties are identified institutionally and professionally, rather than with the human beings who are the focus of its work. The profession is thus free of direct control or review of clientele and within the discipline itself the tolerance for mediocrity and concentration of effort upon traditional areas of application is carefully protected. The range of contribution, the sophistication of effort, and the ethical responsibility to client versus employer are all exceedingly variable. And, as with many other bureaucratic forms, there is little public discussion of either the means of the organization, as these are the prerogatives of the administration, or of the ends, as these are identified by the professional community itself. Thus, the prerogatives of librarians and of library administrators are expressly left to their discretion, with only very limited monitoring by outsiders. Forms of external control are discouraged and thus controversy is played down and overt differences are bureaucratically muted. In librarianship, as in many other comparable occupations, the effect of this has been that where there is disagreement or dissent, and particularly on goals or priorities, such debate has been contained within the institution or within the discipline rather than discussed publicly. The ethical standards of the profession frown upon such public debate— these are matters within the fold and to spread the problems before the constituency is seen as dangerously confusing to them and as a betrayal of professional discretion. No transgression inspires so much venom.[1]

Yet if there is to be leadership toward change, it seems reasonable that public understanding of the nature of the impediments to institutional and disciplinary reconstruction must be furthered rather than constrained. The questions essentially come down to where professional loyalty deserves to be vested. Ralph Nader has put it this way:

> "Employed professionals" are too often the silent instruments of private and public policies which contravene the public interest, destroy the environment and defraud the taxpayer and consumer. Those professionals who have spoken out, within and beyond their

1. The classic case in recent years in librarianship was the article by Daniel Gore, "Mismanagement of College Libraries: A View from the Inside," *AAUP Bulletin*, March 1966, pp. 46–51. The differences over this controversial piece were serious and substantive, but the greatest passion was vented in consequence of the issue of professional betrayal. See *AAUP Bulletin*, September 1966, pp. 283–289.

organizations, have too often been demoted, ostracized, discharged or suppressed when in fact they frequently may be heroic figures.[2]

The drastic measure of soliciting the reporting of violations by librarians to such a body as the newly formed Clearinghouse for Professional Responsibility as part of Nader's public interest group, a new organization soliciting "responsible whistle blowing" by scientists, engineers, and other professional employees of government and corporations,[3] may be too extreme. But the fact is that ethics related to clients must transcend institutional or disciplinary loyalty. Nader is concerned with practices which may be harmful to public or consumer interests. But the principle is the same, whether it is bringing into public focus polluting effects of industrial production or public airing of differences in priorities or goals for such client-committed efforts as library services. For a librarian to bring a case laying out alternatives to the existing structure before the public at this time is seen as a serious breach of his professional responsibility. But this is to continue the conspiracy in which the professionals define their function to suit their own needs, without public or social debate on those terms. What one writer says of medicine obtains as well for librarianship:

> Social policy is coming to be formulated on the basis of the profession's conception of need and to be embodied in support for the profession's institutions. But if those conceptions and institutions no longer conform to the public's conception they have lost their justification, for their justification lies not in their objective truth but in their connection with the values and usages of their society and their clientele. Professional "knowledge" cannot therefore properly be a guide for social policy if it is a creation of the profession itself, expressing the commitments and perception of a special occupational class rather than that of the public as a whole.[4]

Thus the issues, the alternatives, and the options must be made clear to client groups so that the library does not continue to be seen by all in only one way—precisely as it has been and precisely as it has functioned. Those whose professional conscience commits them most strongly to client needs must speak out so that there will begin to be a

2. John D. Morris, "New Nader Group Seeking Tipsters," *New York Times*, January 27, 1971, p. 32.
3. *Ibid.*
4. Eliot Freidson, *Profession of Medicine: A Study of Sociology of Applied Knowledge* (New York: Dodd, Mead and Company, 1970), p. 350.

broadened perception of the possibilities inherent in adapted terms of the services of libraries and of librarians. The human beings for whom the library exists must become parties to the decisions which have traditionally been made by others in their presumed best interests. Only thus are they in a position themselves to evaluate what in fact are their best interests. It may well be that their reading tastes will differ fundamentally from what has been the conventional and long-standing professional view of what is best for them. But it is not until the issue is aired that the stage is truly set for change.

To be responsive ultimately, and particularly in a leadership sense, requires a professionalism which transcends rhetoric and equates genuinely with clients. It is to assault head-on the alternatives, to delineate them, to open the debate without which there can be no sensitivity to reconstructed terms of institutional and individual responsibility to clientele. Traditional librarianship has put power in the hands of few. It has made administration the esteemed contribution and it has demonstrated in every way that the role of professional contribution is of a distinctly low order.

Those with talent are expected to move onward and upward into those administrative realms where power genuinely resides. The field itself decries the futility and irrelevance of the professional contribution and thereby reinforces constantly the fact that it is the institution, the organization, rather than the individual professional who contributes anything. The ultimate consequence is, in the main, an employee culture of passivity wherein many librarians have long since identified the inconsequentiality of their individual contribution. In such a discipline, professionalism could only be enhanced in consequence of open discourse and such discussion might well lead to advancing not only the terms of professional practice but the aspirations of clientele as well.

EDUCATION AND INTELLECTUALISM

In librarianship advances have tended only very uncommonly to be introduced through education and research in the universities. Since the prime route to entry into librarianship is through graduate-level instruction, it seems questionable to accept the pedestrian level of preparation, when in comparable disciplines students are expected to stand on the shoulders of their faculties so as to perceive more clearly and widely the ultimate direction of the field and their own contribution to such development. The limits of recruitment of new entries, albeit perhaps the most crucial ingredient, is only part of the explanation. In a number of ways library education may be compared with graduate study in business administration. In both fields of practice there are individuals who function in work roles in organizations without formal academic preparation. In both instances there is undergraduate education which is not a condition of admission to graduate study. There the comparison ends. Those who aspire to the MBA degree are seen as candidates for ultimate positions of responsibility in their field. To be seen as merely journeymen being trained for inconsequential roles would scarcely be worthy of such an advanced level of academic preparation. To be sure, all may not achieve senior responsibility, but the level of aspiration is such that all are seen as potentially headed in such directions. Thus the graduate experience is one which commits itself to developing habits of mind, problem-solving capacity, and the ideological commitment to a post of responsibility and of leadership.

In library education, aspiration tends to be set at the least common denominator and the demands are more nearly of the order of lower-level technical requirements. In this, for the most part, faculty and student perspectives are shared. It is only the uncommon student who is seen as a potential leader, and the educational process is never geared for him but rather for the more routine functionary. If one aspires beyond the normal levels of library functions, this is seen more nearly as a personal matter and the responsibility to succeed is between the individual and his employing institution. To set its sights on preparing leaders with all that this implies for selection, course standards and content and ideological perspective, would call for a wholly reconstructed framework of library education. Some of the central ingredients might well be the following.

The research climate of the discipline is an essential ingredient. Librarianship is an applied pursuit. Even so, it rests upon insights drawn from the basic disciplines upon which it relies. Ultimately, as in other more mature professional disciplines, it builds upon its own capacity to study its problems by evolving researchers who are equipped methodologically to apply their talents to the specific problems of the field. Eventually a mature discipline develops its own scholars who are capable of analyzing the psychological problems of the organization; its own economic experts for whom the financial affairs of the institution are the focus; its own students of the political process who address themselves to questions of institutional and ecological relationships. In this way, the research enterprise transcends the limits of the purely technical problems of the field. More importantly, the research effort ultimately comes to be more congruent with the fundamental and basic problems of the field. This has seldom happened in librarianship, nor has it generally been the expectation that library education would ever assume such a role.

The habits of mind of those who have come to direct scholarly work in librarianship have influenced the research choices made by doctoral students toward either the historical, the humanistic, and the bibliographic or to the technical questions of arrangement of knowledge and only seldom to the organizational, the political, the social concerns. As a consequence of such a scholarly view, the profession tends to find little insight for contemporary problems. The prime utility of library school research is, for the most part, the passport to a future career in library education or, even more typically, in academic library administration. The effect is to shunt aside the most imaginative and intellectually courageous, to reward the ritualists and the persevering, and so to denigrate the very nature of the research process. Obviously, there must be place for traditional study. It is only a question of proportion. Because doctoral students tend to move gingerly through the process, they will obviously stay with the safest and surest route to the success symbol, even if it implies plodding along in the most marginal and least relevant problem areas.

The nub of the problem of reorienting research in order to more clearly and frequently address basic questions is tied to the way in which academia, and library scholars among them, presume themselves to be disinterested scholars preoccupied solely with looking at phenomena in a way wholly detached from moral consequence. Such a posture reinforces the acceptance of the ongoing values and commitments of the institution and of the discipline and casts the scholar in the role of disinterested observer. Research thus normally starts from the base of existing value choices and commitments. The net effect is invariably to reinforce the established order of things, rather than to threaten its assumptions, or illuminate the range of alternatives. It is this sterility which is decried by those who see such research effort as the servant of power.

An alternative may be found in the development of experimental and laboratory programs as correlates of library education. The institute phenomenon has come to be accepted already at a number of institutions, even if the types of research pursued have in the main centered upon technical problems. Yet the formal institutional structure is less the issue than whether those who hold responsibility for education and research perceive that experimental programs, the testing of innovative alternatives, offer the use of more flexible instruments for both student participant and observation, as well as accretions to the knowledge base of the field. In a time when librarianship is not alone in calling into question the continuing viability of traditional teaching and research processes, it is not surprising to find radical adaptation being called for by disciplines where the emphasis upon research and experimentation has been far more pervasive. In a recent report from the prestigious Columbia University Bureau of Applied Social Research,[5] there is proposed that every university should have several institutes, each oriented to a particular social institutional problem area of society, such as education, urban society, politics, mental health, the family, and race and ethnic relations. Moreover, this report recommends that classroom teaching in the social sciences be abolished after the first year of graduate study so that students can then transfer to a research and training institute of their choice. The representation calls for a full integration of such centers into the formal university structure and the thesis derived in this representation is based upon research evidence that social research centers in the nation's universities are doing a better job of training graduate students than the traditional teaching departments.

To shift the terms to the point where laboratory and experimental programs become the normal and legitimate accompaniment of library education and research calls for the type of imaginative reconstruction of long-held academic perspectives in library education which has divorced education and research from the concerns of practice. And the costs of such experimentation are very high, measured either in human or financial terms.[6] Moreover, the same constraints against the novel and untried obtain in the bureaucratic academic context as in other bureaucratic forms. Innovation remains on trial everywhere in library education as in practice, while the ongoing enterprise is seldom challenged.[7] Still, the prototypal form affords not only the sole device for demonstrating the possibility of alternatives for all who remain unmoved by any but such expression, but also the lure for those who may more nearly be drawn to lend their expertise to efforts committed to the testing of new propositions rather than to the continued reinforcement and perpetuation of the existing order. The experimental base for library education

5. Sam D. Sieber and Paul F. Lazarsfeld, *Reforming the University: The Role of the Research Center* (New York: Columbia University, Bureau of Applied Social Research, 1971).

6. Some of these costs are reflected in the published account of the sequence of problems growing out of the several dimensions of the High John experiment in library education and research. Among the many articles and comments on the High John Project in the library literature in the past few years, see the most recent accounts: R. B. Croneberger and J. C. Welbourne, "Triumph and Tragedy: A Play in Two Acts; the High John Library," *Library Journal*, May 1, 1970, pp. 1705–1708; and Richard Moses, "Hindsight on High John," *Library Journal*, May 1, 1972, pp. 1672–1675; and the notes and comments in *Library Journal*, July 1970, p. 2397, and October 15, 1970, pp. 3416–3418; and *American Libraries*, December 1970, p. 1011.

7. See, for example, Mary Lee Bundy, "Crisis in Library Education," *Library Journal*, March 1, 1971, p. 797.

and research which sees the problem as one of deriving a client response system still in flux and striking out for new ideas, new methods, new perspectives, is a radical departure from an academic base which serves only as replacement training center for an unchanging institutional structure.

GENERATING A NEW BREED OF LIBRARIAN

The role of the change agent is clearly established in the annals of social science. These are individuals who come to institutional forms and social settings with the skills and the knowledge to lead the advance toward next stages in the necessary cultural or technical evolution. While it seems apparent that the discipline cannot neglect the need for change in its leadership perspectives, to prescribe this is not to assure it. One mechanism for lending impetus to a reconstructed sense of institutional and disciplinary striving is to attempt to evolve a new breed of individuals, drawn differently from the pool of human beings who are making occupational decisions and who are then educated in a way which prepares them to function as library professionals with a new focus. To the degree that librarianship continues to appeal to and to prepare individuals in conventional ways, variation is effectively blocked. Moreover, even to the extent that higher value comes to be placed upon technology and on the recruitment of those equipped to handle such technology, the significant needs remain unmet. The traditional efforts of libraries would be improved and made more efficient—and in that sense there would be improvement—but the discipline and the institution might well be basically unchanged. The core of the problem may be seen as one in which the paramount need is for a revised conceptual paradigm for librarianship and for libraries, so that more individuals are drawn in who can help the discipline to become more truly a client response system rather than an inventory system.

For this to come to pass there would need to be more general acceptance, not only among educators but in the practicing community, that the perspectives of the field require revision. One illustration of the difference may illuminate the fundamental nature of the necessary revision. Reference work, as it is taught and as it is practiced in libraries, builds upon the conceptual notion that the normal limits of librarianship are to assist clients by locating existing information needed for problem-solving. Thus the institutional and the disciplinary duty is served at the point when the librarian or the library, following the individual or institutional decision rules about volume of effort to expend on an individual inquiry, assists the user in trying to locate information. There the matter ends. The process is reactive. It is uncommon in the extreme for the professional obligation to embrace the furtherance of information development in areas where information may be lacking, either by generating informational resources or even by promoting their design and development actively through associational or commercial organizations. Nowhere in the ethic of librarianship is there a commitment to respond to client need by going beyond the limits of simply reacting. Interestingly enough, even among those who believe ardently in the need for a reconstructed sense of political engagement in library association affairs and in public affairs generally, there is no translation of this commitment by such actively oriented individuals to the practice of librarianship itself. Even for aroused members of the library community, the active arena of concern is Vietnam or social responsibility. The application of informational expertise to client response terms in ways which would engineer new information resources in the very areas of zeal on the part of the activist are virtually nonexistent.

In large measure, the passive sense of the library role is reinforced by educational norms where reference work is equated with fact seeking as the prescribed role and where an accepting stance within the framework of what exists is seen as the necessary condition of the librarian. Practice then becomes the acting out of the prescribed behavior in unquestioning ways and it is only the uncommon individual, the uncommon library, which transcends such limits. Those efforts which start from the assumption that the response of librarianship is to begin with the client and design, in whatever way feasible, the needed strategy to fulfill need tend largely to be experimental and unusual. Because this is so, individuals with the psychological need to do more than simply serve in sharply proscribed and prescribed ways tend to avoid a career choice which offers such limited outlet for their active contribution and which violates their own sense of self as contributor. Thus the problem is made more acute, for the cycle is circular and exceedingly difficult to interrupt.

To enlarge the outlook of librarianship so as to accommodate new entrants who would strive for altered terms, inevitably requires a wider consensual base about the necessary response of librarianship. In this, it may only be the demonstration, the experimental, the prototypal, in practice as in library education, which can point the way by demonstrating the feasibility of such changed terms. For library leadership now and in the future must revise the perspectives of practice. Social work may provide a parallel instance where a new breed is also being sought, except that the basis of such need seems to be more widely accepted in that discipline. There is coming to be articulated the requirement for a new breed of social worker who goes beyond helping individuals or families in times of crisis or in matters of health, money, or family relationships and who deals rather with people as human beings. Instead of solely attempting to change behavior, the effort becomes one of adapting the institutional structure in order to ameliorate the social conditions which influence behavior. Thus the social worker becomes a social strategist who asks questions about how people get on and off welfare, how to train and find jobs for individuals being released from prisons, how to make cities safe and fit places to live in. In order to find answers to such complex questions, such social workers deal not only with individuals, although some do, but with government at all levels and with a variety of other institutions.

As a potential parallel, librarianship would appeal to individuals for whom the human being as client is the prime purpose for the existence of the profession. In its rhetoric, librarianship conceives itself made up of individuals who like people and books. But the liking has been more heavily on the side of the books than on the side of the people. The relationship between librarians and human beings has tended to be superficial and limited. If there is to be a new breed of librarianship, it will build on a perspective which sees in librarianship the capacity to satisfy the information requirements of human beings. Human problems do not begin with books or their careful description for posterity. They begin with the human being for whom the system exists.

It is clear that educational attitudes must be altered and this comes about best when those not locked into the conventional framework of the field make up part of the faculty. This is not the same as simply identifying the need for more PhDs trained in other disciplines; such an open-door policy invariably draws defectors from other fields, just as does library practice, for precisely the wrong reasons. If the appeal is not that of an applied proving ground for providing the opportunity to aid students to improve their ability to perform responsibly in institutions addressed to human need, such members can prove to be more liability than asset. How to differentiate the purposeful from those attracted to a seemingly softer discipline with reduced strains is analogous to the problem of offering hospitality to dropouts from other fields who shift to librarianship as second or third career choice—except that the educational cadre, since it is so much fewer in number, can afford mistaken choices far less. Moreover, technical contribution from such imports is another necessary element, for the capacity to achieve a reconstructed purpose depends upon the technical sophistication to bring the organizational machinery into place which will facilitate, rather than impede such progression. Still, the crucial nature of the contribution militates for the most judicious choice of such imported talent, lest the luster of their presence bring only enhanced prerogatives for the individuals in the form of new consulting options, rather than impact upon fashioning a new breed of student. The limits of reliance for the generation of a new breed upon those prepared in librarianship itself are fairly evident. Those who receive PhDs in librarianship, despite some modest variation among them, tend to share the views of what their discipline is supposed to cover and how it should be taught and how its frontier should be advanced. Thus the generation of doctorates in librarianship that has been spawned in recent years tends more nearly than not to share the value commitments of the senior administrators in librarianship, a value structure they would not presume to threaten. For the point is that the individuals who tended to gravitate toward doctoral study were, for the most part, drawn from the field and so are like-minded from the beginning. The machinery which existed to move them along in the structure conditioned their remaining like-minded in their value perspectives. There are, moreover, national and regional meetings in librarianship in which doctoral students, faculty members, and practitioners all blend together in ways reinforcing of the ongoing value constructs of institutional practice.

The same cannot be said of those drawn from outside the field because their perspectives and their values and goals have been derived out of disciplinary accommodation elsewhere. The problem, of course, is one of attracting them to a field which has seldom been perceived as calling for the highest qualities of mind and for the most forceful commitment to human ends. Yet in the potential of information as a requisite to human needs in every setting conceivable, there are possibilities in the field which, when fully exploited and detailed, those of an imaginative cast of mind seeking avenues of application for their technical and behavioral capacities might well find attractive. This is as true of potential faculty as it is true of potential young new entrants to the field who are looking for a similar avenue of opportunity.

One of the most significant elements in the attraction of a new breed to librarianship is in the actual experimental, demonstration, and laboratory programs. In such a context there is often the possibility of bringing together many levels of contribution—new recruits, scholars from other disciplines, practitioners, students and faculty drawn from the field—all of whom come together to test and experiment with new models. As the problems are exciting, they hold promise for outsiders; as they identify avenues of opportunity, they attract the young; as they open new options, they appeal to those within the field who seek to change it. All of the components are related, all form part of the same fabric. And all affect each other, and, ultimately, the options of librarianship. To the extent that education and practice are somehow fused in efforts which use as their outlet combinations of laboratory, demonstration, and educational components, all of the crucial elements are present. While the costs of such attempts are great and the lessons hard won, it may be out of such attempts that the needed insights arise to shape the new breed. Again, an illustration may be most germane.

Commonplace in the urban culture of the seventies are new developments oriented toward the assumption of responsibility for providing informational support to individuals in distinct spheres of concern. In every city such programs are springing up. Social-welfare people concentrate upon human needs and aspirations. Legal interests center upon legal information. Health groups focus upon matters relating to physical and mental health. Youth groups have their "hot lines," their warriors against drug abuse, their drug information centers. The public library is dismissed as simply a book collection and its attendants as uncommitted to human need. Some recent experiments have sought to test the efficacy of the public library in ways which would make it more responsive to information requirements which transcend the limits of the physical book collection,[8] but such experiments are scarcely seen as basic to the reason for being of the public library. Even while those associated with the public library profess the fact that they do have information and are equipped to make it available to human beings on matters and in sources not commonly assumed to be within the province of the public library, the fact of the matter is that exceedingly few in the urban or suburban culture accept this rhetoric of the public library. They *know* what a public library is and does.

Part of the problem is that often more than information is sought—counsel, advice, even advocacy. For such a role, not only information is requisite but human compassion and substantive expertise as well. And so new centers are constantly being born. At best, the public library serves only as referral service, redirecting inquiries. Librarianship for the most part shrugs off responsibility. Yet it may be precisely here where the new breed is being born. In such efforts there is coming to be a fusion of information and help which transcends simply handing over a book. Moreover, the expertise of librarianship is a technical value in the context where there is only a problem concern. Here are people who want to help, but are not normally sophisticated about information resources or its handling. Instead of ignoring these phenomena, here is where the library interests might find their greatest challenge. Here is

8. Two such are the Public Information Center (PIC) Project at the Enoch Pratt Free Library and the previously cited Bay Area Reference Center (BARC) at the San Francisco Public Library.

where the schools might be studying information effort in addition to their normal concern with the formal bibliographic institutions. And it is here where students might come more genuinely to understand the modern terms of information need in the public setting.

Moreover, in a complex world in which human information requirements are far from simple, the nature of need may not always precisely match the framework of the particular agency. That is to say, problems do not always neatly fit one context. There may be legal, health, and social ramifications to the same problem. The loose and free-floating information facility which does not correlate with others in related fields may not be serving the interests of those for whom it exists. What may well be requisite is a kind of capping organization of information service and intelligence and here might be the single most important avenue of opportunity for those who would advance the cause, the purpose, and the contribution of the public library.

For a new breed might evolve if education, recruitment, practice, would take part in striking for the means which would link together the public library with the information problem in all its contexts—by study, experiment, demonstration, cooperation, and analysis. In a sense, the public library, at least those with centralized departments and subject collections, has already made a start in this direction. The initiators have sought to build specialized collections of books and journals on distinct subjects which information experts in these areas help to interpret or to aid patrons in negotiating. Information service in other and different discrete fields which have become germane to the requirements of the library's constituency seems only a natural extension of prior effort. The difference would be in transcending the published sources, to the provision of counsel and advice, and on to advocacy effort in behalf of clients of the library. Yet here again, it is only a matter of extension from the subject expert of the literature to the drug expert who advises on treatment, or to the legal advisor who counsels on court procedure. Moreover, the library is not partisan—it is not linked with the motives of any one profession or field with political goals or aspirations and, as such, would have decided advantages and opportunities not open to an institution with a history of political partisanship.

There is, at present, no public agency which attempts to play a coordinating role in rationalizing the full range of information efforts of the community. Here is a task worthy of the best efforts of all those who hold an aspirational view of the public library's future, and an effort which might enlist the best efforts of all those who could contribute to such a reconstructed mission, thereby engendering the kind of new breed of librarian toward which the prior material has been pointing.

To experiment may also be used to avoid the problem or to buy time.

Commonly there is much ballyhoo accorded to only modest effort, hinged largely upon uncommon external funding sources, engaging only a thin layer of competency drawn from a small committed coterie, while bureaucratic business goes on as usual. In this way, the more passionate elements, disciples of new direction and educational practice, take the heat off the educational and institutional structure by carrying out their efforts with little more encouragement than the chance to accept risk. The young or the committed form the vanguard, invest their energies and personal resources, while those who hold power remain carefully on the sidelines, maintaining their neutrality and their routine commitments, tolerating experiment but only within bounds, for such efforts are both fashionable and politically expedient. It is perhaps in the light of the ultimate recognition of such behavior patterns that those who genuinely believe in alternatives become enraged or cynical about the possibilities for change. And under these terms, there can be no new breed.

THE NEED FOR PROTOTYPAL EFFORTS

Leadership needs are inevitably affected by individual organizational situation and structure, by political arrangements, and by stage of development. Those characteristics needed in one situation may be totally inappropriate in another. Dramatic, aggressive leadership forms may fit best in one context, while only gradualism would be tolerable in another. To specify one unique leadership style as universal panacea would be absurd. Moreover, it is even exceedingly difficult to determine the extent to which a change in organizational processes is a condition of the situation or of its leadership. For change may be as frequently engendered by factors having to do with the situation as by leader provocation. Even in discussions with the very individuals involved in a changing structure, it is often difficult to detect where the impetus genuinely arose—out of the situation, through administrative inspiration or due to some combination of the two. The most dramatic illustration may be the special library in which computer applications may be as much the consequence of the availability of computer time and cost-conscious management as of technologically prone librarians provoked to enhance their technical systems. This in spite of the fact that the individual in the situation may quite often develop after the fact an exaggerated sense of his own role in such provocation. This behavior is not unlike the individual reconstruction of historical events by former government officials who, upon retelling the circumstances, frequently attribute to themselves a more significant role than do others who describe the same events.

Different forms of leadership tend to arise out of alternate cultural situations. It is only when conventional institutions are under duress that novel leadership forms tend to emerge. The dilemma of modern-day librarianship is that it stands poised on the threshold of sweeping modification and adaptation, but just as in other bureaucratic forms, clings powerfully to its safe and traditional tenets. Moreover, unlike certain other institutional forms where public sentiment may be more disposed to accept the promise or the need for dramatic metamorphosis (public-school systems may be one illustration), the library is conceived as such a conventional, unchanging, and unchangeable institution, that the possibility of its becoming otherwise is scarcely comprehended. And it is precisely for such a reason that librarianship so very much stands in need of prototypal instances which demonstrate alternative options.

A single Thomas Hoving,[9] to energize and to dramatize the potential of the public library in one great city, as he has the art museum, could profoundly influence the course of American public library history. Yet the problem is that all the classic reasons prohibit the choice of such leadership and the bureaucratic constraints hamper the creative testing of alternative propositions. In essence, the problem is that those with the passion and the aspirations to make libraries otherwise, the charismatic qualities to command a following, if they exist in librarianship at all, are numbered only among the young, the inexperienced, the group not yet seen to hold the potential for leadership. And that those who hold the power to select leadership in all the settings where they function—public, academic, school, and special libraries—because they do not conceive of the necessity for fundamental variation, apply conventional criteria in their choices, using yardsticks such as long years of experience and legitimate professional credentials, all of which conspire to rule out those who might hold more promise. For if new leadership is to come, it will arise more surely from those not ground down by the weight of bureaucratic ritual or from outsiders unburdened by the conventional strictures, who may more clearly perceive the challenge and the opportunity of the library as an adaptable and potentially powerful institutional form.

Prototypal efforts imply risks. For this reason, boundaries and limits are set. Experiment implies unknown outcomes, limits of precision in assessing results, danger from the impossibility of forecasting unforeseen consequences. Hence the adulation of the ritual, the predictable, in spite of flaws and limits. To expect an organizational stance, an organizational leadership, built upon tenets which traffic in zones not subject to traditional patterns in librarianship, where convention is so deeply grained and expected, may be to seek too much. Yet prototypal efforts

9. Director of the New York City Metropolitan Museum of Art.

seem the only practicable means for testing and demonstrating the potential of alternatives. Without such options opened, nothing is changed, nothing can ever change. To force open doorways, in order to attempt alternatives whether at the disciplinary level, the organizational level, the educational level, in order to compel contemplation of variation, is to exercise an option necessary for there to be leadership.

The conceptual framework of librarianship requires some degree of reconstruction. The traditional reactive paradigm is no longer enough. The prime need is for a revised climate in which experiment and laboratory and demonstration efforts receive encouragement at the institutional, disciplinary, and educational levels. For the highest promise of leadership for the next stages of development may more reasonably be sought from those who design and engineer such innovative efforts and who are then called upon to extend the work to a broader and wider base or from those who are attracted to the discipline because of their commitment to the type of activity which holds out the promise of rejuvenating institutional and disciplinary forms. The prototypal milieu may be seen as the seedbed of the libraries of tomorrow, as it is the only hopeful setting from which to look for the emergence of reconstituted leadership for the future. For it is only in such an ambience that there is opportunity to explore the questions of what the organization is, but more significantly, what it wants to become. It is only from the answers to such questions that the principles needed to reform and to reshape the library contribution can be expected. Such a leadership does not perceive disciplinary history as something for which one must accept no responsibility, or over which there is only limited control.

The present condition of libraries is based upon the value choices and the conventional wisdom of the past. The present situation perpetuates the tendencies of another day, supports the rational authority of the historic chain of events in which earlier decisions gave rise to contemporary forms. But it is precisely the characteristic of the leader that he not regard himself as incapable of being anything more than the medium through which the course of the past inexorably flows. For such a logic, pervasive in many institutional forms as well as librarianship, merely rationalizes the myth of neutrality, the choice of passivity, the perpetuation of prior commitments, generated out of an ideological conviction that the modern-day administrative functionary is merely the instrument of an irreversible historical process. Such a shrunken view of autonomy and responsibility eliminates the capacity to exercise new options. Under these terms, the prevailing value structure limits contribution to simply an analysis of the means which will lead more efficiently to the earlier subscribed-to ends. And reason and strategy are thus addressed exclusively to the making of judgments on how to do things rather than on whether or which things. Leadership is absolved of responsibility, control over action is seen as foreclosed, what is cannot be questioned. The status quo is inviolable.

The professed neutrality of such library ideology is spurious. This form of librarianship accommodates to the strictures of prior choices based upon all the political, economic, and social proclivities of the past. To concede that there is no choice left is to deny opportunities to those who have not had them. It is not enough to expect or to hope that the normal processes will deliver the human beings who can lead librarianship forward. The existing administrative generation and those who are to succeed them do not offer such promise. The problems of the times and the problems of the institution require those of spirit and action, who are fired by a vision not of what the institutions and professional practice now are, but what they can become. A new pioneering class not constrained or disabled by the conventions of the field is needed, one which perceives the challenge and the opportunity of the institution and of the information form.

Prototypal designs hold out at least the promise for tampering with, for tempering such designs. They are abundant demonstration that there are choices to be made. They offer potential leadership the proving ground for conjuring the means for modifying the equation of the past, for altering the commitment of the institution from the resources to the client, to new clients, to new services and relationships. It is out of such revised paradigms that there is highest promise for the leadership of the future.

Library administrators appear to want librarianship to change. They would prefer a better world in which improved libraries hold an important place. But their dilemma very frequently stems from the fact that they do not understand the capacity of libraries to be otherwise.

A conversation with a public library administrator inquiring about a student led to a discussion about the crisis of the times and the need for change to come to the entire culture and libraries within it. But this librarian in prescribing change for libraries made very clear how and why it could not be done in his community. It was only a small suburban city. It had a mayor who was really a "construction-worker type." It was run by people who really were not sympathetic or interested in libraries nor would they provide the kind of support necessary. It was essentially the job of the city libraries to make the change because they had the resources and because they had a different climate of interest for their work. Not too much could be expected in his community because after all people there didn't want libraries to do very much more than they really did already, and it was hard to get things accomplished in such a setting.

At the same time that this library administrator was bewailing the condition of libraries and expressing his pious hope that things would change, he was acting out a personal role which made this impossible, without perceiving the incongruity between his words and his action. But libraries will not change through wishful thinking. They will not change until and unless those in posts of leadership responsibility recognize that to bring change about is their responsibility. Not until the effectiveness and the contribution of the organization is seen as the responsibility of leadership rather than the rationalization of inadequacy will change become possible.

Index

Index